BEYOND DESCRIPTION

BEYOND DESCRIPTION

Anthropologies of Explanation

**Edited by Paolo Heywood
and Matei Candea**

CORNELL UNIVERSITY PRESS   ITHACA AND LONDON

This project has received funding from the European Research Council (ERC) under the European Union's Horizon 2020 research and innovation program (grant agreement number 603833). Thanks to this generous funding, the ebook editions of this book are available as open-access volumes through the Cornell Open initiative.

First published 2023 by Cornell University Press

Library of Congress Cataloging-in-Publication Data

Names: Heywood, Paolo, editor. | Candea, Matei, editor.
Title: Beyond description: anthropologies of explanation / edited by Paolo Heywood and Matei Candea.
Description: Ithaca [New York]: Cornell University Press, 2023. | Includes bibliographical references and index.
Identifiers: LCCN 2023003278 (print) | LCCN 2023003279 (ebook) | ISBN 9781501771569 (hardcover) | ISBN 9781501771576 (paperback) | ISBN 9781501771583 (pdf) | ISBN 9781501771590 (epub)
Subjects: LCSH: Ethnology—Philosophy. | Explanation. | Philosophical anthropology.
Classification: LCC GN345 .B38 2023 (print) | LCC GN345 (ebook) | DDC 306.01—dc23/eng/20230213
LC record available at https://lccn.loc.gov/2023003278
LC ebook record available at https://lccn.loc.gov/2023003279

Now every theory tacitly asserts two things: firstly, that there is something to be explained; secondly, that such and such is the explanation. Hence, however widely different speculators may disagree in the solutions they give of the same problem; yet by implication they agree that there is a problem to be solved.

—Herbert Spencer, *First Principles*

Contents

Acknowledgments

We are extremely grateful to all the participants in the workshop "Ethnographies of Explanation and the Explanation of Ethnography: Beyond Ethnographic Foundationalism?" held in King's College, Cambridge, on March 22 and 23, 2018, of which this book is the result. In addition to those who gave papers at that workshop and who have contributed to this book (Jon Bialecki, Joanna Cook, Sarah Green, Tanya Luhrmann, Nigel Rapport, Adam Reed, Gildas Salmon, Richard Staley, and Tom Yarrow), the workshop benefited enormously from the presence of and contributions from Fenella Canell, Harri Englund, Taras Fedirko, Caroline Humphrey, Maryon McDonald, Morten Axel Pedersen, and Alain Pottage.

We are also very grateful to our editor at Cornell, Jim Lance, and to the European Research Council, which funded both the initial workshop and the open-access publication of this book (Grant Number 683033).

BEYOND DESCRIPTION

Introduction

ETHNOGRAPHIES OF EXPLANATION AND THE EXPLANATION OF ETHNOGRAPHY

Matei Candea and Paolo Heywood

What is an explanation? What does it add? What makes it authoritative, clarifying, or misleading? Whom does it serve, and by what means is it produced? These questions lie at the heart of public crises of confidence in expertise and political representation; they echo also within the knowledge practices of disciplines such as anthropology. In a world in which one global political, economic, or indeed epidemiological earthquake after another defies expert predictions of its impossibility, and post hoc accounts can often feel more like rationalizations or special pleading than explanations, competing voices vie for public presence and seek to silence one another in accounting for radical change. At stake in such political, religious, or economic contestations is the particular nature of explanatory speech and its epistemological underpinnings: What visions of truth, if any, underlie such accounts? Who is authorized to provide them, and through which media and technologies? What are the aims, purposes, and ends of explanation and the giving of accounts? Anthropology and the social sciences face such questions too, making contemporary explanatory practice both an empirical and a reflexive challenge.

This book brings together anthropologists, philosophers, and historians of social science to take a double look at the problem of explanation. The book combines ethnographic studies of practices of explanation in a range of contemporary political, medical, artistic, religious, and bureaucratic settings with examinations of changing norms and forms of explanation within anthropology itself—one of the social scientific disciplines in which explanation has been most pointedly and enduringly in crisis. Alongside chapters detailing the explanatory practices required of asylum seekers at the borders of "Fortress Europe" (Green), those of advocates seeking state funding for mindfulness meditation therapy (Cook), the multiple explanations an artist gives of his own "distorted" paintings (Rapport), those of self-defined nonpolitical readers trying to make sense of their favorite author's sympathies with fascism (Reed) or of alt-right bloggers sussing out the minds and argumentative techniques of their progressive opponents (Mair), this book also reflects on anthropological attempts to explain specific classes of phenomena such as miracles (Bialecki) and artwork (Rapport), on anthropology's deployment of and challenge to economic models of behavior (Staley, Salmon), on its attitude to "problems" (Heywood) and "findings" (Luhrmann), and on the tension between the implicit and the explicit in anthropological description, comparison, and explanation (Candea and Yarrow).

The placement of anthropological explanation in the frame in this way is intended as a provocation of sorts. For while, as these chapters show, anthropologists have much to say about expertise, authoritative knowledge, and the mechanics, politics, and ethics of explanation as a thing other people do, the discipline has for some time been rather wary of invoking explanation as a description of its own practice. Anthropology is not alone in this—an anti-explanatory mood has been sweeping a number of social scientific and humanities disciplines. However, anthropology is one of the disciplines in which this mood is perhaps most advanced and all-encompassing. One of its more extreme forms, which we explore in more detail later, is what we will call *ethnographic foundationalism*—the deferral of all epistemological questions to "the ethnography" (Candea 2018; Heywood 2018). Ethnographic foundationalism is not merely the (falsely naïve) claim that anthropologists should suspend explanation and "just describe"; it is the almost mystical belief in the power of ethnographic description to reach back and resolve anthropology's own epistemological dilemmas. But ethnographic foundationalism is only an extreme symptom of a more diffuse anti-explanatory mood we are diagnosing. There seems to be in contemporary anthropology a pervasive sense that *there is a thing called explanation out there and that it is problematic for anthropologists to try to do it.*

On closer examination, however, both parts of that statement are obviously incorrect: there *isn't* a single thing called explanation out there, and anthropologists *do* do it all the time. As for the former, as we outline later, even a cursory look at the literature on explanation generated by philosophers of science shows that there are a number of competing theories and no consensus on what it might mean to explain something, let alone what the proper way is to do it. As for the latter, on almost any definition of explanation, if you look closely enough you will find micro- or meso-explanatory moves woven into the texture of most anthropological texts, even those that purport to be purely descriptive or to reject explanation altogether (see Candea and Yarrow, this volume). We thus want to ask about the forms of explanation present in and possible for anthropology, and what their limits and problems actually are. Even though there may be a case for reclaiming explanation, there may still be compelling reasons to reject it in favor of something else. But if so, why? Can we account for what *is* wrong with explanation, in some or all of its forms?

In sum, this book establishes an inside-out relationship between ethnographies of explanation and the problem of how ethnography is to be explained. From one angle, it proposes a comparative account of forms of explanation in the world, in which anthropology and its crisis of explanatory confidence feature as just one case study among others (albeit one that takes a central place in this book and is examined from multiple perspectives). From another angle, this is a book posing reflexive epistemological questions to anthropology, questions that we feel are best asked alongside and on a par with ethnographic accounts of explanation beyond anthropology. This is not to say that we expect the ethnographic account of others' explanations to resolve the epistemic conundrums relating to anthropology's own explanatory moves. Rather, the book seeks to explore communications and productive tensions between the reflexive problematic of anthropological explanation and the comparative exploration of other explanations in the world. The final section of this introduction, which discusses the chapters in more detail, draws out some of these contrasts and analogies. In the next two sections, however, we will, first, diagnose the anti-explanatory mood that has swept anthropology and cognate disciplines and, second, take a broader look at the notion of explanation and its internal multiplicities in order to reboot our theoretical and ethnographic sense of what explanation might be.

An Anti-explanatory Mood

Our sense of an anti-explanatory mood is partly grounded in the experience of our own training as anthropologists, around a decade apart, in the early years of the twenty-first century. While we each remember being taught about ethnography, description, and critique at various points, we find it hard to recall anyone ever teaching us about explanation, except in one key sense—through a set of worries and warnings about improper attempts to explain. The history of anthropology is often taught as a graveyard of broken explanations and explanatory devices: evolutionism and progress, structuralism and the human mind, Marxism and the laws of history, transactionalism and the maximizing individual, and so on. We remember learning only one thing about explanation as an epistemological problem—namely, that it is a rather dubious and probably irrelevant practice for anthropologists.

On a closer investigation, there were two broad sources for this general anti-explanatory mood, two explicit and articulated challenges to explanation, which, though historically and epistemologically very different, combined to drive home the sense that explanation was a problematic thing to want to do. The first challenge is the one that was recurrently raised against explanation at various points in the twentieth century by proponents of "interpretation." The contrast has a deep nineteenth-century philosophical and sociological pedigree. Social scientists often hark back to Max Weber's critique of narrow historical materialism and crudely functionalist sociology and his claim that "the specific task of sociological analysis . . . is the interpretation of action in terms of its subjective meaning" (Weber 1978, 8).[1] In anthropology a contrast between explanation and interpretation has tended to be rediscovered at regular intervals. In 1950, E. E. Evans-Pritchard savaged the functionalist paradigm, to which he himself had previously subscribed, arguing that anthropology ought to be a historical interpretive endeavor and not seek to provide explanations of society analogous to those of biology. A similar challenge was famously mounted again a couple of decades later by Clifford Geertz, with his claim that anthropology's central object, culture, "is not a power, something to which social events, behaviors, institutions, or processes can be causally attributed; it is a context, something within which they can be intelligibly—that is thickly—described" (1973, 14). This seemingly unavoidable recurrence of the contrast between explanation and interpretation reinforced the sense that anthropology had always been and perhaps would always be riven between "two grand epistemological traditions" (Handler 2009, 628; see also Holy 1987): on the one side lay the explanatory ambitions of positivism, with its cortege of scientism, reductionism, and quantification; on the other, the "understanding" offered by interpretivism, grounded in humanism, hermeneutics, and qualitative thick description. Andrew Abbot (2001; see also Candea 2018) has perceptively analyzed the way in which these paired contrasts operate cyclically in the lives of disciplines as core organizing polarities. For social anthropologists, however, the explanatory side of the contrasts seemed always to be in the past. With a few exceptions (e.g., Bloch 2005), the most recent explicit proponent of positivist explanation who was still recognized as part of the disciplinary canon as we were taught it was Alfred Radcliffe-Brown (1951), whose pitch for anthropology as a "nomothetic" search for social laws came to stand as the classic exemplar of misplaced scientist hubris. While this grand struggle between positivism and interpretivism was already rather passé by the time our training began, it had left behind a tendency to associate explanation with what we will argue is only one, very narrow vision of what contemporary epistemologists might mean by this term.

This provided fertile ground for a far more drastic challenge to explanation, and one that at the time of our training still felt excitingly timely and fresh. This was the radical rejection of any kind of explanation over and above description itself. One of the most forceful proponents of this line of argument was Bruno Latour, whose actor-network theory was fundamentally structured by a profound antipathy for the explanatory ambitions of classic social theories (e.g., Latour 2005). Actor-network theorists were enjoined to "just describe"—to craft forceful accounts that stayed close to the messy contingency of particular assemblages of humans and nonhumans. They were instructed to resist the temptation to reach for the explanatory abstractions that might foreclose the account. This position was informed by Latour's (1988) critique of explanation as either a possibility or a worthwhile aim for the social sciences. Latour defines explanation, in fact, as exactly a measure of the distance between the context of the object and the context of the account. "Powerful explanations" are "empire-building" and "reductionist," imagining that we can hold multiple elements of our object of concern in a handy little receptacle like "capitalism" or "neoliberalism." Even the most basic of explanations, that of cause and effect, is framed as a politics of accusation, an attribution of blame and responsibility, and an error. Latour's ideal explanation is a "throw away" one, a one-off explanation, applicable only to a particular arrangement of elements. An explanation, in other words, that is just a description.[2] As Latour unrepentantly puts it, "I'd say that if your description needs an explanation, it's not a good description, that's all" (2005, 147).

One of the more radical forms that the anti-explanatory mood has taken in anthropology is that of deferring all epistemological questions to "the ethnography." Consider one of the few modern anthropological collections devoted specifically to epistemology in the discipline—a theoretically wide-ranging book by Christina Toren and João de Pina-Cabral. Its contributors are presented in the introduction as being in broad agreement about two things: one is antifoundationalism (Toren and Pina-Cabral 2011, 16), and the other is the fact that ethnography is "the primary condition for anthropological knowledge" (15). At the intersection of those two broadly shared anthropological claims lies the position attributed by the editors to contributor Peter Gow: "Anthropology has no need of any epistemology other than ethnography" (6). The thought is, in effect, that epistemological questions separate from ethnography are quite simply "inappropriate for anthropology" (Holbraad 2009, 81). This is what we are calling ethnographic foundationalism (cf. Candea 2018; Heywood 2018).

Ethnographic foundationalism is more than a simple injunction to forgo explanation for description, à la Latour. More ambitiously, it seeks to find in ethnographic descriptions the solution to anthropology's own epistemological problems. Consider the following questions: How should anthropology understand translation (Viveiros de Castro 2004)? How should anthropologists use examples (Krøijer 2015)? How should they generate politico-economic concepts (Corsín Jiménez and Willerslev 2007)? And how can they reinvigorate their notion of truth (Holbraad 2012)? That is not a list of *potential* problems for an anthropological epistemology to confront. It is, in fact, a list of just a few of the epistemological problems to which various anthropologists have already proposed solutions within the last fifteen years. What these solutions all have in common is that each claims to be derived recursively from the particular ethnographic case the anthropologist happened to be studying. In each case, the solution is for anthropology to adopt some version of what the authors' informants happened to be doing or thinking. So, for example, and in one of the most elegant examples of this maneuver at work, Martin Holbraad finds in the "inventive definitions" of Cuban oracular divination a conceptual apparatus with which to make sense not only of how truth might continue to play a part in anthropological thinking but also of the "inventive definitions" of Cuban oracular divination. Inventive definitions—which is to say, roughly, successful performative speech acts—are both what Cuban diviners do and how to understand it, as the notion of inventive definition is, itself, argued to be an inventive definition. Whether or not one sees such circularity as a virtue or a vice, it closes off the ethnographic from anything extraneous like "theory" or "explanation": the object explains itself.

This offloading of epistemological questions onto ethnography also chimes with a politics of engagement that sees any division between theory and practice as an academic retreat to an ivory tower that, in the words of an editorial in *Anthropology Matters* on the subject, should be made "transparent" (Kyriakides, Clarke, and Zhou 2017). Citing David Graeber as an exemplar, Theodoros Kyriakides and the convenors of the Royal Anthropological Institute postgraduate conference on anthropology's politics of engagement declare that there is no dichotomy between theory and engagement "but rather connections, relations, and multiplicities in the making" (Kyriakides, Clarke, and Zhou 2017). In not dissimilar language but with perhaps more pernicious effect, the British government's Higher Education Funding Council for England demands that our work, in order to have value, have "an effect on . . . the economy, society, culture . . . beyond academia" (Research England 2020). Theory, and in particular that kind of metatheoretical exercise that is epistemology, emerges from these perspectives as suspiciously detached and not "impactful." An antifoundationalist consensus to defer such questions to "the world itself" seems much more palatable.

Of course, we are not here arguing against our shared reference to ethnography as a discipline, which as method and material is surely one of the things that makes us anthropologists, beyond specific sets of research programs. But sharing a reference to ethnography is not the same as finding in it the answers not only to some but to all of the questions we may pose, including questions of research practice and disciplinary philosophy. And it is certainly not the same as thinking that ethnography and description exhaust the proper tasks of anthropology, and that questions such as "How do we explain?" may be safely set aside or ignored.

For to do so is to proscribe (de jure if not always de facto) the sorts of debates and discussions our anthropological forbears had over, for example, the relative worth of deductive or explanatory versus hermeneutic or interpretive models of knowledge and understanding for the discipline. It proscribes them not for the particular answers they might provide but for the very ambition of seeking an answer from beyond the confines of empirical material. It renders the ambition of a book such as this one—to investigate an ethnographic and an anthropological practice without assuming they amount to the same thing—impossible to pursue. It valorizes description and an erasure, as far as is possible, of any distinction or difference between an anthropological account and its object.

More broadly, not only is it the case that we may wish to dispute the specific meanings of foundational concepts, but we may also have different ideas as to their proper relationship. It need hardly be pointed out that empiricism does not suit everybody's politics, and that sometimes the choice between engagement and conceptual invention may be a mutually exclusive one. Neither across anthropology as a discipline nor across ethnographically foundationalist versions of it is any one motivation for such implicit foundationalism dominant. Discussion as to the relative merits of different motivations, however, or indeed as to alternatives to them, and to their relationships, is precluded by their common insistence that discussion of a purely epistemological kind is a waste of our time.

In other words, while many anthropologists seem to agree on the foundational nature of ethnography in our discipline, the origins of such agreement, its purposes and goals, as well as its consequences and effects, are obscured by that very consensus of method.

Our claim is certainly not, then, that it is a problem to believe ethnography as a method unites anthropology as a discipline, nor even is our claim that there is necessarily any problem with any one point of view on what it is that anthropology should be doing. It is that we will be better served in the project of assessing the purposes and underlying metaphysics, the correlations and disjunctures, and the consequences and effects of such justifications by having that discussion openly and explicitly, and without anticipating the answer in our ethnographic findings.

So we have chosen to focus this book on a classic yet long-neglected problem in the epistemology of anthropology, one that also has very clear real-world implications, in its anthropological and its ethnographic varieties. We fully expect that explanation as it is imagined, valued, practiced, or rejected in specific ethnographic circumstances can teach us something about what an anthropological explanation might look like. But we hope also that this book is an opportunity to consider the nature of anthropological explanation as a problem in its own right.

The Multiplicity of Explanation

In seeking to reboot the problematic of explanation, both ethnographically and theoretically, we would be well served by taking a sidelong glance at debates outside the social sciences. Philosophers of science and epistemologists have had profound and long-standing disagreements over what precisely it is to explain, and these debates have generated a number of competing theories and definitions. This section delves into some of these philosophical arguments, definitions, and contrasts, to enrich the often rather one-dimensional discussions of explanation current in anthropology.

In so doing, however, this section is *emphatically not* reaching out to philosophy to define authoritatively what explanation "really is," or to set the ground rules for this book's subsequent discussion. The role of this initial engagement with the philosophy of science is in fact precisely the opposite: not to police the boundaries of what can be called explanation but to expand them. For the core aim of this section is to highlight the multiplicity of ways in which explanation can be invoked beyond the sometimes rather limited implicit understandings current in social scientific discussions, thus challenging the tendency to assume that explanation is a unitary, singular, and clearly defined activity.

This kind of opening-up is a preliminary to the ethnographic explorations in the chapters that follow. In fact, this section might be thought of as a first ethnographic foray into explanation as it is imagined by one particular subset of contemporary Euro-Americans—namely, philosophers of science. This is not an entirely self-contained discourse, of course. Insofar as these "technical" definitions of explanation are often self-consciously drawing on and formalizing commonsense intuitions and understandings, these various philosophical accounts already give us a glimpse of the variety of ways in which explanation is conceived of in the world beyond philosophy.

Overviews of philosophical theories of explanation tend to start with positivists' attempts to map out a "deductive-nomothetic" vision of explanation in the early twentieth century. We will come to this later but would like, for reasons that will become clear as we proceed, to begin in a slightly more unusual place: philosophical discussions of "abduction."

Abduction—also known as "inference to the best explanation" (Douven 2017; Lipton 2004)—is a term originally introduced by C. S. Peirce (1934). It describes a form of inference that is distinct from both deduction and induction. Deduction moves inexorably from known premises to logical conclusions. By contrast, induction and abduction extrapolate likely conclusions from partial knowledge. Induction is usually characterized as a kind of direct "statistical" extrapolation from the known to the unknown. The paradigmatic case is the induction—famously criticized by David Hume—that the sun will rise tomorrow because it has risen every day in my life so far.[3] Abduction, by contrast, is characterized as a form of inference in which a conclusion is reached because it is identified as the best explanation of a state of affairs. An example (Schurz 2008, 207–208) might be inferring the recent passage of an individual on an isolated beach based on the observation of a line of footsteps on said beach. This explanation of the phenomenon (someone has walked across this beach) is only one among many—perhaps infinitely many—possible explanations. For instance, that these footstep-like shapes might have been formed by some coincidental natural process, or by the rolling of a ball with foot-shaped appendages, or, less baroquely, by a large group of people carefully stepping in one another's footsteps. Among these infinitely many possible explanations for a phenomenon, abduction plumps for what seems the best explanation. Another, more commonplace example of abduction might be the thought that someone can read Latin based on the observation of a number of books in Latin on their bookshelf. What is the best explanation for those books being there? The fact that the owner of the bookshelf owns them and might read them. Of course, the books might have been inherited and the current owner might be incapable of reading them, or the owner might have bought them precisely in order to give the false impression of their competency in Latin. In sum, the notion of abduction points to the fact that, in inferring the unknown from the known, we do not always simply extrapolate, following an inductive rule such as "more of the same." Rather, in many cases, such inference involves some kind of more complex explanatory consideration.

For our purposes in this book, philosophical discussions of abduction are interesting for two reasons. The first is that they make a rather convincing case for the ubiquity of explanation in everyday life. By focusing on the structure of micro-judgments and observations such as the ones just discussed, they show that explanations of various kinds are ineradicably woven into our everyday experience, in a way that undercuts arguments "against" explanation in anthropology or elsewhere. The second reason is that starting from this observation about the ubiquity of explanation, philosophers seeking to spell out the structure of abduction—"inference to the best explanation"—are invariably brought face to face with a key problem: contemporary epistemologists have no settled account of what an "explanation" (let alone a "good" or "best" explanation) is. This means that works on abduction (e.g., Lipton 2004) are a great place to look for overviews of the variety of current understandings of explanation in the philosophy of science. It also means that one comes away from them with a refreshing sense that there might indeed be a whole range of different ways of explaining. We argued earlier that anthropologists have tended to act as if there were just one thing called explanation and it was best avoided. The take-home point of philosophical discussions of abduction is precisely the reverse: explanation is ubiquitous and it takes a huge variety of forms.

The first thing to go, from this perspective, is the engrained binary of explanation versus interpretation that has animated so much social scientific methodological discussion. Philosophers of science frequently use the terms *explanation* and *understanding* interchangeably. As Peter Lipton puts it, "The question about explanation can be put this way: what has to be added to knowledge to yield understanding?" (2004, 21). The fundamental contrast to which philosophers of science tend to draw attention is broader than the familiar explanation-interpretation opposition—it is the contrast between describing a phenomenon and adding something further to this description. This extra something is an "understanding" of some sort, and that understanding is what an explanation provides. The contrast between description and "explanatory understanding"—which is central also to the Latourian injunctions to "just describe"—is itself not unproblematic. However, as is often the case, a shift in dualisms has productive effects. Whereas Latourian critiques envision explanation as taking something away from description, curtailing or maiming it in some way, Lipton and others portray explanation as an addition, a "something more." Collapsing the dualism between explanation and understanding is the preliminary to envisioning a wide diversity of forms of explanatory understanding—what are sometimes rather charmingly described as forms of "explanatory goodness" (Godfrey-Smith 2003, 199).

On one canonical and now much criticized view, the "goodness" of explanation lies in relating phenomena to "laws of nature." This deductive-nomothetic (D-N) theory of explanation, elaborated in the mid-twentieth century by logical positivists (e.g., Hempel 1965), is the kind of "explanation" that is usually implicitly or explicitly contrasted to interpretation in the anthropological literature. The D-N model claimed that a phenomenon has been satisfactorily explained when it can be deduced from a set of premises that include a law of nature. For instance, the initially puzzling fact that an oar immersed in water appears to be bent is explained when it has been deduced logically from the law of refraction of light and some contingent facts about the refractive index of water and the position of the oar on that particular occasion. In other words, explanation in this view has exactly the same structure as prediction—it is, as it were, a prediction of things that have already happened. This D-N model of explanation was roughly the one espoused by Radcliffe-Brown in the aforementioned 1951 paper.

A key difficulty with the D-N model of explanation is that philosophers have no settled account of what a "law of nature" actually is, beyond saying that it is a regularity with no known exceptions.[4] And if laws are no more than generalizations of that kind, the D-N "explanation" collapses into saying that some particular thing happens because that sort of thing generally happens. This is rather poignantly illustrated by the meager results of Radcliffe-Brown's own "nomothetic" aspirations for anthropology.[5] Another key difficulty is illustrated in the famous "flagpole" example (Godfrey-Smith 2003, 193–194): according to the D-N theory of explanation, the length of a flagpole's shadow can be explained by deducing it from laws concerning light and a set of contingent facts including the length of a flagpole. This seems broadly unproblematic. However, the D-N theory of explanation also entails that the length of the flagpole can be explained—in exactly the same way—by reference to the length of its shadow. Here, critics of the D-N theory claim that the analogy between *explaining* a state of affairs and *predicting* it breaks down. There is something intuitively wrong about the thought that the length of the shadow *explains* the length of the flagpole.

This something has to do with causality—a sense that while the length of a flagpole causes the length of the shadow, the reverse is not true. This brings us (back) to the broadest and oldest view of what constitutes explanatory goodness, articulated and debated in various ways since at least Aristotle. This is the thought that explanation consists in giving a "causal history"—identifying the relevant antecedent causes of phenomena, events, and states of affairs. In some form or other, this is the theory that most contemporary philosophers of the social sciences tend to associate with explanation (Elster 2015; Runciman 1983). There is little consensus, however, on what kind of thing a "cause" is. In the account of human affairs, this uncertainty about causes is severely aggravated by a host of subquestions about "mental causation" and the distinctive nature of intentions, reasons, and the like (see Dretske 1991 for an overview). Much of the popular social scientific contrast between explaining and interpreting, for instance, turns on a distinction between the mere mechanical causation of behavior, on the one hand, and the identification of intentions and purposes as relevant elements of meaningful action, on the other. And yet Weber himself, to whom this contrast is sometimes traced, saw the endeavors as connected, claiming that "sociology . . . is a science concerning itself with the interpretive understanding of social action *and thereby* with a causal explanation of its course and consequences" (1978, 4, emphasis added).

The criterion of relevance is equally problematic. As Lipton nicely puts it, the big bang is part of the causal history of every phenomenon we know of, but it is hardly "explanatory" in the majority of such phenomena. Causal histories are "long and wide" (Lipton 2004, 32), and the very multiplicity and richness of causal explanation in practice can end up challenging the idea of a clear distinction between explaining and describing.[6] Defenders of causal theories of explanation, however, have sought to respond to these objections by strengthening their notions of cause in a range of ways—by developing statistical or mechanical models of causation, for instance, or by introducing a consideration of counterfactuals (Lipton 2004; Woodward 2019).[7]

However, epistemologists have imagined other versions of explanation beyond the search for laws or the identification of causes. One such contender is the family of "unificationist" theories of explanation (Kitcher 1989; also see Woodward 2019). On this view, a set of disparate phenomena are explained by fitting them under a single, unified account: a coherent theory, an elegant pattern, a systematic structure. One might argue that this is what Darwinism, for instance, in its original version, did. It had very little to say about actual causal mechanisms, nor did it really formulate any fundamental laws of nature. Rather, Darwin's explanation of evolution by natural selection provided a coherent theory to fit a set of very disparate facts—the beaks of finches, the wonderful mechanism of the eye, fossils, and so on—that were suddenly all explained in relation to one another. We could say that—pace Radcliffe-Brown's own claims—anthropological functionalism, insofar as it was explanatory, was actually a unificationist explanation of this kind, rather than a D-N one. None of the most convincing functionalist explanations anthropologists have crafted, such as Evans-Pritchard's explanation of the interrelation of politics and kinship in *The Nuer* (1940) or Émile Durkheim's explanation of the functions of religion in *The Elementary Forms of the Religious Life* (1915), rely seriously on any fundamental appeal to a "law of nature" or even a general "law of society." All of them, however, provide a coherent theory that relates disparate facts to one another and thus makes them make sense. The best structuralist explanations—such as Claude Lévi-Strauss's (1963) account of totemism in the book of the same name or Mary Douglas's (1973) explanation of the underlying logic of the dietary prohibitions in Leviticus—are of this unificationist kind also.

Another family of philosophical accounts of explanation (sometimes character-ized as "pragmatic" [Godfrey-Smith 2003, 199]) departs from those just discussed in attending to the audience-relative and interest-relative nature of explanations. Thus, Bas Van Fraassen's account of explanation starts from the observation that explanations are answers to questions, and questions come in many shapes and sizes. The nature of the question, which is to say also the background knowledge and interests of the questioner, is one of the features that determine whether an answer will count as an explanation in any given case. In other words, to know whether something is an explanation, we need to consider not simply the rela-tion between a theory and a fact (as in classic accounts of explanation) but a relation between a theory, a fact, and a context—which includes the knowledge and inter-ests of the audience for whom one is explaining (Van Fraasen 1980, 156).

This evokes the broader idea that explanation is a matter of "making the strange familiar" (Lipton 2004)—by which account most of anthropology, and interpretive anthropology in particular, is entirely bent on explanation. More surprisingly perhaps, this is also where reductive explanations seem to live—for instance those that explain by translating the purportedly more complex phe-nomena of human behavior into those purportedly simpler and more familiar mechanisms of biology, of biology into physics, of physics into mathematics, and so on. Reductionism and interpretivism make strange bedfellows, but they can both seek to make the strange familiar.

This "familiarity model" of explanation also gives an obvious solution to the difficult problem of how to decide what collection of causes from among the infi-nite causal histories of any given event or phenomenon constitutes an explanation. If explanatory goodness is relative to the interests and background knowledge of the audience, then different causal histories will be explanatory for different audi-ences. This is also why, as W. G. Runciman (1983) notes (see also Candea and Yar-row, this volume), what will to some readers be "mere description" can already be explanation for others. On the other hand, the familiarity model fails to account for explanations—so frequent in scientific accounts—in which the unfamiliar is invoked to explain the familiar, such as when complex psychological mechanisms are invoked to explain familiar behaviors.

Finally—to close this breathless yet far from exhaustive tour of a complex epistemological landscape—Andrew Abbot (2004, 8–10), in a clarifying typol-ogy of explanation, also argues that explanation can be "pragmatic" in a differ-ent sense, in which an account is explanatory if it allows us to intervene in the phenomenon, to concretely influence or shape it.

In sum, discussions of explanation in the philosophy of science on the one hand tend to collapse our familiar anthropological distinction between explaining and understanding: to explain is simply to understand. On the other hand, they propose different theories of what it might mean for an account to provide understanding, to be an explanation.

In order to be an explanation, an account could do one or more of the following (this list is by no means exhaustive):

- relate a specific fact to a general law
- identify the causes of a state of affairs
- answer a specific question about a situation
- translate something unfamiliar into familiar terms
- provide an account of something that enables us to influence or shape it

Philosophers typically go on to argue about the relative merits of these and other theories of explanation, and sometimes about the different merits of different forms of explanation themselves. For our purposes, however, what is interesting is precisely the diversity and richness of forms of explanatory goodness that these debates concentrate. Beyond that core observation, the various overlapping contrasts and typologies discussed earlier are not invoked here in order to bind or limit our discussion, but precisely as an invitation to ethnography. The distinctions and concepts mentioned here have heuristic value in helping us think comparatively across the different chapters in this book, as we will now illustrate in introducing these chapters.

The Chapters

Our contributors describe a range of explanatory practices as both ethnographic objects and analytical strategies. The book is divided into two parts that approach the question from two complementary angles.

Chapters in part I reflect directly on changing norms and forms of explanation within anthropology. The first two chapters, by Heywood and Luhrmann, are both explicitly critical of contemporary anthropologists' refusal of explanation. Heywood points to the disappearance of the classic trope of the "ethnographic puzzle" in anthropological writing, and he roots the move away from explanation in the influence of Ludwig Wittgenstein on anthropologists like Geertz, Rodney Needham, and Edmund Leach. Rather than call for a specific form of anthropological explanation, Heywood points to some of the problems with importing Wittgenstein's philosophical critique of explanation into anthropology. Foremost among these is the fact that Wittgenstein's critique is founded on the idea that philosophical problems are not really problems—they can be "dissolved" by properly rearranging what we know, rather than by adding new information. Such a view may work in philosophy but is inconsistent with any vision of anthropology as being about adding to our understanding of the world.

In chapter 2, Luhrmann argues for a renewed attention to "findings"— observations that call out for explanation. Explanation itself can take various guises: initially it is described as an account of one unfamiliar thing in terms of another that is familiar; later it is far more nomothetic, consisting in generalization or hypothesis that can then be subject to support or refutation. But Luhrmann's key focus is on what leads to the desire for explanation: it is the finding, the question in the world that provokes the need for explanation that is important, rather than of what that explanation consists.

In chapter 3, Bialecki starts from the observation that causal-type explanations are not appropriate in the case of ethnographic objects like miracles. Yet his account of his own and Luhrmann's earlier work on miracles in contemporary America rescues a certain vision of anthropological explanation from them: for Bialecki it is comparison, not only between cases but within them, that allows for "explanation-like effects" to emerge by allowing readers to build a narrative from a certain determinate set of possibilities laid out by the author.

The importance of comparison, and the variety of explanatory effects in anthropological writing, is also at the heart of chapter 4, which consists of a dialogue between Candea and Yarrow, based on the place of explanation in their latest two monographs. Each book is a sort of inside-out version of the other— Yarrow's eschewing "theory" in favor of description, and Candea's a largely conceptual exploration of the place of comparison in contemporary anthropology. At the heart of the discussion is the question of how explicit anthropological explanations need to be in order to be valuable and effective. While the two authors disagree on this point, they find common ground in a notion of "emergent" explanations in anthropology that dovetails in some respects with Bialecki's. At the heart of this vision is the idea that different explanatory effects can emerge for different readers from the same description, if the description itself is sufficiently rich.

The final two chapters of this section focus on the interaction between anthropology and other disciplines in the historical shaping of anthropological forms of comparison. Salmon's chapter 5 looks in detail at a theorist whose focus on agency, strategy, and calculation has sometimes been seen as a strange refraction of economic explanation—Pierre Bourdieu. In particular, Salmon focuses on the tension between Bourdieu's sociological and anthropological explanatory devices and projects, and the respective individualism and holism they each rely on for critical effect. Ultimately, Salmon argues, Bourdieu subordinated anthropological forms of explanation to sociological ones. This move— and one might add, the profound success of Bourdieu's work in influencing anthropology more broadly—is both an effect and a symptom of anthropology's crisis of explanatory confidence.

In chapter 6, Staley tracks complex shifts of meaning in concepts such as "mechanism" and "economy" in physics, economics, and anthropology. Far from feeding into purely causal explanations, the notion of "mechanism" in the work of scholars such as Ernst Mach allowed for explanations to be "economic," in the sense of "tracing uncommon intelligibilities back to common unintelligibilities" in as efficient a way as possible. This in turn influenced Bronislaw Malinowski's vision of explanation as being about accounting for the functional interdependence of different phenomena. Furthermore, by exploring the ways in which certain conceptions of "mechanism" fed into particular political visions of "the economy," Staley shows how academic explanations can also be interest-relative and performative, and feed back into the world around them.

The chapters in part II explore the relationship between anthropology and explanation from the converse angle, by providing anthropological analyses of different forms of explanation in a range of empirical settings. The first two chapters, by Rapport and Mair, provide a hinge to the epistemological explorations of part I: while each starts from an account of practices of explanation outside anthropology, both keep in view very explicitly the reflexive question of anthropological modes of explanation. Rapport's vision of what constitutes anthropological explanation is clearly set out in chapter 7. It is, as he puts it, "to do justice to individual and personal senses of being-in-the-world," to account for action and thought in the context of an individual's worldview, which will itself be multifaceted and internally diverse. In his account of the various ways in which the artist Stanley Spencer explained the distortions in his paintings, we find a number of our explanatory styles: all the explanations provided render something troubling and unfamiliar into something we might make sense of; some are unificationist (the distortions emerge from a desire to bring objects together within a single scheme); some are nomothetic (the distortions played a part in a larger design); and some are causal (they are the result of the appearance of certain emotions in the artist).

Mair, in chapter 8, also addresses the need to pay attention to our interlocutors' explanations. More specifically, he invokes a form of context-based explanation in which people set their actions within the wider universe of their beliefs, just as anthropologists do in their accounts of them. In his exploration of Vox Day, an American alt-right blogger and author, we also find other forms of explanatory practice in Day's attempts both to persuade his readers and to explain why his point of view is the right one: nomothetic explanations are prominent ("Social Justice Warriors always lie"), yet, as Mair highlights, this is also a pragmatic, interest-based explanation, because Day is happy to admit that this "law" is in fact rhetorical hyperbole, useful for persuasion as well as for explanation. Mair notes that discourses such as those of Day are routinely bundled under the social scientific and popular explanatory category of "post-truth." But this neat label tends to divert attention from the often extensively worked-out epistemological theorizing of these actors themselves. By contrast, in his account of anthropological explanation, Mair argues that it is important to bear in mind the relationship between anthropological explanation and the explanations of our interlocutors, even if these are not always isomorphic.

In sum, both Rapport and Mair reflect on the necessary relationship between anthropological explanation and the explanations that anthropologists' interlocutors themselves provide. Yet neither collapses ethnography and explanation in the manner we have described as "ethnographic foundationalism." In neither case is the "object" of the anthropological account left with the task of explaining itself (and resolving anthropology's epistemological troubles into the bargain). Rapport, in his insistence on the primacy of doing "justice to individual and personal senses of being-in-the-world," might seem to come close. But this endeavor itself is justified by an extensive and explicit general account of the nature of human experience, which frames and situates Spencer's own multifarious and fragmentary explanatory moves. As for Mair, his account of Day is clearly not intended to replicate Day's explanations of the rhetorics of "Social Justice Warriors." Yet there is something of the pragmatic, interest-based flavor to his own explanation of Day, as part of his aim is to better equip us to argue with Day's form of rhetoric-cum-dialectic.

The final three chapters explore ways in which a range of actors take upon themselves the task of explaining, or find this task is thrust upon them. Green, in chapter 9, describes the immense difficulties faced by migrants entering Europe in explaining why they deserve asylum. She shows how they are trapped between the territorial logic of human rights (based on agreements between states) and the universal logic of humanitarianism (based on hospitality for those suffering). Here we see a version of explanation in which context is key: the landscape of asylum has changed drastically as the number of migrants has increased because the tension between human rights and humanitarianism renders the refugee a necessarily exceptional figure. To be seen as genuine, an explanation of asylum seeking must be exceptional. When the number of migrants rises, the exception disappears, and border authorities assume all migrant explanations must be fake. Yet in the concluding paragraph of her account we find an almost nomothetic, "in principle" explanation superseding this context-based account: the refugee, caught between territoriality and universality, will always, in some respects, be a paradoxical, exceptional figure.

In chapter 10, Cook introduces us to a group of experts. Members of the All-Party Parliamentary Group producing a report on the efficacy of mindfulness in the United Kingdom, they are called on to explain why mindfulness-based interventions should be funded and promoted by government. She shows how their first attempt at this—based on a unificationist-like explanation of the universal and holistic benefits of mindfulness as a spiritual technique—failed to convince those to whom it was addressed. In its place, they were obliged to substitute a much more obviously causal and mechanical account of the precise ways in which mindfulness would benefit particular population groups for specific reasons and in specific ways. One of the broader points that can be drawn from the chapter is the interest-relative nature not only of explanation but of explanatory practice: unificationist explanation was simply not fit for purpose in this case, whereas more straightforward causal explanation accomplished what was required.

In the final chapter of this book, Reed explores the ways in which members of the Henry Williamson Society are called on to explain the fascist politics of their favorite author—politics that many of them only discovered upon joining the society. The case illustrates the ubiquity of the role of "expert": membership in the society suddenly puts everyday people, who would not otherwise claim the mantle of being historians, psychologists, or political scientists, in the role of quasi-experts who bear the responsibility of explaining Williamson's admiration for Oswald Mosley and Adolf Hitler. One of the ways in which they manage this tension is by shifting between what Reed calls different "scales of explanation." Williamson Society members alternate "big" monocausal explanations of Williamson's political proclivities with "little explanations"—a variety of small "becauses" that don't seek to add up to a single grand conclusion—and with occasional attempts to reject explanation altogether (for instance by claiming the autonomy of literature from the author's biography). It is not only explanation here but also the ability to hold explanation in abeyance that emerge as interest-relative.

Conclusion

These chapters all neatly exemplify the two points we have been making throughout this introduction: that explanation is ubiquitous, in the world and in our own writing, and that it is also varied and diverse, taking a range of forms.

We also learn a number of other things about explanation from these contributions: for instance, the problems of explanation we find ourselves encountering today have extensive roots. By historicizing both ethnographic and analytic debates over explanation, our authors show that the present "crisis of expertise" is far from the first time that explanation has appeared problematic or difficult.

We learn, too, that explanation is often motivated by values and ethical investments, including when it emerges from technical expertise, whether that of anthropologists or mindfulness gurus. We also learn that it is not only those with technical expertise who have the demand for explanations thrust upon them: asylum seekers and members of little-known literary societies must also explain themselves. Indeed, perhaps more broadly, and pace Latour, we learn that while explanation may well be a powerful weapon (as in Mair's discussion of Vox Day, for example), or an unquestioned entitlement—as in some critiques of "overreaching experts"—it can also be a requirement, a demand, or a burden, as in Green's and Reed's contributions. Cook's contribution adds an extra layer of complexity here, in that it may be not only explanation itself that is required of actors but also specific forms of explanation, a fact that should be all too familiar to anthropologists and other academics coping with various mechanisms of bureaucratic accounting.

This observation brings us back to a point from which this introduction began. The difference in approach between the two parts of this book might seem stark, with part I devoted to epistemology whereas part II is devoted to ethnography, and yet these are really two sides of the same coin. The chapters in part II are not merely anthropological accounts of other people's explanations—they are also themselves reflexive instances of anthropological explanation in action. Read in the light of Candea and Yarrow's discussion in particular, the chapters in part II illustrate how anthropological explanatory strategies range across a continuum from explicitly showing one's workings (see, for instance, Mair) to allowing description to do its work (see, for instance, Reed)—and some unexpected combinations of the two (for instance in Rapport). Conversely, the chapters in part I add up to an account of explanatory forms in one empirical setting, the discipline of anthropology. Reading the chapters of part I in light of part II, for example, one can see the ways in which anthropologists, too, oscillate between, on the one hand, claiming the right and authority to explain and, on the other, finding explanation thrust upon them as a—sometimes onerous—duty by various external agents. The double dynamic of explanatory power and explanatory demand applies forcefully to anthropology as a discipline. Insisting that anthropology should not be in the business of explaining because of the potentially pernicious consequences of doing so ignores the fact that we are very often *required* to explain, by publics, by our political commitments, by institutionalized accounting, and by our "findings" or "problems," in Luhrmann's or Heywood's terms. Given this fact, a more exciting question, we believe, than *whether* to explain is *how* we might explain. As the contributions in this book attest, that question has a range of potentially productive answers.

NOTES

1. However, to invoke Weber in this way is to consign to the background the extent to which he saw interpretation and explanation as connected—more on this later.

2. Yet, with characteristic panache, we find Latour in a note at the end of the text happily admitting that his own account is not self-exemplifying in the manner he demands of his readers. For Latour's account is of course an explanation in itself of his vision for the social sciences, and it is one that demands we accept a specific vision of politics, of discipline, and of epistemology without further argument.

3. Another example might be the induction that Mr. Smith, who lives in Chelsea, is rich because most people living in Chelsea are rich (Douven 2017).

4. Even proponents of the D-N model have struggled to articulate solid distinctions between "laws" and mere "generalisations" (Hempel 1965, 338; cf. Woodward 2019).

5. For all its bombastic reference to laws of social statics and social dynamics, the only actual "law" suggested in the 1951 paper is a pretty tautological affair—namely, the "law" that wherever there exist moieties in society, these are in what Radcliffe-Brown (1951, 18) terms a relation of "opposition"—a union of opposites. Since Radcliffe-Brown derived the notion of opposition from the example of moieties, this is a faint law indeed—little more, in fact, than a broader reformulation of one aspect of the very notion of moiety itself (see Candea 2018, 86).

6. These metaphysical problems with the notion of causation were part of the prompting behind the elaboration of the D-N theory, which, broadly speaking, bypasses the question of causality. The D-N model doesn't so much reject causality as reformulate causal explanation by claiming that to identify a cause is implicitly to claim that there is an underlying law that stipulates that such causes always bring about such effects. However, as we noted earlier, the nature of what might count as a law is equally disputed.

Incidentally, this tension between causal and D-N visions of explanation at midcentury also explains a fact that might strike contemporary readers as odd in Radcliffe-Brown's 1951 piece. There, the author characterizes his own "nomothetic" position as a search for understanding, by contrast to historical explanation. This is because the vision of history to which he is contrasting his own (D-N) approach is not the interpretive kind of history proposed by Evans-Pritchard (1950) but history as a form of causal explanation of a kind he attributes to Franz Boas and his followers: "One is the 'historical' method, by which the existence of a particular feature in a particular society is 'explained' as the result of a particular sequence of events. The other is the comparative method by which we seek, not to 'explain,' but to understand a particular feature of a particular society by first seeing it as a particular instance of a general kind or class of social phenomena, and then by relating it to a certain general, or preferably a universal, tendency in human societies. Such a tendency is what is called in certain instances a law" (Radcliffe-Brown 1951, 22).

7. Lipton (2004, 30–54) notes, for instance, that causal explanations are often contrastive in practice—that is to say, they tend to ask not simply, "Why this?" but rather, "Why this, rather than that?"

REFERENCES

Abbott, A. 2001. *Chaos of Disciplines*. Chicago: University of Chicago Press.

——. 2004. *Methods of Discovery: Heuristics for the Social Sciences*. New York: W. W. Norton.

Bloch, M. 2005. "Where Did Anthropology Go? Or the Need for 'Human Nature.'" In *Essays on Cultural Transmission*, edited by M. Bloch, 1–20. Oxford: Berg.

Candea, M. 2018. *Comparison in Anthropology: The Impossible Method*. Cambridge: Cambridge University Press.

Corsín Jiménez, A., and R. Willerslev. 2007. "'An Anthropological Concept of the Concept': Reversibility among the Siberian Yukaghirs." *Journal of the Royal Anthropological Institute* 13:527–544.

Douglas, M. 1973. *Natural Symbols: Explorations in Cosmology*. Pelican Anthropology Library. Harmondsworth, UK: Penguin.

Douven, I. 2017. "Abduction." In *The Stanford Encyclopedia of Philosophy*, Summer 2017 edition, edited by E. N. Zalta. Metaphysics Research Lab, Stanford University. https://plato.stanford.edu/archives/sum2017/entries/abduction/.

Dretske, F. 1991. *Explaining Behavior: Reasons in a World of Causes*. New ed. Cambridge, MA: MIT Press.

Durkheim, É. 1915. *The Elementary Forms of the Religious Life*. Translated by J. W. Swain. London: George Allen and Unwin.

Elster, J. 2015. *Explaining Social Behavior: More Nuts and Bolts for the Social Sciences*. 2nd ed. Cambridge: Cambridge University Press.

Evans-Pritchard, E. E. 1940. *The Nuer: A Description of the Modes of Livelihood and Political Institutions of a Nilotic People*. Oxford: Oxford University Press.

———. 1950. "Social Anthropology: Past and Present." *Man* 50:118–124.

Geertz, C. 1973. *The Interpretation of Cultures*. New York: Basic Books.

Godfrey-Smith, P. 2003. *Theory and Reality: An Introduction to the Philosophy of Science*. New ed. Chicago: University of Chicago Press.

Handler, R. 2009. "The Uses of Incommensurability in Anthropology." *New Literary History* 40:627–647.

Hempel, C. G. 1965. *Aspects of Scientific Explanation: And Other Essays in the Philosophy of Science*. New York: Free Press.

Heywood, P. 2018. "Making Difference: Queer Activism and Anthropological Theory." *Current Anthropology* 59:314–331.

Holbraad, M. 2009. "Ontography and Alterity: Defining Anthropological Truth." *Social Analysis* 53:80–93.

———. 2012. *Truth in Motion: The Recursive Anthropology of Cuban Divination*. Chicago: University of Chicago Press.

Holy, L. 1987. "Description, Generalization and Comparison: Two Paradigms." In *Comparative Anthropology*, edited by L. Holy, 1–21. Oxford: Blackwell.

Kitcher, P. 1989. "Explanatory Unification and the Causal Structure of the World." In *Scientific Explanation*, edited by P. Kitcher and W. Salmon, 410–505. Minneapolis: University of Minnesota Press.

Krøijer, S. 2015. "Revolution Is the Way You Eat: Exemplification among Left Radical Activists in Denmark and in Anthropology." *Journal of the Royal Anthropological Institute* 21:78–95.

Kyriakides, T., H. Clarke, and X. Zhou. 2017. "Introduction: Anthropology and the Politics of Engagement." *Anthropology Matters* 17. https://doi.org/10.22582/am.v17i1.472.

Latour, B. 1988. "The Politics of Explanation: An Alternative." In *Knowledge and Reflexivity: New Frontiers in the Sociology of Knowledge*, edited by S. Woolgar, 155–176. London: Sage.

———. 2005. *Reassembling the Social: An Introduction to Actor Network Theory*. Oxford: Oxford University Press.

Lévi-Strauss, C. 1963. *Totemism*. Boston: Beacon.

Lipton, P. 2004. *Inference to the Best Explanation*. 2nd ed. London: Routledge.

Peirce, C. S. 1934. *Collected Papers of Charles Sanders Peirce*. Vol. 5, *Pragmatism and Pragmaticism*. Cambridge, MA: Harvard University Press.

Radcliffe-Brown, A. 1951. "The Comparative Method in Social Anthropology." *Journal of the Royal Anthropological Institute* 81:15–22.

Research England. 2020. "How Research England Supports Research Excellence."
    https://re.ukri.org/research/ref-impact/.
Runciman, W. G. 1983. *A Treatise on Social Theory.* Vol. 1, *The Methodology of Social
    Theory.* Cambridge: Cambridge University Press.
Schurz, G. 2008. "Patterns of Abduction." *Synthese* 164:201–234.
Toren, C., and J. de Pina-Cabral. 2011. "Introduction: The Challenge of Epistemology."
    In *The Challenge of Epistemology: Anthropological Perspectives*, edited by C. To-
    ren and J. de Pina-Cabral, 1–18. Oxford: Berghahn.
Van Fraassen, B. C. 1980. *The Scientific Image.* Oxford: Oxford University Press.
Viveiros de Castro, E. 2004. "Perspectival Anthropology and the Method of Controlled
    Equivocation." *Tipiti* 2:3–20.
Weber, M. 1978. *Economy and Society: An Outline of Interpretive Sociology.* Berkeley: Uni-
    versity of California Press.
Woodward, J. 2019. "Scientific Explanation." In *The Stanford Encyclopedia of Philosophy*,
    Winter 2019 ed., edited by E. N. Zalta. Metaphysics Research Lab, Stanford Univer-
    sity. https://plato.stanford.edu/archives/win2019/entries/scientific-explanation/.

Part 1
ON ANTHROPOLOGICAL EXPLANATIONS

ARE THERE ANTHROPOLOGICAL PROBLEMS?

Paolo Heywood

In 1946, at a meeting of the Moral Sciences Club in a room of the Gibbs Building in King's College, Cambridge, Ludwig Wittgenstein and Karl Popper had such a heated disagreement over Popper's talk (entitled "Are There Philosophical Problems?") that Wittgenstein is alleged to have brandished a poker in Popper's face. Subsequently immortalized in the book *Wittgenstein's Poker* (Edmonds and Eidinow 2001; see also Popper 1952), the episode is illustrative of a basic cleavage in late twentieth-century analytic philosophy in relation to its nature and proper task.

To summarize their disagreement all too briefly: Wittgenstein thought that most, if not all, philosophical problems were not really problems. Long before Bruno Latour's comparable argument for the social sciences, Wittgenstein was inveighing against explanation: "I want to say here that it can never be our job to reduce anything to anything, or to explain anything. Philosophy really is 'purely descriptive'" (*The Blue and Brown Books*, 18).[1] He took this position as a consequence of his belief that philosophy is not a set of theories or a body of doctrine but an activity, an idea also to be found in some modern visions of anthropology (e.g., Ingold 2013). Philosophy is an activity—or several different sorts of activity, perhaps—rather than a body of doctrine because it concerns language and the world but is also part of language and the world, and cannot therefore be said to represent either as whole objects, or to represent their limits (hence dooming metaphysics, logic, ethics, and aesthetics, as they had largely been conceived, to "silence"). This is evident in the final parts of the *Tractatus* (1922) and, famously, becomes yet more pronounced in the *Philosophical Investigations* (*PI*), in which it is argued (or, more properly, "shown") that language does not derive meaning from any capacity for representation, but from its use (*PI*, 43). Hence philosophical doctrines that attempt generalizing or representational explanations are to be avoided, and the proper task of philosophy consists of showing how what appear to be problems are in fact consequences of the improper use of language. As an activity, philosophy is thus meant not to solve problems but to dissolve them: "Philosophical problems should *completely* disappear" (*PI*, 133, italics in original). That is also why the *PI* itself takes the form that it does: an eclectic collection of aphoristic discussions of particular examples, in contrast to the systematic propositional structure of the *Tractatus*. The *PI* is itself designed to "show," rather than to tell, and so even the claims it makes regarding meaning and use are themselves not explanations but descriptions, illustrations, and therapeutic interventions (see Crary and Read 2000). We might say, then, that where other philosophers had identified "problems," Wittgenstein saw confusions of linguistic and conceptual categories that required dissolution, rather than resolution.

Popper, on the other hand, thought that there were indeed genuine philosophical problems. Not that these would be purely philosophical—that is, containing no factual or empirical components. Indeed, he thought that the very idea (itself a dogmatic philosophical one) of "purely" philosophical problems was responsible for the mistaken notion that the task of philosophy was to therapize them away. Instead he thought genuine philosophical problems always have urgent, nonphilosophical roots (1952, 130).

I begin with this dispute in order to distinguish between what I take to be two correspondingly different visions of the nature of anthropological problems, to paraphrase Popper. The first, which I think the more prevalent in contemporary anthropology, is broadly Wittgensteinian in form. By this I do not mean that it necessarily draws directly on Wittgenstein, although early examples did—such as Rodney Needham (see later in this chapter). I mean simply that it adopts the view that what may at first sight appear to be anthropological problems (or "ethnographic puzzles," as anthropologists used to call them) are really only artifacts of our perspective or approach. That is, their resolution—or better, their dissolution—may be achieved simply by a reconfiguration of our conceptual or linguistic categories. To this way of thinking, a successful account will reframe its initial question such that the question itself now seems absurd or misposed. It is due to the prevalence of this way of thinking, I suspect, that the once-popular category of the ethnographic puzzle has now largely disappeared from view in anthropological writing.

That older notion of the ethnographic puzzle gestures to a Popperian alternative vision of the nature of anthropological problems, in which there are empirical problems, as well as conceptual ones. Despite the prevalence of the

Wittgensteinian view, a great many works of anthropology begin precisely from a real problem (an ethnographic puzzle, even if it is no longer referred to as such), whether that be about the continued existence or origins of matriliny, prescriptive patrilateral parallel cousin marriage, or feuding, or about whether there is a cultural pattern to the ways in which people experience God (e.g., Richards 1957; Schneider and Gough 1961; Malinowski 1932; Weiner 1976; Needham 1958; Evans-Pritchard 1940; Gluckmann 1955; Luhrmann 2012, this volume).

In this chapter I will endeavor to describe these two visions of what constitutes an "anthropological problem." To the first, in its purest forms, there are no anthropological problems, only conceptual tangles requiring dissolution. To the second, there are problems also requiring explanation. My suggestion will be that rarely do these approaches find themselves in serious debate with each other, with or without pokers, and that rarely are clear and explicit justifications of either particular vision formulated. Many anthropologists may find themselves in sympathy with aspects of both, depending on the situation in which they find themselves, as is reasonable.

However, the contemporary prevalence of the Wittgensteinian form is in large part responsible, I suspect, for the knee-jerk antipathy to explanation Matei Candea and I identify in the introduction to this book. In making the link between this implied Wittegensteinian vision and our attitude to explanation, I want to argue that this negative attitude to explanation stands or falls on the question of whether there are anthropological problems, requiring resolution, or only confusions, amenable to dissolution. In other words, this negative attitude to explanation is fully sustainable only if one thinks the answer to the question, "Are there anthropological problems?" is "No."

I will suggest that that cannot be a sensible answer. In our efforts to purge the discipline of any vestige of "scientism" (e.g., Ingold 2014), we have spent a great deal of time waving anti-explanatory pokers at Popper's ghost. But Wittgenstein may be no better a friend to anthropology than Popper. His vision of philosophy may be perfectly coherent, and indeed correct. But as Popper pointed out, its consequence is to purge philosophy of any interest in empirically answerable questions, or novel data and facts. That cannot be a consequence to which anthropology should aspire, as I illustrate with the help of an ethnographic puzzle drawn from my fieldwork on fascism in Italy.

"Problems Should *Completely* Disappear"

The claim that there are no anthropological problems might sound like an improbable proposition, but there are coherent and defensible reasons for which people might declare explicitly or imply such an answer. Take, for instance, the commonplace that writers should be in the business of "showing," not "telling," and its implication that description trumps explanation or interpretation. This is occasionally applied explicitly to ethnography (e.g., Gullion 2016), but almost any understanding of ethnographic writing will rely, to some degree or another, on the importance of narrative and imagination. "Imagine yourself suddenly set down . . ." is an attempt by Malinowski to bring his readers along with him, to evoke, not just to state or aver a set of ethnographic facts. Despite Malinowski's stress on the importance of collecting and presenting a "scientific" array of statistical and observational data in ethnographic writing, he was also no stranger to the importance of engaging the reader's imagination in order that they "conceptualize . . . what the text could not present in full" (Thornton 1985, 8), hence his notion of "imponderabilia." In a slightly different vein, Evans-Pritchard suggested that an anthropologist's "theoretical conclusions" should be "found to be implicit in an exact and detailed description" (1973, 3). Though that may have a distinctly Latourian ring to a twenty-first century ear, it follows a series of arguments about the necessity of possessing a general theoretical framework within which such a description would make sense: "One cannot study anything without a theory about its nature" (2). The notion that ethnographic writing must involve some degree of "showing" is of course not the same as the claim that "showing" exhausts what ethnographic writing should be doing. That latter claim implies that objects of ethnographic writing require no further elucidation than to be "shown"; they are in themselves revealing of whatever it is that is to be revealed. They are not problems requiring solutions. They need only be properly depicted or described for their nature to be understood.

A related but much more philosophically rigorous justification of this sort of position returns us to Popper's adversary in his argument for the existence of problems in philosophy, for it is in Wittgenstein that it finds its greatest exponent. Wittgenstein's views need no lengthy exposition, and I am far from capable of doing them justice here, so a brief summary must suffice:

> It was true to say that our considerations could not be scientific ones. It was not of any possible interest to us to find out empirically "that, contrary to our preconceived ideas, it is possible to think such-and-such"— whatever that may mean . . . and we may not advance any kind of theory. There must not be anything hypothetical in our considerations. We must do away with all *explanation*, and description alone must take its place. And this description gets its light . . . from philosophical problems. These are, of course, not empirical problems; they are solved, rather, by looking into the workings of our language, and that in such a

way as to make us recognise those workings: *in despite of an* urge to misunderstand them. The problems are solved, not by giving new information, but by arranging what we have always known. (*PI*, 109)

What are the "scientific considerations" that Wittgenstein thinks philosophy should avoid? They are, broadly speaking, general and reductive explanations, which are "the real source of metaphysics, and lead . . . the philosopher into complete darkness" (*The Blue and Brown Books*, 18). Famously, for example, we do not grasp the meaning of a word by possessing a mental picture of a general idea. We do not know how to point to a "leaf" because we have a general idea of a "leaf" (18), or to a "yellow ball" because we have a picture of "yellow": "To see that this is not *necessary*, remember that I could have given . . . the order, 'imagine a yellow patch.' Would you still be inclined to assume that he first imagines a yellow patch just *understanding* my order, and then imagines a yellow patch to match the first!" (11–12). So here we have a vision of problems that are absolutely not amenable to empirical resolution. Nothing—according to Wittgenstein, in any case—can answer as a matter of fact the question of what goes on in someone's mind when ordered to point out the yellow ball, a thing that we call "understanding." What resolves this puzzle instead is linguistic clarity. When we use the word *understanding*, we often imagine it to exist as a full-fledged mental state, complete with mental picture of the general idea of a phenomenon. But Wittgenstein shows us—note the showing, rather than explicit telling—that this makes no sense of our ordinary use of the word *understand*: nobody would require that possession of a mental picture of a yellow patch be a prior requirement to correctly fulfilling the order to conjure up a mental picture of a yellow patch. And in fact, in practice, it is the correct fulfillment of such an order that we take to constitute "understanding" in everyday life—we say the man has "understood" the order if he picks out the yellow ball, not (usually) by checking to see if he has the right mental picture.

It is not difficult to imagine anthropological equivalents of this vision in which terms require rearrangement and clarification for the puzzle to dissolve. Indeed, almost any anthropological argument that relies on some version of the "category mistake" problem (itself a Wittgensteinian notion that comes from Gilbert Ryle [1949]) does this to some degree or another. When Hawaiians killed Captain Cook, were they killing a man, a god, or a chief (Obeyesekere 1992; Sahlins 1985, 1995)? We might put that question on one end of the scale, given the amount of empirical data mustered in support of the various positions. Is paternity a physical, biological relationship of which one can be ignorant, or a conceptual, social relationship that expresses cosmological meaning (Delaney 1986; Leach 1966; Spiro 1968)? This latter is a "purer" Wittgensteinian position, in which it is clearly stated that the "problem" of virgin births is a product of misconstrued meaning and the misposing of questions (Delaney 1986, 494). Are Ifá oracular pronouncements meant to be representational claims about the world, or "inventive definitions" that transform their objects (Holbraad 2009, 2012)? This last example is perhaps as clear an example as is to be found in anthropology, and it has been accompanied by a whole theoretical movement that explicitly figures anthropology's main task as one of reconfiguring concepts in order to render "alterity" sensical (Holbraad and Pedersen 2017).

"His Look Was Fleeting, and He Saw Very Little"

It is not my intention to dispute any of these particular arguments, and the broader "category mistake" framework is probably a fundamental and unshakable form of anthropological reasoning, though it is not always uncontested. Evans-Pritchard's *Azande* is in a sense a response to the category mistake–type argument of Lucien Lévy-Bruhl on primitive mentalities. How can otherwise rational people believe in witchcraft? The Levy-Bruhlian answer would be to find this question misposed, assuming as it does that "rational" and "magical" thought are part of the same set. Evans-Pritchard's (1937) argument and ethnography demonstrate instead just how perfectly possible it is for otherwise "rational" people to attribute causality, in a certain specific sense, to witchcraft.

Similarly, Wittgenstein's views have not been without their critics in philosophy. Popper aside, Ernest Gellner wrote a famously scathing critique in *Words and Things* (1960; see also Gellner 1988); more relevant to present purposes is *The Grasshopper*, by Canadian philosopher Bernard Suits, who framed his argument as follows: "'Don't say,' Wittgenstein admonishes us, 'there must be something common or they would not be called "games"—but look and see whether there is anything common to all.' This is unexceptionable advice. Unfortunately, Wittgenstein himself did not follow it. He looked, to be sure, but because he had decided beforehand that games are indefinable, his look was fleeting, and he saw very little" (1978, x).

The rest of *The Grasshopper* is a highly engaging series of logical demonstrations to the effect that games are indeed definable, but I raise Suits's critique because of what it suggests about Wittgenstein's method and object. I have already noted that the *PI* is not intended to be explanatory, but illustrative or elucidatory. What Suits makes clear is that the thing on which it is performing that operation, whatever one calls it, is not the category "games," and certainly not any actually existing game. An alien wishing to learn about, to have something explained to them of, or elucidated on, football or boxing would do better to pick up Eduardo Archetti (1999) or Loïc Wacquant (2004), and even one simply wishing to learn about the category "games" would probably learn more from Suits than from Wittgenstein.

As far as Wittgenstein goes, this is unsurprising and unobjectionable, since clearly the *PI* is not meant to be a book about games, but about language (or language-games, perhaps, but the point remains). His anti-explanatory method, in other words, is applied to a particular kind of object. He was not, as Suits suggests, actually "looking [at] and seeing" "games" but rather looking at language. As Wittgenstein himself puts it, "Philosophy just puts everything before us, and neither explains nor deduces anything. Since everything lies open to view there is nothing to explain" (*PI*, 126). It concerns, in other words, things—language, above all else—that "lie open to view": "The problems are solved, not by giving new information, but by arranging what we have always known" (109). In other words, his method demands that he can only be "looking [at] and seeing" something he already knows—like language—not something to which new information would be relevant.

While that view of philosophy may have much to recommend it, transposed to anthropology it becomes much more difficult to maintain consistently. Philosophy as an activity may well be the resolution of puzzles to which we already know the answer, in which "everything lies open to view," but it is harder to imagine that all of the objects of anthropology are known to us already in this way, and that in no cases are new empirical data helpful in resolving our problems. The classic vision of the ethnographic puzzle had an ethnographic (i.e., empirical) solution, as in Audrey Richard's various examples of concrete resolutions of the conflict between matriliny and patriarchy. Sometimes "ethnographic puzzles" may well turn out to be Wittgensteinian puzzles, of the sort requiring dissolution rather than solution. But often they concern situations in which everything does not lie open to view, and are thus much more like the "problems" Popper hoped to identify for philosophy: they require explanation.

In the remainder of this chapter, I am going to suggest that these two different perspectives on the character of anthropological problems have very different consequences. I do not suggest that *all* anthropological problems are problems requiring explanations. But neither do I think it sustainable to take the position that *no* anthropological problems have this character, and that position is a logical consequence of the notion that anthropology should not be in the business of explaining. In other words, I think that to inquire about and to make claims for or against "explanation" is not just a question of approach, method, or writing but also necessarily a question of objects. Whatever we are doing (explanation, interpretation, understanding, description, analysis), are we doing it to things we already know, or things about which we wish to know more?

To explain my position more clearly, I proceed to treat an example of what we might think of as an ethnographic puzzle, one focused on a topic that is quite closely related to explanation—namely, "definition." Definition is an especially happy example to discuss for two reasons, beyond its kinship with "explanation" as an allegedly "reductive" activity.

First, it was problems of definition that led anthropologists such as Edmund Leach (1961) and, building on the same ideas, Needham (1971, 1975) to problematize in turn the possibility of explanatory generalization, although neither of them, in fact, wished us to abandon generalization altogether (Leach 1961, 1; Needham 1975, 365). Leach famously, in "Rethinking Anthropology," described the categorizations that led anthropologists to "problems" such as that of matriliny as instances of "butterfly-collecting," declaring that the "problems" originated in the arbitrary categories ("matrilineal society"), not in the world (1961, 2–3). Elsewhere Leach (1984, 17) acknowledged the influence of the later Wittgenstein on his vision of anthropology, but this is much more pronounced and explicit in Needham, who, making a very similar argument a decade later than Leach, in "Remarks on the Analysis of Kinship and Marriage" (1971, 2), cites Leach and Wittgenstein in the same breath as inspirations.

Second, we have, once more, Wittgenstein in general and Needham in particular to thank for the notion that it is not only our anthropological categories that escape definition but also most ethnographic ones we are likely to encounter. Needham's article on the Wittgensteinian notion of "polythetic categories" is famous, like its predecessor, for the argument that the class of societies we once termed "matrilineal" or "patrilocal" in fact contain no single shared predicate that justifies their definition as a set (1975, 365). Worse, even more general categories such as "descent," "marriage," or "kinship" are equally unable to pick out substitutable objects, or equivalent meanings. For these reasons Needham argued that we treat such categories as "polythetic," or as what Wittgenstein would call "family resemblance terms," like the category "games." Polythetic categories and family resemblance terms are not united by any essential quality or predicate that all members of the category share but are instead woven together like a rope, in which different fibers create the stability of the entity, rather than any single one (350). But Needham not only believed that most of our analytical terminology was polythetic in nature; he also believed—unsurprisingly given the influence of Wittgenstein—that ordinary language was too. That is, not just "our" ordinary language but any instance of ordinary language that an anthropologist was likely to encounter, no matter what the indigenous perspective on such a matter might be—"alien concepts" are polythetic, "in a fashion that is similarly unrecognized by those whose modes of thought we want to comprehend" (367).

My intention is not to indict Leach or Needham, who both actually defended explanatory generalization of their own preferred relational form (Needham 1975, 365), but only to indicate that in treating a problem of definition, I am treating a problem central to the question of anthropological problems, as well as one that is also, in some sense, a quintessential example of what a nonproblem looks like to a certain sort of anthropology. That is, if you take the position that all concepts and categories are polythetic in nature (i.e., that they share no single quality or predicate), then any problem of definition is—by definition, as it were—not in fact a problem. If you know already that definition is impossible for you as well as for your interlocutors, then you need not worry about explaining—rather than describing—any given instance of it beyond stating that fact.

To illustrate how this may be unsatisfactory, I will describe a problem of definition I have encountered in the course of recent fieldwork on fascism in Italy. Before doing so, however, I want to do a little more to characterize the Wittgensteinian approach to definitions in anthropology, drawing on Needham in particular.

The Puzzle of Definitions

Any specific practice of definition that may appear to give rise to a problem, as I have just suggested, has a very easy answer if you take the position that going in search of definitions is necessarily a fruitless endeavor. Or rather, such a problem is dissolved because what is in fact going on is clearly something other than a practice of definition as we might be wont to imagine it—what is going instead are moves in a game, say, or perhaps the manipulation of terminology to suit a particular set of aims. In other words, we may know already, having read Needham or Wittgenstein, that defining words or categories in the way we imagine definition to work is impossible because words or categories do not consistently pick out the same objects or sorts of object in the world, being rather tools or devices with which to intervene in that world, the objects in which, in any case, do not possess essential qualities or properties that could be picked out by words. Knowing this, we may concern ourselves instead with describing instances of definition, with what they do, with their context, their tone and inflection, with the intentions we may or may not be able to read behind them, et cetera.

I hasten to add at this point that arguing for explanation is not the same as arguing against description. Clearly such description is a necessary condition for an anthropological account of whatever one wishes to call the activity of trying to define a concept. I am going to suggest, though, that it may not always be a sufficient one.

Consider the précis of the kind of account I have just provided. Here we have what some (Popper and Gellner, for instance) would call a doctrine, an explanation, a theory, or a "telling," and what others might want to call an illustration, an elucidation, or a "showing," but which in either case is performing an operation on "definition" qua definition as a philosophical question. The nature of that explanation/elucidation is to tell/show that definition is impossible. Then you have a descriptive activity that shows some particular (pseudo-)definition in action as composed of all of the contextual factors that really matter to it.

We can see this sort of account in action in Needham's "polythetic categories" article. Needham's explanatory/elucidatory object in that paper was the broad question of how categories function. Like the notion of "family resemblance," his account of the concept of a polythetic category tells us something near the maximal level of generality about the way in which language works and provides us with a tool with which to describe—but not to explain—the uses of such categories in any given and specific circumstance. So his account requires a (monothetic) definition of "monothetic" and "polythetic" categories, but from that point further requires no such definitional practice, as any given term can be described as either one or the other, the majority of course being "polythetic" and amenable to description, not explanation. He is not attempting to explain what any particular category means, so further ethnographic nuance has no particular use.

But the effect of such an account—though eminently suited to Needham's goal for it—is to erase the level in between that of maximal philosophical generality (an explanation of how language works) and minimal ethnographic particularity (a description of how any given polythetic term is actually deployed). The only form of explanation or definition it permits is the—by definition, as it were—universal, generic explanation and definition of something as a "polythetic category." Like the *PI*, its object is language as an object we already know, rather than any particular or specific problem originating in something we do not already know. It tells us about language, rather than about games, or matriliny, or marriage, or descent.

That would be one way to treat an ethnographic problem of definition, roughly corresponding to the method of "dissolving" it, against which Popper was arguing. The punch of the resolution—its dissolution—comes in rearranging our perspective on a thing we already know ("definition" as a generic activity) such that it no longer comes to appear as a problem. Martin Holbraad's work on Cuban divination is a highly convincing anthropological example of exactly this sort of approach to questions of definition, about which I have written elsewhere

(Heywood 2018a, 2018b; Holbraad 2009, 2012). This is not the only way in which one might treat such a problem, however, as I suggest later. An alternative, and more straightforwardly explanatory, approach would look for resolution in the concrete specifics of the problem.

"Dogs and I Do Not Know What Else"

The specific problem I deal with here is a fairly general one, rather than one that is highly ethnographically specific, although it does arise from my current field-work. That generality does not change its form as a problem to be resolved empirically, however; it merely expands the relevance of that resolution, I hope. As I have been suggesting, one consequence of the foregoing approach to anthropological knowledge—quite explicit in Leach (1961), for example—is that it erases the possibility of what we might think of as "restricted generalizations," or indeed "comparison" of a certain form (cf. Candea 2018, 101–103, on "caveated generalizations"). Both Leach and Needham, for instance, make universal generalizations (Needham in linguistic form and Leach in structural, mathematical form), and obviously they leave open the possibility of particular description in any given case. What they close off is what we might—albeit not altogether happily—think of as the level in between: any invocation of a classificatory analytic term that ties it to a particular sort of context (whatever the nature of the context) and distinguishes it from others. We cannot employ the category "matrilineal" to distinguish some societies from others. Of course, as Candea points out, we continue to do this "with a pinch of salt" all the time (2018, 209–211).

The problem I will address is one raised in my own field site, but it is certainly not confined to that context. It runs as follows: Why does it appear to many people in Europe and the United States that, as George Orwell put it in 1944, "of all the unanswered questions of our time, perhaps the most important is, 'what is fascism?'" To be clear, then, my problem is not the definitional problem of "What is fascism?" but the explanatory problem of "Why do people continue to put so much energy and passion into looking for definitions of 'what fascism is'?"

Trying to define fascism is a particularly fraught endeavor. Historical and political arguments over the proper meaning and definition of fascism have been taking place since it first emerged as a phenomenon in the 1920s and show no immediate sign of cooling off. A range of definitions have been proffered by eminent historians of the subject in search of a "fascist minimum" (Eatwell 1996), while at least one prominent scholar became so frustrated by the ambiguous use of the term that he famously called for it to be banned from historical discourse (Allardyce 1979). Orwell, in raising the question of "what fascism is," was making nearly the same point in remarking that he had heard the word applied to "farmers, shopkeepers, Social Credit, corporal punishment, fox-hunting, bull-fighting, the 1922 Committee, the 1941 Committee, Kipling, Gandhi, Chiang Kai-Shek, homosexuality, Priestley's broadcasts, Youth Hostels, astrology, women, dogs and I do not know what else" (1944). Historians and other academics have defined fascism as, among other things, a petit-bourgeois response to the development of socialism (see, for instance, Poulantzas 1974; Trotsky 1944), a psychological phenomenon resulting from a kind of mass hysteria (Reich 1933), a species of "developmental dictatorship" (Gregor 1979), a palingenetic form of ultranationalism (Griffin 1991), and a sort of religion masquerading as a political movement (Gentile 1990), to name only a few such definitions.

Recently these debates have become yet more fraught by, as it were, coming alive. They have moved from residing largely or entirely in the realm of scholarly journals and academic conferences into the world that such journals and conferences aim to investigate, from the abstract to the concrete, from analysis to object (*Slate* magazine, for example, printed an excerpt from Kevin Passmore's *Fascism: A Very Short Introduction* as part of its academy series on fascism, suggesting readers consult the extract to determine whether they were living in a "fascist state" [Onion, Thomas, and Keating, n.d.]; the *Atlantic*, noting the "elusiveness" of definitions of fascism, interviewed Robert Paxton in search of a checklist of features to assess the extent to which Donald Trump is a fascist [Green 2016]). The pages of international news and commentary are filled with speculation as to whether and how far France's National Front, Germany's Alternative for Germany, or Austria's Freedom Party "count" or do not "count" as "fascist," and the word was even in the running to be *Merriam-Webster's* "word of the year" in 2016.

Fascism is in some sense an obvious candidate example of a family resemblance term or a polythetic category. Since its coinage at the end of the First World War, it has provoked virulent argument and debate over what exactly it means and how it should be defined, debate that shows no signs of abating at present, and which is in fact increasing in volume as various contemporary political figures and movements are labeled with the term. Part of the reason it provokes such debate is that such figures and movements, both past and present, do not appear to share any single predicate that qualifies them for membership in the class (see, for example, Allardyce 1979). Of course, this might be said to be true of other political movements (and I have described "communism" in Bologna in a similar fashion [Heywood 2015]). But the problem is exacerbated by a number of factors in the case of fascism, including the lack of any clear doctrinal text, inconsistency of practice and policy on the part of "fascist" regimes, an apparent aversion to ideological or theoretical self-definition on the part of self-declared fascists themselves (at least some of whom might well have approved of the notion of fascism as a "family resemblance"), and the peculiar fact that fascist movements have been, if they have been anything, usually ultranationalist in character while also—arguably—forming a supranational object of some form.[2]

All of these factors, as well as more traditional problems of definition, combine to make it extremely difficult to define *fascism*, while apparently doing nothing to dispel—and indeed perhaps fueling—the appetite of historians, political scientists, journalists, commentators, and ordinary people for attempting to do so.

One such attempt is an article in the *New York Review of Books* by Umberto Eco (1995), which lists many of the aforementioned problems with defining fascism and concludes that it is, in fact, an excellent example of a family resemblance term. The term *family resemblance* also recurs frequently in modern newspaper and magazine accounts of the rise of the Far Right in Europe and the United States, in arguments both for the fact that Donald Trump and Marine Le Pen are in some sense parts of the same phenomenon and for their further inclusion within an "ur-fascism" that would also cover its historical manifestations (e.g., Esposito 2015; McDougall 2016).

Eco's specific suggestion is that, like *game* in Wittgenstein's original argument, "fascism became an all-purpose term because one can eliminate from a fascist regime one or more features, and it will still be recognizable as fascist" (1995). There is clearly a sense in which *fascism* is indeed an "all-purpose term," the same sense that makes Eco's argument compelling for many historians and contemporary political commentators worried about the (mis)application of the term.

But for precisely that reason, Eco's analogy is slightly misleading. For many of the people he is addressing, that audience of historians, political commentators, and indeed many contemporary Italians, the word *fascism* is not at all like the word *game*, in that its proper definition and application are *exactly* what they are concerned with. That is from whence Eco's argument derives its power: it sounds like it is a description of how a word is being used but is in fact a prescription for how it ought to be used. It competes with, rather than explains, other attempts at definitions of fascism, in the same way in which I have suggested the concept of "polythetic categories" was explicitly intended by Needham to compete with people's practices of monothetic definition, and in the same way in which Suits points out of Wittgenstein that he knew already that games were indefinable, without in fact having to "look and see." It might explain "what fascism is" in ordinary language terms, but what it certainly does is to explain away why that question matters to people in the first place. It is a form of "therapy" in the sense that Wittgenstein intended philosophy to be, in that it aims at the dissolution of the problem of defining fascism by pointing to the mistaken premise of the problem—namely, that fascism has or should have a definition.

To sum up, then, I am suggesting that it is perfectly possible to see the question, "What is fascism?" as a sort of Wittgensteinian puzzle, amenable to dissolution. But I am also suggesting that such a reading risks missing something worth explaining, not about definitions but about fascism—namely, the problem of why it is that people appear so concerned to define it in the first place. In other words, it may or may not be true that "What is fascism?" is a misposed question. But whether it is or not is entirely immaterial to the question of why people we might study keep on asking it. It would be relevant if we saw our task, as Wittgenstein did, as being the therapeutic one of correcting such misposed questions. But this would be an unusual position for an anthropologist to take, to say the least, and it is not mine here. Mine, again, is the question of why the search for definitions persists in the case of fascism.

Debates of a comparable intensity and range do not go on over the proper meaning of *socialism* or *liberalism*, for example, and users of those terms—at least in English—do not usually feel the need to consult experts in order to assess whether their usage is correct (which is not to say that such consultation would be always unhelpful). One clear difference between *fascism* and those terms is that there are comparably fewer people involved in such debates who would define themselves with the word, though, as I will describe, there are some. One might then think that the inability to rely on oneself as a yardstick of meaning, and the comparable dearth of self-declared exemplars of fascism to whom one might turn instead, is a factor contributing to the continuation of such arguments, and this is no doubt correct, though I think not the whole story. Another important and related difference is the fact that *fascist* is more often used as a term of disapprobation than comparable terms, though this fact alone is again not enough to explain a craving for definition, given that everyday terms of disapprobation are habitually used without the least interest in whether they technically apply to the people they are employed to describe (someone may be a "bastard" without us needing evidence that they were born out of wedlock).

To take another academic example, one that combines the characteristics of lacking self-declared referents as well as that of being used as a term of disapprobation: *neoliberal* and *neoliberalism* are notoriously nonspecific in meaning. Far from those characteristics leading to a clamoring for clarity or extensive debates over proper usage, in other words, scholars who use the terms seem to revel in their ambiguity and the capaciousness of their referential universe (see, e.g., Muehlebach 2012). It is usually those who, for whatever reason, do not tend to use the terms who demand some greater precision of meaning (see, e.g., Eriksen et al. 2015; Ferguson 2010; Heywood 2014).

As I have described it thus far, the problem I have been treating is why *fascism* appears to attract a certain sort of definitional or indexical attitude. That is, a wide range of people have, since its inception as a political movement, worried or theorized about the question, "What is fascism?" as Orwell succinctly put it, and in doing so they have often proffered specific answers to that question, such as a palingenetic form of ultra-nationalism (Griffin 1991) or resistance to transcendence (Nolte 1966), to give two quite specific instances, and they have also tended to do so in full awareness of the fact that others have proffered alternative, but often equally specific, answers. They have, in other words, treated *fascism* as if it were, in effect, a sort of natural kind term, or a species of rigid designation.

Originating in the work of post- and, in at least some sense, anti-Wittgensteinian philosopher Saul Kripke, a rigid designator is a word that is used with what Hilary Putnam calls an "indexical intention," in that it is designed persistently to pick out the same sort of object, regardless of the knowledge the user has about the nature of that object (Kripke 1980; Putnam 1975). The paradigm case is the way in which we tend to use proper names: roughly speaking, if I say, "Nixon was the president of the United States," then I use the word Nixon intending to pick out one and only one particular object in the world, and then I attribute to that object a description, in this case, "was the president of the United States." If I likewise say, "Nixon may not have been president of the United States," my intention is to speak about a possible world in which that description does not apply, but the whole point of the usage of the name Nixon in that context is that it still denotes the same person. I use the name, in other words, to rigidly designate the same object no matter what description is also true of the object. This is also often the case with very clearly indexical terms such as pronouns (*you, he, she*) and words like *now, today,* and *yesterday,* which are usually not used as, even though they can be read as, disguised descriptions.

A subspecies of rigid designators is legal terms, like *theft, murder, arson,* and so on (Marmor 2013, 581–587). These words, when used in legal contexts, are often intended to designate a special sort of act, and no other. Newspapers refer to "alleged" crimes until those crimes have been proved in court, and we habitually refer to "joyriding," for instance, rather than theft when discussing the crime of taking a car for the purpose of cruising around in it rather than for the purpose of depriving the owner of it (even if we do not properly understand the legal distinction). As Paul Dresch has put it in regard to the importance of categories in legalistic thinking, "One has to have an idea of, for instance, 'kinsmen,' and of what they should do, as distinct from experience of my particular brother or cousin, before one can complain of them not doing it. Legalism makes such categories explicit" (2012, 12). Note also how this framing runs decidedly against the grain of Wittgenstein's arguments about generalism and mental pictures.

Fascism has a historical existence as a legal term of art across Europe. In Italy, for example, in the closing stages of the Second World War and subsequently, the Allies and the postfascist Italian government institutionalized a range of measures designed to "de-fascistize" the Italian state (see, e.g., Domenico 1991). They issued lengthy questionnaires to state employees in an attempt to evaluate exactly how "fascist" they were; they criminalized attempts to reconstitute the fascist party in the postwar constitution by specifying some of the means by which this might be recognized. In the case of the Nuremberg Trials, the rigid designation employed was even more specific, and the court declared membership of the leadership corps of the Nazi Party, of the SS, and of the Gestapo and SD to be a criminal offense in and of itself, notwithstanding other offenses they may have committed.

The success of such attempts at rigidly designating what it means to be a fascist is a different question. Much of the modern anxiety over the term no doubt stems from the sense that these attempts were highly unsuccessful, that we ought to be able to say why Donald Trump, for example, is, in fact, a fascist, and that the right form of rigid designation would allow us to do so. This would also explain the current fascination with a search for "experts" on fascism, and the hope that a historian of, say, Vichy France could provide us with a way of pointing at figures such as Trump and stating why they are fascist. I have written elsewhere of the lack of success these attempts have had in Italy, in particular, and how that explains the persistence of a personality cult of Benito Mussolini centered on Predappio, the site of my current fieldwork (Heywood 2019, 2020).

My point for present purposes is merely that the historical status of *fascism* as a legalistic rigid designator is a candidate explanation for a problem ("Why are we in search of definitions of fascism?") that does not require us to reconstrue the meaning of one of its terms (*definition*). People look for essential and defining features of fascism because they imagine it in the same way in which they imagine *murder* or *theft*. This explanation may of course be mistaken. But to say instead only that *fascism* has no definition because it is a polythetic or family resemblance term is not to explain the fact that people search for definitions but to explain it away. It is to add no new information about "fascism" the concept (or the object in the world), only about *fascism*, the word.

Conclusion

Reshuffling our conceptual categories is no doubt frequently a helpful exercise. But it cannot be the only one we pursue. It leaves the facts of the matter unchanged, when closer investigation of those facts may yet yield valuable results. Had Evans-Pritchard left interest in Azande rationality and witchcraft at the level of a "category mistake," we would have none of his specific insights on the particular nature of Azande thought on causality, nor the insight that that thought resembles our own in certain surprising respects.

Most anthropology undoubtedly occupies both the Wittgensteinian and Popperian modes at different points. But in order to do that, it must explain, as well as describe. Not all questions simply dissolve in good description. That conclusion follows necessarily from the fact that anthropology's objects are not only objects about which new empirical information is irrelevant. The Wittgensteinian position on philosophy as "pure description" only makes sense because the description in question already takes understanding for granted. The famous "look, and see" injunction, as Suits argued, is really unnecessary because part of the point is that the reader *already knows*, in some sense, the truth of Wittgenstein's claims, because they are descriptions of how the reader themselves ordinarily uses language.

The objects of anthropological knowledge are often both more and less than this. They are "more" in the sense that we do not possess understanding about them in advance, such that all that is required to grasp them is the correct slotting of them into place in an already-existing conceptual schema. They are "less," if you will, because they are usually far more specific than, say, "language." To take Needham as an example one final time: "The outcome of analyses of this kind should not be seen merely as a local or technical rectification of European academic argument, but as pointing to a general hazard of language which presumably afflicts men in any tradition when they classify their fellows and their nature" (1975, 367). The whole structure of this sort of argument obligates it to explain— or show, more generously—something universal about language, while denying it the ability to explain anything more specific, because the universal fact shown is that explanation is impossible. Anthropologists usually "look, and see" a little more closely than this.

Beyond the specific question of the enduring value of explanation, the "dissolution versus explanation" distinction outlined here may also be a useful heuristic in thinking through the sorts of questions that any ethnographer is likely to face. Resolving a problem by declaring the question to be misposed may often be very tempting, but before doing so it is worth asking not only whether in fact an empirical resolution is imaginable but also what sort of object one wishes to treat: a great strength of the dissolution orientation is that dissolving a problem often reveals something illuminating about anthropological categories, as Needham did, for example; an equivalent strength of explaining the resolution of a problem is that it is arguably more likely to yield some substantive ethnographic and empirical insight. Unlike Popper, who makes his disapproval of questions of disciplinary method and epistemology clear despite addressing such questions at length in his Moral Sciences Club paper (1952), I have no intention of suggesting that illuminating anthropological categories is an inappropriate aim. Only that it does not serve us when we confuse it with that of actually answering an ethnographic question.

NOTES

Acknowledgments: I am very grateful to all the participants in the workshop on explanation from which this chapter and book result, and to Matei Candea for organizing that workshop with me. I am also grateful to Simon Blackburn, Harri Englund, and James Laidlaw for their very helpful thoughts and comments on this chapter, and to the participants of the social anthropology seminar at Oxford University for their comments and questions on an earlier version of it.

1. Unless otherwise noted, all citations are from Wittgenstein 1998.

2. This is with the exception of the extremely short entry in the *Italian Encyclopaedia* of 1932, which was at least partly devoted to rejecting the notion of "doctrine."

REFERENCES

Allardyce, G. 1979. "What Fascism Is Not: Thoughts on the Deflation of a Concept." *American Historical Review* 84:367–388.

Archetti, E. 1999. *Masculinities: Football, Polo, and the Tango in Argentina*. London: Bloomsbury.

Candea, M. 2018. *Comparison in Anthropology: The Impossible Method*. Cambridge: Cambridge University Press.

Crary, A., and R. Read. 2000. *The New Wittgenstein*. London: Routledge.

Delaney, C. 1986. "The Meaning of Paternity and the Virgin Birth Debate." *Man* 21:494–513.

Domenico, R. 1991. *Italian Fascists on Trial, 1943–1948*. Chapel Hill: University of North Carolina Press.

Dresch, P. 2012. "Introduction: Legalism, Anthropology and History: A View from Part of Anthropology." In *Legalism: Anthropology and History*, edited by P. Dresch and H. Skoda, 1–37. Oxford: Oxford University Press.

Eatwell, R. 1996. "On Defining the 'Fascist Minimum': The Centrality of Ideology." *Journal of Political Ideologies* 1:303–319.

Eco, U. 1995. "Ur-Fascism." *New York Review of Books*, June 22, 1995. http://www.nybooks.com/articles/1995/06/22/ur-fascism/.

Edmonds, D., and J. Eidinow. 2001. *Wittgenstein's Poker*. London: Faber and Faber.

Eriksen, T., J. Laidlaw, J. Mair, K. Martin, and S. Venkatesan. 2015. "The Concept of Neoliberalism Has Become an Obstacle to the Anthropological Understanding of the Twenty-First Century: Debate." *Journal of the Royal Anthropological Institute* 21:911–923.

Esposito, F. 2015. *Fascism, Aviation and Mythical Modernity*. London: Springer.

Evans-Pritchard, E. 1937. *Witchcraft, Oracles, and Magic among the Azande*. Oxford: Clarendon.

——. 1940. *The Nuer: A Description of the Modes of Livelihood and Political Institutions of a Nilotic People*. Oxford: Clarendon.

——. 1973. "Some Reminiscences and Reflections on Fieldwork." *Journal of the Anthropological Society of Oxford* 4:1–12.

Ferguson, J. 2010. "The Uses of Neoliberalism." *Antipode* 41:166–184.

Gellner, E. 1960. *Words and Things*. London: Penguin.

——. 1988. "The Stakes in Anthropology." *American Scholar* 57:17–30.

Gentile, E. 1990. "Fascism as Political Religion." *Journal of Contemporary History* 25:229–251.

Gluckmann, M. 1955. "The Peace in the Feud." *Past and Present* 8:1–14.

Green, D. 2016. "The Elusive Definition of 'Fascist.'" *Atlantic*, December 18, 2016. https://www.theatlantic.com/politics/archive/2016/12/fascism-populism-presidential-election/510668/.

Gregor, A. 1979. *Italian Fascism and Developmental Dictatorship.* Princeton, NJ: Princeton University Press.

Griffin, R. 1991. *The Nature of Fascism.* London: Psychology Press.

Gullion, J. 2016. "Show, Don't Tell." In *Writing Ethnography*, 75–78. Rotterdam: Sense Publishing.

Heywood, P. 2014. "Neoliberal Nation? Mobbing and Morality in Italy." *Journal of the Royal Anthropological Institute* 20:151–153.

——. 2015. "Equivocal Locations: Being 'Red' in 'Red Bologna.'" *Journal of the Royal Anthropological Institute* 21:855–871.

——. 2018a. *After Difference: Queer Activism in Italy and Anthropological Theory.* Oxford: Berghahn.

——. 2018b. "Making Difference: Queer Activism and Anthropological Theory." *Current Anthropology* 59:314–331.

——. 2019. "Fascism, Uncensored: Legalism and Neofascist Pilgrimage in Predappio, Italy." *Terrain* 72:86–103.

——. 2020. "Ordinary Exemplars: Cultivating the Everyday in the Birthplace of Fascism." *Comparative Studies in Society and History* 64:91–121.

Holbraad, M. 2009. "Ontography and Alterity: Defining Anthropological Truth." *Social Analysis* 53:80–93.

——. 2012. *Truth in Motion: The Recursive Anthropology of Cuban Divination.* Chicago: University of Chicago Press.

Holbraad, M., and M. Pedersen. 2017. *The Ontological Turn: An Anthropological Exposition.* Cambridge: Cambridge University Press.

Ingold, T. 2013. *Making: Anthropology, Archaeology, Art, and Architecture.* London: Routledge.

——. 2014. "That's Enough about Ethnography!" *HAU: Journal of Ethnographic Theory* 4:383–395.

Kripke, S. 1980. *Naming and Necessity.* Cambridge, MA: Harvard University Press.

Leach, E. 1961. "Rethinking Anthropology." In *Rethinking Anthropology*, 1–28. London: Athlone.

——. 1966. "Virgin Birth." *Proceedings of the Royal Anthropological Institute of Great Britain and Ireland*, no. 1966:39–49.

——. 1984. "Glimpses of the Unmentionable in the History of British Social Anthropology." *Annual Review of Anthropology* 13:1–23.

Luhrmann, T. 2012. *When God Talks Back: Understanding the American Evangelical Relationship with God.* New York: Alfred Knopf.

Malinowski, B. 1932. *The Sexual Life of Savages.* London: Routledge.

Marmor, A. 2013. "Meaning and Belief in Constitutional Interpretation." *Fordham Law Review* 82:577–596.

McDougall, J. 2016. "No, This Isn't the 1930s—but Yes, This Is Fascism." The Conversation, November 16, 2016. http://theconversation.com/no-this-isnt-the-1930s-but-yes-this-is-fascism-68867.

Muehlebach, A. 2012. *The Moral Neoliberal: Welfare and Citizenship in Italy.* Chicago: University of Chicago Press.

Needham, R. 1958. "The Formal Analysis of Prescriptive Patrilateral Cross-Cousin Marriage." *Southwestern Journal of Anthropology* 14:199–219.

——. 1971. "Remarks on the Analysis of Kinship and Marriage." In *Rethinking Kinship and Marriage*, edited by R. Needham, 1–34. London: Tavistock.

——. 1975. "Polythetic Classification: Convergence and Consequences." *Man* 10:349–369.

Nolte, E. 1966. *Three Faces of Fascism*. New York: Halt, Rinehart, and Winston.

Obeyesekere, G. 1992. *The Apotheosis of Captain Cook: European Myth-Making in the Pacific*. Princeton, NJ: Princeton University Press.

Onion, R., J. Thomas, and J. Keating. n.d. "Fascism: A Slate Academy." Slate. Accessed January 3, 2023. http://www.slate.com/articles/slate_plus/fascism.html.

Orwell, G. 1944. "What Is Fascism?" *Tribune* (London). https://www.orwell.ru/library/articles/As_I_Please/english/efasc.

Popper, K. 1952. "The Nature of Philosophical Problems and Their Roots in Science." *British Journal for the Philosophy of Science* 3:124–156.

Poulantzas, N. 1974. *Fascism and Dictatorship: The Third International and the Problem of Fascism*. London: Verso.

Putnam, H. 1975. "The Meaning of 'Meaning.'" *Minnesota Studies in the Philosophy of Science* 7:131–193.

Reich, W. 1933. *The Mass Psychology of Fascism*. London: Souvenir Press.

Richards, A. 1957. *Chisungu: A Girl's Initiation Ceremony among the Bemba of Northern Rhodesia*. New York: Grove.

Ryle, G. 1949. *The Concept of Mind*. London: Hutchinson.

Sahlins, M. 1985. *Islands of History*. Chicago: University of Chicago Press.

——. 1995. *How "Natives" Think about Captain Cook, for Example*. Chicago: University of Chicago Press.

Schneider, D., and K. Gough. 1961. *Matrilineal Kinship*. Berkeley: University of California Press.

Spiro, M. 1968. "Virgin Birth, Parthenogenesis, and Physiological Paternity: An Essay in Cultural Interpretation." *Man* 3:242–261.

Suits, B. 1978. *The Grasshopper: Games, Life, and Utopia*. Toronto: University of Toronto Press.

Thornton, R. 1985. "'Imagine Yourself Set Down . . .': Mach, Frazer, Conrad, Malinowski, and the Role of Imagination in Ethnography." *Anthropology Today* 1:7–14.

Trotsky, L. 1944. "Fascism: What It Is and How to Fight It." Marxists Internet Archive. https://www.marxists.org/archive/trotsky/works/1944/1944-fas.htm.

Wacquant, L. 2004. *Body and Soul: Notebooks of an Apprentice Boxer*. Oxford: Oxford University Press.

Weiner, A. 1976. *Women of Value, Men of Renown*. Austin: University of Texas Press.

Wittgenstein, L. 1922. *Tractatus Logico-philosophicus*. London: Kegan Paul.

——. 1998. *The Collected Works of Ludwig Wittgenstein*. Edited by G. E. M. Anscombe, G. H. von Wright, R. Rhees, and H. Nyman. Oxford: Blackwell.

2

ON ANTHROPOLOGICAL FINDINGS

Tanya M. Luhrmann

An explanation is an account of one thing in terms of another thing that makes sense of the first thing for an audience familiar with the second thing. We explain the news differently to a child than to a friend. A doctor explains test results differently to a patient than in an academic talk given to her peers. Explanation depends on audience, and in anthropology, the expectations of the audience have shifted substantially since the discipline was founded. We used to see cultural differences, and those comparisons became the crux of what we wanted to explain. No longer.

We know the story well. Margaret Mead and Bronislaw Malinowski set out to use the comparison of people living differently elsewhere to show that the assumptions Americans and Europeans often made about human nature were sometimes wrong. Then came the tumult of the 1960s. Chastened by critiques about power and exploitation, anthropologists began to think about anthropology not so much as a field about explanation through comparison between societies but more as a means to witness the injustices inflicted by some societies on others (Robbins 2013). They became more hesitant to talk about direct comparison, because they became so aware of the many ways comparison can go astray. In one paper, a group of young anthropologists write, "Of all the social and historical sciences, anthropology is perhaps that which is most formally aligned with the very idea of the comparative. . . . Yet in practice, social and cultural anthropology may be one of the least comparative disciplines" (Miller et al. 2019, 284). "Where have all the comparisons gone?" bemoans a more senior group (Borofsky et al. 2019). "Where did anthropology go?" asks Maurice Bloch (2005, 1).

The time has come to bring back comparison. Elsewhere (Weisman and Luhrmann 2020), I give a reasoned philosophical and methodological account of this argument. Here I want to explain why comparison can feel liberating for an anthropologist, and how anthropological comparison can open up new vistas in which to think and to explain.

I arrived in Cambridge to study anthropology in 1981. For me, Cambridge was a lot like Hogwarts. By late October, the streets went dark before late afternoon, and the leaves skittered across the flagstones in the damp wind. It was damp; it was always damp in Cambridge, and it was easy to believe that there were ancient secrets in the old stone walls. In their shadows, anthropology seemed like something very new. In fact, early founders of the discipline still lunched in college. Meyer Fortes, Edmund Leach, and Audrey Richards sometimes came to the department's Friday seminar. E. E. Evans-Pritchard's niece sold fabric at the end of the street. Where anthropology had seemed like one major among others at my undergraduate American university, at Cambridge anthropology seemed like a young, brash discipline that challenged tradition with mud-splashed truths.

In that heady world, the queen of the social sciences was philosophy, not economics (as people sometimes said back home). Down the corridors where John Maynard Keynes had walked, the ghosts that seemed to matter to the anthropology department were philosophical ones. I read through Ludwig Wittgenstein my second year in graduate school the way young American anthropologists now read Giorgio Agamben, with the sense that these were the texts that serious students mastered (see Heywood, this volume). I attended Elizabeth Anscombe's last lectures as if they were glimpses of the grail. She was perhaps Wittgenstein's best student, and she had translated the version of *On Certainty* that I read. One day in class, she was struggling to ferret out the meaning of a sentence in the text. Why, she asked us, had Wittgenstein used the direct article for this noun? There was a long pause in which she looked thoughtfully at her notes. Then she said suddenly, "Ah! I mistranslated that sentence." Another day, a timid young scholar poked his head into the room and asked us whether this was a class on the philosophy of knowledge. Anscombe gave him a long, measured look. "You could say that," she responded. "But that is not what you mean."

There was a clear sense that the philosophers were the smart, respected cultural insiders and that anthropologists were slightly scrubby outsiders. The sharpest anthropology students went to talks by Bernard Williams and Quentin Skinner and they read Willard Quine and Saul Kripke. The department turned out almost to a person when Richard Rorty came to town. When Jack Goody retired, the department hired a man trained as a philosopher, Ernest Gellner, to take his place. He became my adviser. My generation—Pascal Boyer, James Laidlaw, Simon Coleman, Henrietta Moore—all started out writing as if our ultimate goal was to persuade analytic philosophers to think differently about belief, just as Evans-Pritchard had done.

The problem, of course, was that while the philosophers loved having a direct source of sublunary Martians, as Clifford Geertz so splendidly observed, they weren't very interested in anthropology. They no longer read books by anthropologists. And the anthropologists were not, in general, much good at philosophical argument. That was not just because philosophers use language in very special ways, honed by years of training. (Here a comment by Wittgenstein comes to mind. A group of men are seated under a tree, he wrote, discussing whether the tree exists. They are not mad, he explained. They are doing philosophy [1969, 120, n.467].) It was because the kind of thing that the philosophers were doing—their basic philosophical project—was not anthropological. The philosophers were ultimately interested in the language game of coming up with a compelling description of words like *belief*. The anthropologists were trying to explain what was going on when their field subjects sacrificed a cow. As a result, the anthropological work on belief was becoming increasingly frustrating, culminating in Rodney Needham's (1973) book on the subject, which managed to argue that no one believed anything at all.

Meanwhile the problem with Wittgenstein—and with Michel Foucault, Agamben, and the other philosophers young anthropologists read today—was that their questions were so big that no empirical research could answer them (see Heywood, this volume). These authors invite us to reflect on what we know already about human life and to think about it differently, rather than setting us empirical puzzles we can solve. They ask, What is the nature of human understanding? rather than, Why do the English bury their dead and the Zoroastrians leave their bodies to be picked clean by vultures? This was also the era when Clifford Geertz was arguing that anthropology was more like literary criticism than it was like science. That suggested that the details of what fieldworkers discovered weren't particularly important as discoveries (although one could say that this was not quite what Geertz had meant). After all, the task of a literary critic is to interpret novels readers have already read, and to help readers into a different understanding of them. Literary critics deliver new understandings, not new data. Then Geertz's postmodern critics took him to task for his arrogance in claiming to represent the Other. The new intellectual environment— the crisis in representation, the postcolonial critique, the comparison to literary criticism—led many of us to think of ethnography more as interpretation than as discovery research. To be sure, we all understood that our goal was to have a question that fieldwork could answer. But the climate invited us to imagine that our goal was to evoke and to challenge rather than to do what other social scientists did, which was to find out something new and explain why it mattered.

In fact, back in the day, as a young graduate student emerging into an intellectual world shaped by the postmodern and postcolonial critique and by Geertz's lush prose, I imagined that the goal of the book of the research—the ethnography as published—was to provide an account of another world that would capture that world perfectly in a literary way and as elegantly as Geertz had done. One's goal was surely to write a book that would live forever, just as the books of Evans-Pritchard and Fortes had done. It would have to be a humble book, acute in its understanding of the limits of observation, because that was how the critique had schooled us. And because it was humble, it would explain something in particular—that other world—but nothing in general. This was the chastening effect of critique. The effect was to shift one's ambitions away from empirical argument (what *was* the social effect of literacy?) to imagining the ideal book as a gem: compelling, precise, complete. Such a book would stand on its own to challenge the reader's assumptions. It would make the strange familiar and the familiar change; it would present a complete picture of its ethnographic topic; and nothing more needed to be said.

And of course, this way of imagining the ethnographic book sets the bar impossibly high. If the goal was to astonish, the job had already been done. Once we have the Azande, how many more sublunary Martians do we need? If the goal was to write a perfect gem, it was always easy to see the need for a sharper cut. In many ways, the intellectual climate of the day set up young ethnographers to feel like failures.

It wasn't until I began to spend time with an interdisciplinary group at the University of Chicago that I began to think of my own intellectual task differently. The Chicago Templeton Network mostly comprised academic psychologists and biomedical researchers—scientists whose papers were often very short and centered on tables and graphs. They simply didn't believe me when I told them what I had seen from my ethnographic research—that some people were better at prayer practice than others, and that prayer shaped the way that they experienced their world. The group wanted different kinds of evidence to support the claim. This annoyed me. After all, I had spent many years collecting those ethnographic observations. It made me so annoyed that I set out to prove my point. I did some more structured research and found that the outcome supported my ethnographic observations. When I gave my presentation, beginning with my years of ethnographic research and leading up to my first quantitative finding, they listened patiently until the first scatterplot went up on the screen. Then someone smiled at me and said, "Data!"

This also annoyed me.

Yet the work liberated me because it shifted my focus from perfection to puzzles. The specific attempt to compare people with one another systematically raised as many questions as it answered. I had demonstrated that people who differed in ways measured by a standardized scale were more likely to enjoy praying and more likely to experience what were supposed to be the fruits of prayer—a real relationship with God, a sense of a back-and-forth conversation with him, even a sense that God was sensorially present. I had been able to show that some people were better at prayer than others, and that these differences seemed to change how they experienced their world in the most concrete way.

I had done this by using a scale that measures something called absorption, which asks people whether certain statements are true for them—whether they like watching clouds change shape in the sky, whether they sometimes experience things the way they did as a child, whether they can change noise into music just by the way they think about it (Luhrmann, Nusbaum, and Thisten 2010; Tellegen and Atkinson 1974). The scale seemed to probe the way people experienced their inner and outer senses. It seemed to ask, Do you enjoy getting caught up in your imagination? Do you like to pause and drink in the morning? The work suggested that the way people were oriented toward their mental experience was quite important to their experience of prayer.

Let me pause here. My decision to use a scale might seem peculiar to many anthropologists. Scales probably seem like dead tools that reduce the complexity of human experience. And of course, they do reduce the complexity. But in an anthropologist's hands, they also help to open up the work. Scales, after all, are really just tools to help us to compare: to say that this group, compared with that group, owns more land, or respects their teachers more, or spends more time in meditation. Anthropologists create scales—structured interview protocols— all the time without using the term. A structured list of questions also helps you to see differences between experts and nonexperts. These people seem more interested in narrative, more focused on detail, than those people, and maybe that difference is important. When we ask systematically about the differences, it helps to build an argument. It gives us confidence in what we see. Standardized scales are created by other people who have used them many times and have confirmed that they work in similar ways in at least some different settings. In this case, I had an intuition; I used a standardized scale, and it supported the intuition; I felt bolder when I gave a talk, because I was more confident in what I had to say. In anthropology, these tools are usually called mixed methods, and they were far more part of the early ethnographies than many of us now remember. Margaret Mead collected an extraordinary amount of data of many different kinds, using all sorts of methods. We might remember her for the Samoan girls she wrote about, but her work on the Arapesh is a dense compendium of mixed-methods data.

Why was this liberating? Because I was no longer aiming for the definitive account, the perfect gem. I had identified a puzzle, and it was clear that many people would chew over it and shake it back and forth like a dog with a rope toy. What, after all, *was* absorption? Was it an individual trait, somehow encoded in a body? Or a cultural invitation, encouraged by different social practices? I knew what the scale's authors thought—but I wasn't sure I agreed with them. Now what I was doing was more like detective work, not like literary criticism. Now the details mattered, because it was suddenly clear that no one actually knew them. No one knew whether the absorption scale would pick up similar religious phenomena in other countries, and what it would mean if it did or it did not. No one knew what it meant that people high in absorption had funny little hallucination-like experiences, nor, for that matter, whether it followed that they were like people with schizophrenia. This was fun. It was not because I had added a quantitative dimension to my work. It was because I had a clear sense that there are real puzzles, and empirical research can help to solve them.

To be clear, I still believe that the basic research method of anthropology is ethnography. I still spend long hours with people. I sit in the park with people who hear voices that taunt them. I go on weekends with people who talk with the dead. But I have now begun to think about the goal of ethnography differently from the way I did in the days before my interdisciplinary encounter. I think differently about how and what I want to explain. These days, I think of myself as having findings.

Findings are empirical observations that call out for explanation by generalization. The generalization is a hypothesis, which later findings will support or challenge. Findings are news in the way that the general idea that Moroccans, say, are Moroccan is not. They offer puzzles that need to be solved.

Here is an example. I have begun to spend time in psychiatric settings outside the United States, chatting with patients and doctors, learning about how people find their ways into an inpatient ward. What I do these days that I did not do when I was younger is to ask those patients systematic questions about what they hear. That means that I can compare them with what other patients say elsewhere.

In the Accra General Psychiatric Hospital, I found that people who meet criteria for schizophrenia often reported that the voices who speak to them come from God. On average, they reported that their voices are more positive than those reported by a comparable group of Americans. In Chennai, similar subjects more often said that they heard their kin. They more often said that they heard the disembodied voices of people they already know in the flesh. Not one person in my American sample told me that their dominant voice-hearing experience was positive, and only three Americans out of twenty told me that they heard the voice of someone they actually know (Luhrmann et al. 2015a, 2015b). Why? I think it might have something to do with the social worlds in which they begin to hear those voices. That's important, because how harsh the voices are seems to have something to do with how well people recover—and if the content of the voices can be shaped by culture, it suggests that medication ought not to be the only way our clinicians intervene.

I think if anthropologists went back to empirical comparison, the field would feel liberated, just as I did. If we as a field did empirical comparison with the aim of observing different patterns of behavior and developing theories that explain specific differences—findings—in such a way that we could say whether those theories are better or worse, we would have so much to say, and to so many people. Empirical comparison does not need to be an assertion of arrogance, as the postmodern critique sometimes assumed, but a concession of humility. Claims based on findings are necessarily limited. They are partial attempts to explain a puzzle. Once presented as such, the ensuing debate keeps one more humble still. They are contributions to a conversation in which one is one of many players.

And findings matter. If I can show that the voices heard by people with psychosis are different in different countries, I am able to argue that voice-hearing responds to learning. That paves the way to think differently about what we should do for those who want to experience their voices differently. Explicit comparison enables us to make claims about the way specific cultural features may have specific consequences. And that, as Mead urged long ago, is how anthropology could change the world.

Now I want to say more about my most recent foray into comparison.

Some years ago I wrote a book, *When God Talks Back* (Luhrmann 2012), about the evangelical Christianity practiced by maybe a quarter of Americans. In these faiths, people seek out a personal relationship with an interactive God. In these faiths, God talks back. Those who worship imagine God as actively, supernaturally powerful, and as intimate. Such a God cares about humdrum worries; he wants to hear about them and to talk about them. He can and may step in to improve the quality of a haircut. The challenge of the research was to understand how a human was able to experience an invisible other in dialogue. One cannot foreclose the possibility that the supernatural is present (see Bialecki, this volume). But the supernatural is, by definition, nonnatural: nonordinary, not materially available to the senses. In this kind of Christianity, people talk about hearing God "speak." I wanted to know what they meant in uttering that sentence and what that experience was like.

What I saw was that knowing God in this way was not so much a matter of belief but a matter of skill—something that you learned to do—and that the main vehicle for the learning was prayer. People usually prayed informally, and in that prayer, they conducted daydream-like conversations with God in their minds. The church invited people to develop these daydream-like dialogues in particular ways.

First, the church invited them to think about their minds not as private but as containing thoughts and images and sensations they might once have understood to be internally generated but were in fact communications from God. Not all thoughts counted: people were encouraged to attend to the "texture" of thought, or the "topography" of mind, and pick out thoughts that were "stronger" than others, or felt more spontaneous.

Second, the church invited them in to practice their dialogue with God by in effect pretending that God was present: by going for a walk with God, or by asking God what shirt he wanted them to wear. They did not consider God to be imaginary, nor did they think that they were doing "mere" pretend. C. S. Lewis entitled one of the chapters of *Mere Christianity* "Let's Pretend" to suggest that we pretend in order to experience as real. That is what the church intended.

Third, the church invited them to practice being loved unconditionally by God in a variety of ways. People learned to talk to God as they might to a therapist, and waited to hear what this wise, sensible person might say. They learned to remind each other to see themselves from God's point of view—not as the weak, inadequate person they felt themselves to be, but as a loving and empathic observer would see them. And they stood in for God within the prayer circle, praying out loud to someone the words they felt that God was giving them to say.

Newcomers to this kind of church would begin by saying that God didn't talk to them. Yet after some months they would sometimes report that they could recognize God's voice the way they recognized their mother's voice on the phone. Sometimes they reported that they heard God speak in a way they could hear with their ears. This experience of an audible voice was not a common occurrence— these were not psychotic voices—but they were important to those who experienced them.

One could see, then, that there was learning, and that the learning was not just about learning to say certain things—to adopt a certain discourse—but that it changed something about the experience of mind. My next methodological move came out of my new respect for findings and my burning desire to answer my critics. I added experimental methods to see if I could replicate these ethnographic observations by other means. We brought in over a hundred people and randomized them to prayer practice or to lectures on the gospels. Those in the prayer group were more likely to report more vivid mental images; they seemed to use mental images more; they reported more unusual sensory experiences and more intense spiritual experiences; they experienced God more as a person, felt his presence more, and interacted with him more often (Luhrmann and Morgain 2012; Luhrmann, Nusbaum, and Thisted 2013).

Why bother with the experimental work? Because fundamentally this was a claim that depended on individual differences: on differences between before and after, between trained and untrained. *When God Talks Back* argued that paying attention to what one imagines makes the world of the mind more vivid, and that this was central to understanding imagination-rich prayer. The big claim is that paying attention to inner events alters someone's awareness of those events to the extent that the attention can alter their decision about what they perceive to be true—a human experience that explains something about how prayer works in different cultural settings. The ethnographic data presented phenomenological findings that demonstrated general patterns of experience; the experimental data demonstrated that proclivity and practice shifted those patterns in predictable ways. Ethnography is good at capturing general patterns, the underlying grammar of experience. But the most persuasive way to identify individual differences between those who pray and those who do not involves comparison within a group of subjects, and that is most easily achieved by experimental design.

Yet it also seemed that there was something about the experience of hearing God that was hard for my Christian subjects—and this was an *ethnographic* observation about a specific cultural world. These Christians would talk about struggling to experience God as real in their thoughts. They would say things like, "You'll think I am crazy," or "You don't need to send the white coats for me." The fear of being crazy was even more pronounced when they reported hearing God speak with their ears. These hesitations seemed to have to do with the secular context and the psychological model of mind among middle-class Americans.

That suggested that there was a scholarly and scientific story not only about the consequence of giving inner experience increased significance through prayer but also through the way that inner experience was understood in a specific social world. In other words, it seemed that there was a story not only about attention in general but about the particular way people learned to pay attention in particular social worlds. It seemed likely that different social groups encourage people to attend to their mental activities in different ways—that they imagine mind differently, that they imagine thought differently, that they have different assumptions about what happens when you think and whether that matters and how people learn. That is a hypothesis about cultural variation in theory of mind.

Psychologists have demonstrated that the basic presumption that the mind is separate from the world is one of the most definitive achievements of childhood development. By the age of three, more or less, toddlers understand that mental states can explain behavior. The classic experiment is the "false belief" task. A child and the child's mother watch an experimenter hide a toy. Then the mother leaves the room, and the experimenter moves the toy to a new hiding place. When the mother returns, the experimenter asks the child where the mother thinks the toy will be. (This is often represented by dolls, as in the "Sally Ann" tasks.) Very young children point to the second hiding place, because that is where the toy actually is. They presume that all people know what they take to be true about the world. Older children understand that the mother does not know that the toy has been moved, and so they point to the first hiding place. They have developed what psychologists call a theory of mind. They understand that what people think they know may be different from what has happened in the world (Wellman 2013).

Yet what the observer really observes is that the child draws inferences about knowing, believing, wanting, and intending. "Mind" is the name for the container we imagine for those acts. And anthropologists know that different social worlds represent that container differently, although we as a tribe have not done much with that observation. In 1988, the psychologist Angela Lillard pulled together these anthropological findings (Lillard 1998). Euro-Americans, she pointed out, imagine the mind as the seat of mental processes; as located in and identified with the brain; as private but knowable; and, judging by the size of the vocabulary used to describe it, as extremely important. In Euro-America, the mind gives an individual his or her identity. Your feelings, your beliefs, your ideas—in Euro-America, they make you you.

Many other cultures locate the mind not in the brain but in the heart, as the Ilongot (a tribe in the Philippines) do (Rosaldo 1980). Among the Ilongot, many of the mind's features are attributed to social interaction. "What is important for Ilongots is not what goes on in the rinawa [the closest word for their conception of mind] but between people" (quoted in Lillard 1998, 12). The clear distinction Euro-Americans make between mind and body is more muted in other social worlds. The Japanese, for example, make no simple distinction between the two and do not identify self with mind (Lebra 1993). And mind is often less elaborated outside the Euro-American context. Signe Howell (1981) made determined efforts to describe all mental process terms among the Chewong, a tribe on the Malaysian peninsula. She found five (*want, want very much, know, forget,* and *miss* or *remember*). There was, she reported, no word for *think*.

Indeed, in many parts of the world, people resist interpreting what is in other people's minds. This tendency is so pronounced in the South Pacific and in Melanesia that anthropologists have come to speak of "opacity of mind" (Robbins and Rumsey 2008). Mayans also privilege the description of behavior over mental states but seem to be more concerned with the accuracy of the world-word relationship. Eve Danziger has found that Mopan Mayans explicitly disregard mental states and de-emphasize fantasy and pretend play (as Suzanne Gaskins also demonstrates for Yucatec Mayans) because what counts is the direct correspondence between speech and fact—not whether the speaker, at the time of uttering, believed that the spoken claim was accurate (Danziger 2006; Gaskins 2016). Danziger, like Lillard, uses this example to demonstrate that the standard psychological theory of mind is culturally Euro-American. The Mayan child is not behaving in the way that many theorists have suggested, explicitly formulating models of mental states. The child does draw the correct inferences, but in a way different from the Euro-American expectations of the mind.

In 2011, we organized a conference that brought together anthropologists and psychologists to see whether we had sufficient evidence to argue for local theories of mind.[1] We identified at least six such theories:

The Euro-American Modern Secular Theory of Mind: In this theory of mind, people treat the mind as if there is in effect a clear boundary between what is in the mind, and what is in the world. Entities in the world, supernatural or otherwise, do not enter the mind, and thoughts do not leave the mind to act upon the world. The assertion that they do is seen as a symptom of mental illness (thought insertion and thought withdrawal). What is in the mind is not real in the way that tables and chairs are real; one can speak of "mere" imagination. At the same time, what is held in the interior of the mind is causally important. Intentions and emotions are powerful and can even make someone ill.

The Euro-American Modern Supernaturalist Theory of Mind: This theory can be found undergirding charismatic Christianity, contemporary spiritual healing, alternative bereavement practices, paganism, and other practices that are sometimes identified as "new age." Here people treat the mind as if it conformed to the modern secular theory, except in specific respects. The mind-world boundary becomes permeable for God, or for the dead person, or for specific "energies" that are treated as having causal power and, usually, their own agency. The individual learns to identify these supernatural presences, often through implicit or even explicit training. Other features of the secular theory apply. The training becomes important because the secular model of mind is the default model with which these individuals work.

The Opacity of Mind Theory: This theory is found in varying forms throughout the South Pacific and Melanesia. Its most striking feature is the insistent refusal to infer what other people are thinking unless they verbalize their intentions. In these societies, asserted intention is taken to be causally powerful in a way that felt intention is not. That is, whatever one's actual intention may be, the intention one asserts (or is taken to have asserted) is taken to be causally powerful. The impropriety of inferring privately held intention is so great that it can be impolite to look directly into another's eyes. At the same time, the boundary between the mind and the world is often porous, so that spirits (or the Holy Spirit) pass back and forth across it.

The Transparency of Language Theory: In these societies, for which our best examples come from Central America, language is understood to align with the world rather than to express interior states. Fiction may be frowned upon; play by children may be tolerated but not encouraged. The vocabulary to describe mental states may be thin or near-nonexistent. Most notably (to ethnographers) beliefs that happen to be false but are not understood to be false by the speaker may be identified as "lying." When an utterance is assessed, what matters is its truth-relationship to the world rather than its relationship to the intention of the speaker.

The Mind Self-Control Theory: Our best example of this theory locates it in Thailand, but it can be found in different versions throughout Asia. In Thailand, the most important concern around the mind is how well it is controlled. One can have a well-controlled mind, or one that is less well-controlled. When the mind is poorly controlled, emotions and intentions become powerful and can enter other poorly controlled minds as ghosts or spirits. Thoughts thus are real in a way that is quite different from the Euro-American model. One's mind can be unbunched, and can wander. Thoughts can act in the world and on other minds in ways that are only partially related to those that first thought them.

Perspectivism: This theory suggests that the world is dependent on the perspective one takes on it. Many Amazonian peoples are held to conceptualize theoretically the world as if it is seen from a particular perspective: a human's or a jaguar's, for example. Here there is a great deal of interest in the idea that what appears to be blood to a human may seem to be beer to a jaguar (for instance). There is an expectation that a human can become a jaguar and vice versa. The most important feature of a mind seems to be that it can migrate from body to body. People sometimes fear ending up in a non-human form permanently. People can make claims that they have seen other people becoming non-human, or been with humans who become non-human. (Luhrmann et al. 2011, 6–7)

This list is not exhaustive. It may not be accurate. It does not imply that everyone in these social worlds thinks about the mind in the same way. The sheer existence of the list, however, supports the general claim that there are striking cultural differences in the way distinctive social groups imagine the map of this human terrain of knowing, intending, desiring, and feeling—the hilly, pockmarked terrain of human awareness.

Do these differences matters? That is what I set out to answer five years later, drawing on my initial comparative work in the San Francisco South Bay; Accra, Ghana; and Chennai, India (Luhrmann 2017). The Mind and Spirit Project (funded by the John Templeton Foundation) set out to ask, Is there a relationship between the way people think about thinking (their local theory of mind) and the way they experience the supernatural?

To be clear, this is a question about the relationship between the way a social group *represents* the domain of what we Western English speakers call the mind—what we call their local theory of mind—and the way people actually *experience* what they identify as the divine or supernatural. There is of course no strict distinction between experience and representation. Decades of philosophical and ethnographic analysis have taught us that. But there is a difference in the target of the research. We set out to identify models of mind across different social worlds and experiences of what William James called the "more"—that which exceeds a materialist understanding of the world as we know it (1935, 501). Our aim is to ask whether there is a systematic relationship between the two.

Why should there be? Much of what humans deem spiritual, to use Ann Taves's (2009) useful phrase, involves the identification of what a skeptical Anglophone observer would call mental events: an impression or thought, a quasi-sensory voice, an awareness. American charismatic Christians seek for the voice of God within their minds. They expect to hear God speaking back through their thoughts. They must, then, be able to identify a thought—and that is a culturally shaped act. Bruno Snell (1960) and Maurice Leenhardt (1979) each describe a social world (archaic Greece, early twentieth-century New Caledonia) in which people do not have the vocabulary to describe inner experience and in which the gods act in concrete ways; Julian Jaynes ([1976] 2000) argued that the one was responsible for the other.

How do we compare? We chose five countries that, because of existing historical and ethnographic research, we thought encouraged different representations of the relationship between mind and world: China, Ghana, Thailand, the United States, and Vanuatu. (My primary coconspirators here were Christine Legare and Kara Weisman.) We appointed ethnographers competent in the local language and experienced in local research to spend nine months in the field and two years (and more) on the project. (They were Felicity Aulino, Josh Brahinsky, John Dulin, Vivian Dzokoto, Emily Ng, and Rachel Smith.) We found an "apple" for an apple-to-apple comparison: an urban charismatic church with specific features—charismatic experience, aspirationally middle class, with a theological expectation that God would speak back to each of his worshipers. All churches are different, but Pentecostal and neo-Pentecostal congregations are at least presumed to have more similar—more portable—cultures than many (Freston 2013; Robbins 2004).

In each setting, we did a set of intensive, semistructured interviews—one on the mind, another on spiritual experience, each usually one to two hours in length. Each fieldworker did twenty such interviews in each site. We did similar interviews with related groups—a rural variant of the urban church, and an urban and rural faith of local importance (Methodism in the United States, Buddhism in Thailand). To minimize the problems caused by having different interviewers, our team spent four months together reading, talking, developing, and piloting the interviews before the work began. To see if our observations would be consonant with other groups in the same country, we also collected other kinds of data: one hundred shorter interviews in each setting in a location like the local department of motor vehicles; packets of pen-and-paper surveys on mind and spirit with local undergraduates; developmental experiments with children and adults. We have more than one way to compare.

The hard part was deciding what to ask. What serves as an object that can be compared like to like? This is a matter that involves choice, compromise, and limitation. There were three issues. First, time is finite. One cannot talk to everyone about everything, or even to one person about very much. Second, not all questions are worth asking. Some events are so rare or so difficult to describe that asking about them generates mush. I am willing to grant that there is something like a mystical experience with the characteristics William James ([1902] 1935) thought were so important. But in my long experience of asking people about spiritual events, I have found that when I ask people whether they have experienced a remarkable event with qualities of ineffability, transience, noesis, and passivity, people often say, "every afternoon." That answer is undoubtedly wrong for the rare events James described. We left mystical experiences off our list, although we did ask people to describe their most remarkable spiritual experience and so left room for them to describe such an event. Third, there are unknown unknowns. There are events not thought of in our Euro-American world that do exist in others. In our four-month preparation, one fieldworker—Rachel Smith, who went to Vanuatu—kept asking how we would ask about small blond dwarves. At first I took this as a metaphor for all we did not know to ask. Then it turned out that in Vanuatu, people do indeed report small blond dwarves. So we created a question we could use everywhere that we hoped would lead people to talk about the dwarves in Vanuatu.

That introduces a basic rule: conversation, conversation, conversation. Our interview protocol was built on my own experience in talking with charismatic Christians in Chicago and then on the San Francisco South Bay peninsula. Then we talked and talked about the way those questions might be received by Christians and non-Christians in our different settings. We piloted in the United States, and when the fieldworkers arrived in their sites, we piloted again.

We chose to ask about two kinds of spiritual events: general events deemed religious, particularly about the way that spirit spoke or communicated, and what the folklorist David Hufford (1982) calls "core" experiences. These are events that appear to occur in many cultures; that occur in some people independently of prior expectation; and that appear to form distinct patterns with stable traits. These are events such as voices, visions, a sense of presence, out-of-body events, and sleep paralysis. They are often described in the medical and historical literature. I think of core experiences the way psychiatric researchers these days think about psychiatric diagnoses—that they are somewhat fictional but useful categories that more or less pick out differences in human experience.

Then there is the mind. What on earth is the mind, "the thing that thinks," in René Descartes's phrase? There is nothing about which we have more privileged knowledge and about which at the same time we know so little. No one has access to what Augustine called the vast choirs of our memory, and yet when we search for thoughts we sometimes find ourselves grasping shadows in a mist. James ([1890] 1950, 179) described the resistance to describe the mind on the grounds that the concept of mind is hard to describe precisely as "spiritual chloroform." So we proceeded.

We began with a heuristic: an analytic distinction between the human experience of thinking, intending, believing, wanting, feeling, and the awareness of those mental acts, and the culturally specific representations of those acts. We distinguished them as terrain and map: the first as the phenomenological experience common to humans, and the second as the way those phenomena are represented in a local social world. We presume that not all the human terrain is locally mapped as mind—that specific kinds of mental events, such as anger, might be mapped more as part of body or of spirit. We also presume that the local mapping changes the experience of the event. But we do not presume that the map is a cookie cutter that completely determines human experience.

We set out to identify the way our local communities mapped this terrain by asking our interview participants about a series of stories we hoped would capture the way they imagined what thoughts and feelings could do and how and why; whether thoughts and feelings should be shared, and with whom and when and why; and whether what the mind invents out of whole cloth is real, and should be encouraged, and why.

We have a long way to go, but we appear to have a finding: that when the terrain of the mind is mapped so that it is imaged as more porous, more permeable, so that thoughts cross back and forth across the mind-world boundary to affect the world directly, people report more bodily spiritual events. When the terrain is mapped in a more bounded way, as Charles Taylor (2007) described—when the mind is imagined as an epiphenomenon of the brain, when thought is supernaturally inert, when feelings like anger affect one's own body but not the material world beyond—spiritual events are less sensory and more thought-like. God speaks into the mind, rather than with a voice one can hear with the ears. When people represent thoughts and feelings as potentially potent, as when ideas about witchcraft and sorcery are salient, or when people imagine the mind as vulnerable to thoughts and feelings from elsewhere, as in divination, they are more likely to describe moments in which they see spirits with their eyes or hear them with their ears.

What constitutes an explanation here? The paradoxical point is that the more we emphasize the finding as something that needs to be explained, the less important, in some ways, the explanation becomes. In some sense, an explanation is always emergent. Our current explanation (Luhrmann 2020) is that these ideas about thought affect the way thought is experienced: as more substantial, as more viscous, as more thing-like. We think that these expectations may alter experience so that sometimes, thought-like events pop out into the world and are experienced as more external. As we learn more, as we do more work, no doubt our explanation will change. What we feel we have achieved so far is the observation of something. There are different models of mind, and something about them seems associated with more vividly sensory spiritual experience. We have an empirical finding that *calls out* for explanation. We do not have a polished gem that describes something in particular deeply but generalizes nowhere. We have a puzzle, and we hope that it provokes debate.

NOTE

Acknowledgments: With grateful thanks to Paolo Heywood, Matt Candea, and the participants at the conference from which this emerged.

1. Lemelson conferences are funded through the Society for Psychological Anthropology by a personal gift from Robert Lemelson. Some portions of this chapter have previously been published as "On Finding Findings," *Journal of the Royal Anthropological Institute* 26 (2020): 428–432.

REFERENCES

Bloch, M. 2005. *Essays on Cultural Transmission*. LSE Monographs. London: Berg.

Borofsky, R., L. Nader, M. Candea, and J. Friedman. 2019. "Where Have All the Comparisons Gone?" Member Voices, *Fieldsights*, September 10, 2019. https://culanth.org/fieldsights/series/comparison.

Danziger, E. 2006. "The Thought That Counts: Understanding Variation in Cultural Theories of Interaction." In *Roots of Human Sociality: Culture, Cognition and Human Interaction*, edited by S. Levinson and N. Enfield, 259–278. Oxford: Berg.

Freston, P. 2013. "The Future of Pentecostalism in Brazil: The Limits to Growth." In *Global Pentecostalism in the 21st Century*, edited by R. Hefner, 63–90. Bloomington: Indiana University Press.

Gaskins, S. 2016. "Pretend Play as Culturally Constructed Activity." In *The Oxford Handbook of the Development of Imagination*, edited by M. Taylor, 224–247. Oxford: Oxford University Press.

Howell, S. 1981. "Rules Not Words." In *Indigenous Psychologies*, edited by P. Heelas and A. Lock, 133–144. New York: Academic Press.

Hufford, D. 1982. *The Terror That Comes in the Night*. Philadelphia: University of Pennsylvania Press.

James, W. (1890) 1950. *The Principles of Psychology*. New York: Dover.

——. (1902) 1935. *The Varieties of Religious Experience*. New York: Longmans.

Jaynes, J. (1976) 2000. *Origins of Consciousness in the Breakdown of the Bicameral Mind*. New York: Houghton Mifflin.

Lebra, T. S. 1993. "Culture, Self, and Communication in Japan and the United States." In *Communication in Japan and the United States*, edited by W. B. Gudykunst, 51–87. Albany: State University of New York Press.

Leenhardt, M. 1979. *Do Kamo: Person and Myth in the Melanesian World*. Chicago: University of Chicago Press.

Lillard, A. 1998. "Ethnopsychologies: Cultural Variations in Theories of Mind." *Psychological Bulletin* 123 (1): 3–32.

Luhrmann, T. M. 2012. *When God Talks Back: Understanding the American Evangelical Relationship with God*. New York: Knopf.

——. 2017. "Knowing God." In "Infrastructures of Certainty and Doubt," edited by Morten Pederson. Special issue, *Cambridge Journal of Anthropology* 35 (2): 125–142.

——. 2020. *How God Becomes Real: Kindling the Presence of Invisible Others*. Princeton, NJ: Princeton University Press.

Luhrmann, T. M., R. Astuti, J. Robbins, J. Cassaniti, J. Marrow, J. Lucy, K. Geurts, et al. 2011. "Toward an Anthropological Theory of Mind." Position papers from the Lemelson Conference. Includes introduction, individual essay, and edited collection. *Journal of the Finnish Anthropological Association* 36 (4): 5–69.

Luhrmann, T. M., and R. Morgain. 2012. "Prayer as Inner Sense Cultivation." *Ethos* 40 (4): 359–389.

Luhrmann, T. M., H. Nusbaum, and R. Thisted. 2010. "The Absorption Hypothesis: Learning to Hear God in Evangelical Christianity." *American Anthropologist* 112 (1): 6–78.

——. 2013. "'Lord, Teach Us to Pray': Prayer Practice Affects Cognitive Processing." *Journal of Cognition and Culture* 13:159–177.

Luhrmann, T. M., R. Padmavati, H. Tharoor, and A. Osei. 2015a. "Differences in Voice-Hearing Experiences of People with Psychosis in the USA, India and Ghana: Interview-Based Study." *British Journal of Psychiatry* 206 (1): 41–44.

——. 2015b. "Voice-Hearing in Different Cultures: A Social Kindling Hypothesis." *Topics in Cognitive Science* 7 (4): 646–63.

Miller, D., E. Costa, L. Haapio-Kirk, N. Haynes, J. Sinanan, T. McDonald, R. Nicolescu, J. Spyer, S. Venkatraman, and X. Wang. 2019. "Contemporary Comparative Anthropology—the Why We Post Project." *Ethnos* 84 (2): 283–300.

Needham, Rodney. 1973. *Belief Language and Experience*. Chicago: University of Chicago.

Robbins, J. 2004. *Becoming Sinners: Christianity and Moral Torment in a Papua New Guinea Society*. Berkeley: University of California Press.

——. 2013. "Beyond the Suffering Subject: Toward an Anthropology of the Good." *Journal of the Royal Anthropological Institute* 19:447–462.

Robbins, J., and A. Rumsey. 2008. "Introduction: Cultural and Linguistic Anthropology and the Opacity of Other Minds." *Anthropological Quarterly* 81 (2): 407–420.

Rosaldo, M. 1980. *Knowledge and Passion: Ilongot Notions of Self and Social Life*. Cambridge: Cambridge University Press.

Snell, B. 1960. *The Discovery of Mind*. New York: Dover.

Taves, A. 2009. *Religious Experience Reconsidered*. Princeton, NJ: Princeton University Press.

Taylor, C. 2007. *A Secular Age*. Cambridge, MA: Harvard University Press.

Tellegen, A., and G. Atkinson. 1974. "Openness to Absorbing and Self-Altering Experiences ('Absorption'), a Trait Related to Hypnotic Susceptibility." *Journal of Abnormal Psychology* 83 (3): 268–277.

Weisman, K., and T. M. Luhrmann. 2020. "What Anthropologists Can Learn from Psychologists, and the Other Way Around." In "Mind and Spirit: A Comparative Theory," edited by T. M. Luhrmann. Special issue, *Journal of the Royal Anthropological Institute* 26 (S1): 131–147.

Wellman, H. 2013. "Universal Social Cognition." In *Navigating the Social World: A Developmental Perspective*, edited by M. Banaji and S. Gelman, 69–74. Oxford: Oxford University Press.

Wittgenstein, L. 1969. *On Certainty*. Oxford: Basil Blackwell.

ON (NOT) EXPLAINING THE DOMESTIC MIRACLE

Jon Bialecki

The Ontological Challenge of the Domestic Miracle

There is, to be blunt, something off-putting about the miraculous, or at least there is for anthropological imaginaries. We can intuit this fact that the sort of miracles discussed, and often (at least allegedly) performed in Protestant and Pentecostal churches in the United States, the United Kingdom, and swaths of northern Europe, are inopportune objects by the way that modern ethnographies go right up to the edge of the miracle, only to stop analysis and description when it comes to actually having to confront the object. We can see this in the proliferation of ethnographies of various Anglo-American Christianities, ethnographies occasioned in part by the advent of a self-conscious anthropology of Christianity, and in part by the increasing political activism of various politically conservative Christian movements (these two phenomena, I should mention, are not themselves unrelated). Multiple ethnographies have captured the political and semiotic aspects of these collectivities that are quite open about their endorsement of a supernaturally inflected understanding of the world (see, e.g., Bielo 2009; Coleman 2000; Elisha 2011; Engelke 2007; Harding 2000; Strhan 2015). But like someone whistling past the graveyard, the miraculous is often just skated by. The miracle is mentioned only in passing, usually in a neutral voice that studiously avoids either skepticism or surprise, and used only as evidence for some other puzzle regarding issues such as personhood, the private-public divide, or the structure and effects of evangelical rhetoric. These are important concerns, to be sure. But the miracle never appears as an object in its own right, and the question of how the miracle is constituted goes equally unanswered.

As we will see, there are good reasons for this: miracles pose even more of an ethnographic puzzle on their face than one might expect. This situation may especially be the case in a book that has taken up "explanation" as its central thematic, considering that one of the inevitable backdrops for such a conversation in contemporary anthropology and ethnography will be some form of what the editors of this book refer to as "ethnographic foundationalism." This term was coined as a placeholder for the tendency in the discipline to refrain from using anthropological categories to explain ethnography; the fear is that the importation of these nonindigenous logics would be a form of intellectual violence. Rather, ethnographers should derive their models for whatever phenomenon they happen to be attending to from the narratives of their informants.

We see an example of this, for instance, in the monograph by Joel Robbins (2020), a very influential figure in the anthropology of Christianity. In that book, Robbins argues that anthropologists writing on Christian populations would be well served by deriving their theoretical models at least partially from theology because theology in considerable measure is a clarified and rationalized expression of the account that Christians would themselves give of how both religious practice and divine agents shape and order their lives. But while there has been a great deal of attention to theology in the anthropology of Christianity, I would argue that theological thought does not stand as the chief representative of ethnographic foundationalism in the subdiscipline. Rather, when the miracle as a category is discussed, I would suggest that a certain attitude toward an ontological framing is more prominent. Specifically, there is a general tendency to implicitly or explicitly assume the ontology of one's Christian interlocutors when discussing the miracle, sometimes in the form of something called the ontological turn, which is the more common form when anthropologists discuss Christianity. The ontological turn is a species of ethnographic foundationalism on steroids. It argues that anthropologists must wholeheartedly accept the ontology of their field interlocutors when they write. Doing so, it is claimed, not only avoids the intellectual violence that troubles practitioners of ethnographic foundationalism but also is the only means of producing what is truly anthropological thought, in that treating field ontologies as if they are valid means creating novel concepts that "fit" these ontologies. (Holbraad and Pedersen 2017). Now, to be clear, I am not claiming that all anthropologists who write on Christianity in an ontological vein are Christians, though there are those believing anthropologists who do share their informants' understanding of reality and see the ontological turn as salutatory (see, e.g., Meneses 2018; Merz and Merz 2017). But additionally, there are also anthropologists who adopt the ontological turn writing in what we might want to call a "secular" genre (Scherz 2017; Vilaça 2015, 2016; Willerslev and Suhr 2018). It is true that there have been voices that, with different levels of adamancy, have criticized foregrounding local ontology as a theoretical frame in the anthropology of Christianity (Bialecki 2018; Marshall 2014). But to the degree that the miracle is engaged with at all, it is through an ontologically inflected ethnographic foundationalism.

Either despite or because of the way that the miracle is more generally avoided, the oddness of the ontological miracle as a topic may not be initially apparent on the surface. This is surprising. The miracle seems to be exactly the sort of received-rationality-breaking ethnographic "wonder" (Scott 2013) that the ontological turn is seen as popularizing; a metaphysical event that purposefully runs counter to the type of naturalistic reason that is perceived as endemic to the West in general and to the academy in particular. This is so much the case that addressing the miracle may even seem like cheating, a lazy turn to low-hanging ontological fruit. To use the categories developed in an article by Matei Candea (2016), all one has to do to engage in what he calls "frontal" comparison—the contrasting of some other society or culture with our own, whether as a form of contextualization, critique, or estrangement—is to juxtapose the miracle with the conceptual logic of some secular Euro-American society. One then congratulates oneself on having dealt a blow to a constipated, hyperscientistic image of thought, for having struck an ethnographic coup that bravely opens the way to new postsecular imagination.

There is something probably (slightly) unfair about the picture that I'm painting here. I think that even though I'm talking down ontological discussion of the miracle, there is something seductive about such a theoretical maneuver, and I certainly have not always been above trying to pull it off in my own work. But a little reflection on the ease with which this theoretical move can be done suggests that there may be something facile, and perhaps even illicit, in the maneuver, at least when talking about miracles. Not all iterations of this maneuver suffer from this fault, I wish to be clear. To the degree that one accepts the premise of an ontological-methodological framing in the first place, or for that matter of any sort of "frontal" comparison, I think there are instances of "miracles" in social and cultural milieus that are informed by sensibilities so different from ours that such a contrast can be productive. The problem comes, however, not when one is working with the miracle in the form of an apparition of a ghostly horseman or some bleeding icon somewhere in the Middle East, just to choose examples from anthropological literature resplendent with the miraculous (see, e.g., Heo 2018). Rather it comes when one is thinking about the miracle a bit closer to home. The contemporary Anglo-American Protestant miracle breaks ontology as a method, and leaves other attempts to "explain" the miracle in a bad position. Which is to say that other attempts to explain away the miracle will find themselves taking up stances that are not necessarily intellectually invalid, nor unethical in the strict sense of the term, but that would leave many ethnographers with a bad taste in their mouth, considering the ethical debt that the anthropologist is supposed to hold toward his or her informants.

The problem with ontological attempts to assail the miracle is that when one is dealing with the "domestic" miracle (for lack of a better phrase), the frisson that comes with a moment of critique manufactured through a juxtaposition of our intellectual conceits to the alien thought of the other is unearned. That is because the miracle is already a form that is indigenous to the West, and as such it can't be contrasted with Western metaphysics in an attempt to tax our understanding to some breaking point. To return to Candea's language, the domestic miracle therefore cannot be juxtaposed to our own indigenous understanding because the miracle is already present in our world and is already a feature of the intellectual hinterland that makes the contrast with some other mode of thought possible in the first place. Thus, the seeming encounter with alterity contained in ethnographically addressing the miracle is a false one, because there is no alterity in the first instance.

I will dwell a bit longer on the indigeneity of the miracle, since I suspect this will be a contentious claim. To be blunt, the miracle is an outsize part of our intellectual inheritance. Of course, some would say that this is not a problem, and we can still take on objects like this. As just one example, contemporary programmatic statements regarding ontology have been open to turning to much more slight gradations of difference. We can think of the call to work "beyond the relation," for instance, and expand the ontological methodology's scope to take on ethnographic milieus that are not predicated on the dividual logic of parts and wholes. However, it is one thing to be open to using an ontologizing methodology to unpack social forms that are incrementally closer to our own framework, as Martin Holbraad and Morten Pedersen (2017) have advocated. The difference here, though, is that the domestic miracle is not just close to us. It is the very precondition of our form of thought.

Some may complain that the miracle is cognitively exterior to us because it is exactly what is rejected by contemporary social-scientific logic, but it is the very act of rejection that makes the miracle unalienable. The miracle serves as a self-defining other in intellectual constellations as diverse as apologies for the natural science and garden variety anti-Catholicisms. And after David Hume and Baruch Spinoza, one might even say that it is a striking-through of the miracle (though importantly a striking-through without erasure or foreclosure) that serves as the possibility condition of contemporary discussions of religion and reason. Furthermore, it arguably still exists in our society as a "positive" entity in the internal critique of various forms of secularism and scientific reason. Of course, we could always stipulate an artificial hinterland, some intellectual caricature of a rationality, rather than any actual mode of rationality as we use it in the wild. This positing of an artificial hinterland is not an unusual move, as Candea reads more recent trends. (He gives examples of such stipulated intellectual faux locales as "Western 'liberal' understandings of freedom" and "Eurocentric notions of modernity" [2016, 195].) This creation by fiat of a purely ideological hinterland makes the miracle seem external to ourselves by drawing an artificial border between us and it, no matter how close we are situated in regard to that concept. Alternately, we could always take another angle and argue that while we may have a conceptual alacrity with the domestic miracle, it is experientially distant enough from us moderns that we can count it as other (which is, of course, to put to the side the issue of the relationship between experience and the ontological methodology). We could plead that, to use Charles Taylor's (2007) term, today we have buffered and not porous selves, and the miracle is just the kind of magic that we have been trained to lock out.

This leaves us suggesting that there may be two semilegitimate moves to allow us to at once rescue and alienate the phenomenon: that of creating a purely hypothetical and hence somewhat thin and intellectually brittle home ground to hold against the domestic miraculous other, or that of back-projecting an experience-near "hinterlands" requirement as an addendum to the ontological turn's platform. To be honest, both arguments sound like special pleading to me, but even if they are convincing to others, we still need to go on to ask, who would "us" be in this exercise anyway? When we are discussing the position of anthropology vis-à-vis the domestic miracle, the answer to that question is not so clear. As the historian Timothy Larsen (2014) has observed, some of the most noted twentieth-century British social anthropologists were also noted religious believers, adherents to an often supernatural form of Catholicism (see similarly Engelke 2002). The fact that many of these anthropologists also had long and fruitful sojourns in the United States suggests that this religious "fifth column" may not be particular to the United Kingdom alone. We also would have to deal with an increasing theological interest in anthropological reasoning and ethnographic methods (see, e.g., Lemons 2018). Given all this, formulating even a straw-man secularism that we would simultaneously identify with and use as a foil may be at best inexact and at worse disingenuous or dangerous, presuming allies and identities that are not as we imagine; as the punchline to the old joke goes, "Who do you mean 'we,' kemosabe?" Finally, there is the possibility that we might always be dealing with an anthropological case of "Je est un Autre." By this, I mean the fact that even academically trained nonbelieving anthropologists fall into miraculous and religious thought at times. This is something that is usually not spoken about. But every so often, you will have anthropologists owning up to particular life moments as bordering on or crossing into the miraculous, even if they don't habitually think in terms of either miracles or divinity as actual causal agents or events. (One particularly well-written example that I can point to is Ellen Badone's [2013] personal essay on religion, anthropology, and death in Janice Boddy and Michael Lambek's *Companion to the Anthropology of Religion*.)

This problem of locating the miracle in our conceptual topography is not the only difficulty we face. Even if it doesn't cross any bright lines, explanation of the miracle at least courts ethical risk and intellectual vapidity. Let's take vapidity first. While explanation retains a certain tension when juxtaposed to ontology, we should not forget that ontologically oriented anthropology is itself not antithetical to an explanation of a kind. "Powder is power" (Holbraad 2007), for instance, may serve as an axiomatic, or an instigation to the production of novel analytic concepts. But it is also an explanation (at least within a particular framework) of the capacities and causal chains that power/powder exhibits. That, though, is not the case across the board. Consider again the domestic miracle. Even if the conceptual location of the domestic miracle didn't short-circuit any attempts to ontologize it, the internal logic of the domestic miracle would still foreclose any explanation set in the ontological key, or that of any other frontal comparison. That is because the essence of the domestic miracle is that it *defies* explanation. The miracle is marked not by an internal organizing logic but rather by a break with logic, a suspension of natural law. Of course, there are limits to the autonomy of the miracle. There is usually an assumption of some kind of ethical charge to the miracle (the "satanic miracle," for instance, seems like an oxymoronic formulation, unless you are Aleister Crowley or in a Finnish black metal band). Another limit to the miracle is in the degree of variety that it can tolerate. One of the striking things about the domestic miracle is that it appears that God may be sovereign, but he is not very imaginative. Particularly in its Pentecostal and charismatic forms, the miracle seems to have a somewhat limited range of variation, usually remaining stuck in a healing/tongues/prophecy/deliverance-from-demons rut. And we should notice that in many accounts of the miracle, the effective monotony of the miracle and its moral valence seem to not be unrelated (recall C. S. Lewis's [1947] observation that even if the miracle and nature are different orders, they are different orders crafted by the same author, suggesting that these orders cannot be entirely dissimilar). But neither this relatively truncated miraculous possibility space nor the ethical value either carried or communicated by the miracle in any way explains the miracle.[1]

Now, of course, it is possible to save the situation by not presenting an ontological study of the "domestic" miracle at all. One could argue that because of the miracle's native-born resistance to ontologically oriented ethnographic methodology and other modes of "frontal" comparison, and due to its hostility to any explanation that occurs "on its own terms" (that is, using the internal logic of this ethnographic phenomenon), it is an inopportune object that must be approached through more conventional modes of explanation, ones addressing physiological, cognitive, and perceptual engines that strain to produce phenomena that then get coded as "miracles."

The downside of this turn to a different explanatory mode, though, is that such a move does not differ from domestic explanations. But it does run wildly counter to the understandings of the people that truck in these sorts of miraculous. Such an explanatory tactic threatens to rely on mechanisms that would overwrite the (lack of) causal narratives that are brought to this issue, replacing a divine hand with an evolutionary or cognitive spandrel. One could object that this makes it seem as if the believers who participate in the domestic miracle are having their ontological cake and eating it too. They get to claim that their logical construct is internal to "our" logic (again, with some lack of clarity regarding who is included in "our logic"). And at the same time, they can claim special privilege to only have themselves define the miracle, rather than having to tussle around about its meaning with others. First, we should remember that this is an anthropological problem and not a problem across the board. Other disciplines can still take up attempts using these other explanatory frameworks if they care to do so. Second, as has been noted in discussions of why it took so long for a self-conscious, for-itself anthropology of Christianity to get off the ground, this simultaneous proximity to and distance from the analytic mechanisms of social science is one of the frustrating things about relations between "Christians" and "anthropologists" (Robbins 2003). This is certainly also the case when considering the interrogation of the domestic miracle as an ethnographic object. But we should remember that the miracle as a *concept* and the miracle as a *social fact* are two different things, and that by choosing a naturalist explanation, we are interfering with or even openly attacking the latter, while not changing the status of the former. In short, if we choose to overwrite the meaning of the miracle, we then endorse the assumption that our informants are at best mistaken and at worst either gullible or culpable. Even more, we insinuate that we have a privileged access to reality that they do not. Whatever we think of the ontological turn, we can at least agree that it tried to make a virtue of not engaging in the hierarchical ranking of expert accounts over indigenous knowledge. While the ontological claim of being the "first to take their informants seriously" is questionable, we can at least agree that they *try* to take their informants seriously in this regard.

In the end, the danger is that we will be read not as making statements about the constitution of particular events or sets of events that are read as "miraculous" in the modern day but rather as making statements about the existence of miracles tout court, or even worse, about the existence of God. The anthropological formulations of "experts" are knowledge of a different kind, and due to methodological and epistemological regimentation, they should not be seen as being the fungible equivalent of other forms of knowledge. That would be to play with the kind of blind relativism that corrodes the capacity to claim that any form of knowledge has its own ethical and analytic distinctives and capacities. But when we cross over into topics that strain any kind of empirical account, and that appear to be at best at the far border of the anthropological remit, we should remember that there will be those both inside and outside the discipline who will counsel us that "whereof one cannot speak, thereof one must be silent."

Fractal Comparison and "Explanation-Like Effects"

This leaves us in an unenviable position when it comes to the domestic miracle. We cannot mine the miracle for novel concepts, as proponents of an ontological methodology and other frontal comparatives would have it, because the miracle, at least in its domestic form, is already part of our intellectual furniture. And attempts to have us claim otherwise would leave us at best in denial about the role of religion and of religious believers in contemporary social science. Further, the internal logic of the miracle disables our ability to "explain" it, since one of the chief determinants, if not the chief one, of what is and what is not a miracle is whether it can be explained. And trying to explain it using logics alien to those who endorse the reality of the domestic miracle is an attempt at demystification. And this suggests that believers in the miracle are either credulous or implicated in a semiconscious or conscious fraud.

I do not believe that this dilemma is inescapable. I believe that there are *two* ways (or rather, two books) out of this thicket that have already been explored, even if these two approaches do not look like each other, and if they go their separate ways after needling through this narrow pass. The two paths through this problem share the same ethnographic object: a single contemporary American charismatic or evangelical movement called the Vineyard, a rapidly grown set of over 2,400 congregations worldwide, known for its celebration of miraculous acts such as prophecy, deliverance from demons, speaking in tongues, and healing. One of these books has the virtue of being widely received and acclaimed; I am thinking here of *When God Talks Back* (*WGTB*), by Tanya Luhrmann (2012; also see this volume). The other book has the equally singular, but slightly less prestigious, distinction of being mine (Bialecki 2017). Despite this difference,

I want to suggest that they share something beyond ethnographically engaging with the same religious group. My argument here is that both these books square the circle, producing something *like* an explanation. They present narratives that have "explanatory-like" effects but that are not ultimately structured as explanations. (This is despite the language both authors use in their books; each uses the word *explain* and many of that word's synonyms quite freely.)

I will . . . explain? . . . what I mean by "explanatory effects without explanation" and "participating in the miracle" later in this chapter. But first I want to defend putting these books alongside each other in the first place. Placing these books side by side is a bit cheeky for numerous reasons. One reason why this alignment is a bit presumptuous is that these books have had disparate impacts. Luhrmann's book is double-voiced in that it is at once a thorough ethnography and an exercise in public anthropology of the like that has become quite rare in our discipline as of late, and it was the center of a great many critical popular media discussions at the time of its release. By contrast, while my book has received a few kind reviews, I suspect that it got misplaced somewhere on its way to the *New York Times* mailroom and will not end up catalyzing much general public media disputation. This is not to be understood as griping—as we will see, I believe that Luhrmann's capacity to write an ethnographic monograph that is capable of triggering this kind of reception is part of how the argument of her book operates.

Regardless, for our purposes, reception is not the most critical distinction between these books. A more pertinent difference is that these books are, in a sense, only *proximately* concerned with the domestic miracle. This is not to say that the miracle doesn't dominate each one. Rather it is to say that what motivates the investigation of the miracle in the first place is not the same in each monograph, and that each conversation concerns a different set of problems that constitute their further horizons. *WGTB* takes up the issue of the ease of belief in the current secular dispensation, a time when most nonbelievers presume that belief is binary, and that believers effortlessly adhere to faith. Luhrmann's explicit goal is to complicate this flat picture by seeing belief as something that is always vulnerable and difficult even in those moments when it is (temporarily) achieved. It is not that believers are blind to the reasons that feed the skepticism of agnostics, atheists, and other "nones." Instead, it is that they train themselves to perceive the world in ways that allow what could easily be presented as an absence to be seen instead as divine plenitude, in part through reading their sensorium in different ways, and in part by modifying that sensorium. In this way, *WGTB* is also a reaction to various almost fundamentalist scientisms. The book is pushing back against evolutionary psychological explanations of religion as merely a side effect, false positives caused by an overly sensitive agency detector; such a theory makes belief in supernatural actors both quick and easy, as it is better to intuit an entity that isn't there than it is to not identify one that is. But *WGTB* also undermines medicalized accounts of miraculous phenomena, accounts that presume this behavior could only be rooted in psychiatric pathology. This medical explanation is "contraindicated" by the fact that these believers do not show the psychic pain, disordered thoughts, and disrupted lives that are usually associated with the sort of mental illnesses that cause someone to hear "voices."

Diagram's stakes are different. The book is concerned mostly with a way to discuss difference within and between Christian movements, as a response to nominalistic provocations that would reject a comparative anthropology of Christianity by claiming that the pure amount of variation found in the category "Christian" suggests that there is no underlying commonality, or at least no commonality outside of historical accidents. It tries to counter the claim by finding one structure common to multiple different Vineyards—that is, the domestic miracle—and showing that seemingly quite different instances of the domestic miracle can be seen as expressions of a single malleable, but still determinable, set of relations (called a diagram, after the sense used by Gilles Deleuze). It then attempts to see other Vineyard practices, such as stewardship of funds, care for church presentation, and the reading of the Bible as an authoritative text, as also being mutations of this diagram, where agency, obligation, and temporality take different forms, and hence have different effects. It closes by reading other contemporary forms of Pentecostalism, charismatic Christianity, and even evangelicalism as also being expressions of the diagrammatic set of relations claimed to be found in the Vineyard. The argument is that both variations in intensities of forces and temporalities, alongside the effects of having these expressions occur in different environments and realized through different material, can account for the differences between these different modes of religiosity, while still seeing something not unlike a genetic continuity underlying them all.

What I may have just laid out in my précis of *Diagram* may sound a great deal like an "explanation," which is something I will need to return to. But first I want to close off this discussion by saying that these different stakes result in the object that is interrogated being presented in different ways. There is the old cliché that most intellectual activity can be reduced to lumping or splitting. Like other academic clichés, there is something tired about it, but there is also something true. In this case, each book does both, though in a different sequence. *WGTB* lumps, so as to address a wider fact of splitting, and *Diagram* splits, but only so it can lump later on. For *WGTB*, the Vineyard is treated as "a" thing. This is not done blindly, or without an open acknowledgment of light amounts of intellectual violence: *WGTB* understands that there is difference between various Vineyard churches and between various Vineyard believers, but for the book (as it is for more Vineyard believers the book concerns itself with) the Vineyard is "one" thing. *WGTB* works similarly with the domestic miracle. The miracle is a single thing: the act of "hearing from God." And this is regardless of whether the miracle occurs through coincidence, through a sense or a concept popping into one's head, or even (for some) through an audible voice. This lumping of the miracle into a single object is done because *WGTB* wants to say something about a broader American evangelical Christianity, and it can only do so by making the Vineyard not a special case with features that are particular to it but rather an exemplar, an object that might stand out a bit, but only because it exhibits some commonality in clearer and more robust ways, allowing for a more colorful depiction of something that may be expressed in other Christian groups only in shades of gray.

This is not how *Diagram* operates, however. It proliferates miraculous forms, distinguishing between divine messages experienced through the act of reading the Bible, and suddenly recalling scriptural passages as a form of receiving prophecy. It sets aside hearing from God as a spontaneous phenomenon from hearing from God as a result of exposure to practiced pedagogues; it even suggests that the latter is linguistically expressed in three different styles. It sets apart sharing a message from God to someone privately from doing the same in a public space. Speaking in tongues is set apart as well, and healing is given its own subcategory (with variations depending on proximity or closeness to the individual being prayed over, and the different manner of divine healing that is being interceded for). This is not to say that this material is absent from *WGTB*, but rather to say that in the latter book, they are treated as different tokens of the same type, with each instance having its own character, but all being, in essence, a moment in a longer conversation with God.

These differences are motivated differences, as pluralizing the miracle or seeing it in the singular allows for different *comparative* operations to be mobilized, and for the creation of different "explanation-like effects." What I mean by "explanation-like effects" is best illustrated by sketching out how they occur in each book. And this can only be done by returning to the issue of comparison that began our discussion of what is problematic about the domestic miracle for the ontological turn (and other frontal comparisons). Comparison, as Candea notes in his already referenced article, is not only between the hinterland and the foreground; anthropology also has a long tradition of what he refers to as "lateral" comparison, where the juxtaposition of different ethnographic cases is used to set stakes, fashion arguments, and test claims. Since the disciplinary epistemological crises of the 1980s, this axis of comparative methodology has not enjoyed the primacy that it once did. Despite this, Candea argues that lateral comparison is still a legitimate and necessary part of anthropological thought, and of the evaluation of ethnographic material.

At the risk of straining Candea's metaphor, though, I would like to observe that there can be finer gradations of comparison. If we are not going to presume that the boundaries of the cases are necessarily isomorphic with the boundaries of already problematic entities like "cultures" or "societies," then lateral comparisons—or, as I will argue shortly, both lateral comparisons and comparisons that are *akin* to lateral comparisons—can be made where the differences are much slighter. Indeed, there is no reason why they cannot be made from separate instances that are "within" the ethnographic author's case. And the resonances between these cases give birth to "explanation-like" effects, by which I mean groups of patterns that open the way for readers to select a causal account from a somewhat determinate set of possibilities inherent in the author's presentation of the pattern, but do not mandate the adoption of any specific *particular* account, and hence do not explain. To differentiate them from Candea's more classical sense of comparison, we can call these *fractal* comparisons, inasmuch as they either reiterate or anticipate the more classical lateral comparative operations that occur at a greater conceptual scale, and between different authors.

I'll start with *Diagram*, since the case there is relatively quick to make. What is being compared and the warrant for the comparisons is more obvious, and the absence of explanation more clearly laid out than what is found in *WGTB* (which, as we shall see, does not conversely mean that *WGTB* obfuscates what it is doing or otherwise acts in bad faith—the problem there is a function of a fundamental undecidability). As just noted, *Diagram* proliferated the miracle, but the reason that the miracle was proliferated was so that its various instantiations of it could be laid alongside each other. This laying alongside each other is an important part of the argument. This parallelism is how *Diagram* argues for the existence of a common pattern. Without this maneuver, it would be hard to allow the already referenced set of relations to come to the surface. What is more, it is only through setting various instantiations of it alongside other instances that important elements of the pattern can be presented. The juxtaposition of differences, as well as similarity, not only allows for arguments such as the relatively "strata-independent" aspect of the underlying pattern (which is to say, it can be exhibited through numerous linguistic and nonlinguistic modes, and at scales that range from the individual to the nation). This also allows for a discussion of how the various aspects set in relation to one another can vary in their intensity, with intensity here not just meaning strength but also referencing qualitative aspects. This allows not only the similarities between various instantiations of the miracle to become apparent but the range of variation as well. Finally, this multiplicity of micro-comparisons allows for the jump in scale, where we cannot speak of variations on types and expressions of the Vineyard miracle, and instead compare the Vineyard miracle as a swath of possibilities against other neocharismatic and neo-Pentecostal groups, which is the moment when this fractal comparison shifts into becoming more akin to the forms of lateral comparison that concern Candea.

Depending on how you think of this sort of operation, it either produces or unveils a set of patterns. What it does not produce or unveil is an explanation. There are two reasons why *Diagrams* cannot be said to explain anything, or rather, to be more exact—since the form of the miracle "explains" some otherwise odd behavior in charismatic evangelical political and economic concepts and actions—why the miracle itself cannot be explained even as it explains other things. The first reason is that this structure cannot be thought of as a cause. The diagram of *Diagram* does not compel forces to behave in any way. Instead, it is just one pattern that affects and precepts can fall into if they are pushed that direction by other forces that are prior in logical or actual causation. To the degree that the pattern has any causal features, it is at best as something along the lines of a quasi-cause, an effect that retrospectively appears to be responsible for the very forces that brought that effect into being.

Under *Diagram*'s logic, though, the true nature of those forces cannot be addressed at any depth, which is the second reason while the miracle cannot be explained even as it explains. Some of the forces, such as intermediary sense perceptions, can be described, but the production of any longer causal narratives involving them is cut off by the fact that these forces inevitably lead off into other domains outside the miracle, and it is not clear that there is a consistency as to the direction that various individual causal accounts of specific miracles would be heading. Given the importance of the modular nature of the miracle for *Diagram*, the source of these forces cannot be addressed in advance, or at least not in a manner that is not at best merely probabilistic. This modular construction speaks not only to the source of forces but also to their character. There is a ban, established in *Diagram* by theoretical fiat, on "looking behind" the miracle. The logic of this across-the-board ban is that reading this through a sociological, psychological, phenomenological, or for that matter theological lens introduces new actors into the equation and transforms the content of forces, thereby denaturing the miracle. This is not a rejection of any of those analytics across the board. Rather, it is merely a statement that taking up a theoretical claim involving "looking behind" changes the nature of what is being looked at, and the question of the capacities of the miracle as an object becomes a different conversation.

Which brings us to *WGTB*. That book, with its focus on the psychological capacities of absorption, and its deep-seated enmity to reductionist evolutionary psychological approaches, may seem to be working against *Diagram*'s sensibility (or perhaps, considering the sequence in which they came out, it would be better to say that *Diagram* tries to retroactively legislate *WGTB* as being invalid). If anything would be a case of looking behind the miracle, one might reason, it must be this act of tying the miracle to a specific human cognitive faculty. This, of course, would be to ignore the different ultimate horizons that these books are working toward; *Diagram*'s ban on looking behind the miracle only makes sense in light of its original project of focusing exclusively on charting the variability of the miracle. But even more to the point, seeing *WGTB* as looking behind the miracle would be to miss out on what I feel is probably one of the subtler, and yet one of the most audacious, aspects of that book.

The nature of *WGTB*'s achievement stems from how it engages in comparison. The book uses comparison in a way that is radically different from the way that comparison is deployed in *Diagram*. As stated, *WGTB* treats the miracle as a single object, so it may seem that the kind of fractal comparisons *Diagram* makes are impossible, and that only more standard forms of frontal and lateral comparison are possible. It is certainly true that despite *WGTB*'s interest in the domestic miracle, there are moments of frontal comparison. This frontal comparison, though, is done merely to set up the stakes of Luhrmann's project, to underline the degree to which the sensorial world of Vineyard believers stands in stark relation to the consensus sensorium of most nonbelievers. And lateral comparison is important to the book as well. In *WGTB*, the Vineyard is discussed in relation to other forms of first-world ecstatic religiosity and early modern spiritual exercises. More central to the argument about the difficulty of first-world contemporary supernaturalized faith are the contrasts between the Vineyard's mode of dealing with more-than-human agents and forces and the way that "never seculars" deal with the same actors. "Never seculars" are believers who do not have nonbelief laid out as a possible alternate position, and therefore whose reasoning regarding supernatural entities is not informed by a corrosive knowledge of consociates who, when it comes to God, "have no need of that particular hypothesis" (to quote Pierre-Simon Laplace's most likely apocryphal statement). But I would argue that the pivotal form of comparison that informs this book is one that no spatial metaphor can shoehorn into Candea's template. That is because it is my argument that *WGTB* engages in the work of comparing the miracle *with* the miracle *itself.*

This comparison of the miracle with itself is achieved through *WGTB*'s continual juxtaposition of a psychologized depiction of the miracle as a model of sensory attunement with the more experience-near accounts of her informants learning to identify God's voice (with these accounts drawn from either particular informants or ideal-typical general statements about what "the Vineyard" does). These are not two different sets of miracles, but rather the same process, differently framed. It is the contrast between these frames that gives rise to what I might want to call a naive reading of *WGTB* as an exercise in psychological reductionism. Under this reading, *WGTB* is about middle-class Americans training their imaginations to such an extent that they can spontaneously, unconsciously, and convincingly confabulate an unreal God as a conversation partner. While I suspect that this "village atheist" version is the most common academic reading of the book, it is not without problems. The first problem with the naive reading is that *WGTB* states that neither ethnographic methods nor anthropological thought are capable of "disproving" (or for that matter, proving) the existence of God. Of course, hypothetically showing that Vineyard believers are caught up in hallucinatory practices would not prove that God does not exist, it would merely show that whether or not he exists, this set of his adherents are not in communication with him in the way that they imagine themselves to be. But the implicit logic of *WGTB*'s claim of anthropological agnosticism is that this particular study, while it may not endorse Vineyard beliefs about speaking with God, does not impeach them either.

This idea of an implicit agnostic logic in *WGTB* might seem less speculative when we add the claim that the juxtaposed accounts of the miracle themselves have no single causal structure. This is to say that when reading the book, *it is literally undecidable whether the psychological techniques described in the text encourage either the capacity to imagine a God who isn't there or the ability to listen to a God whose presence is obscured.* We are told at times that speaking to God is like having an imaginary friend—that is, an entity that is not there and whose features are purely granted by the person conjuring him up. But at other times, we are told that this is like learning the vocabulary of wine tasting, something that, despite all its pretense, is a way of describing an object that is there and that does have definite features. But what is not going on here is some kind of ambivalence. These moments that seem to lean one way or the other on the existence of God are capable of being rehabilitated for the alternative position. Rather, the argument that I am making here is that *WGTB* can be understood *either* as endorsing a logically prior human imagination that creates a flawed, unreal God or alternately as endorsing a logically prior God who is only approachable through exercises of a flawed imagination that has a tendency to be "unreal" in the sense that it is also prone to creating false positives.

This feature of the book became clear to me when, as preparation for writing this chapter, I reread *WGTB*, but from the hypothetical position of someone who took the existence of God as already given. Reading the book through that prism did not produce moments of frustration or disagreement with the book's narrative. Rather, it shifted discussions that previously read like psychological compensation for social isolation as being instead discussions on why a relationship with God is a healthier mode of being in the world than the self-imposed alienation of the nonbeliever. Moments that naïvely read as fantasy and playacting instead read as the use of human imagination to dilate the senses such that the ever-present but subtle cascade of divine signs could become both perceptively apprehensible and cognitively legible. It felt as if I had come across a second esoteric text hidden in plain sight on the exoteric surface of the first.

But understanding *WGTB* in this way would be to hypothesize some kind of duplicity or bad faith. The bad faith, however, was my own. That is, neither reading is the "message" of the book, and I had merely taken my presumptions (either my original nonbelieving understanding or a later "as-if" religious understanding) and introjected them into what I thought was the book's argument. But recall, the book is not arguing that God is entirely a symptom of a hypertrophied capacity for absorption, or that psychological self-development is the royal road to God. Rather, the book is working against a claim that belief in the contemporary world is not a precarious achievement but merely an unthinking and untroubled endorsement of faith that is blind to evidence. The act of comparing the miracle to itself, or couching the same process in two different parallel framings, achieves that (incidentally, I should note that it is this labor that causes the presence of causal language in *WGTB*). But this achievement is a negative achievement—not the presentation of an explanatory framework but rather the undermining of another.

Is it possible to argue that *WGTB* not only "explains" the miracle but does so twice over by offering two frameworks for the miracle that can be set in relationship to each other in two different ways? I would imagine that the answer to that provocation depends on how one understands explanation. It seems that the presence of two different readings that threaten to vitiate each other, and that are presented by the text in a way that makes it impossible to use textual evidence to decide between them, cannot stand as an explanation. Indeed, a multiplicity of explanations that cannot, on their own terms, collapse into a single explanation seems to foreclose explanation to the same degree that *Diagram* does through its ban. The reasons behind this foreclosure of explanation of the miracle in each case, I would argue, are those discussed in the first half of this chapter: the foreclosure of frontal comparisons, the inability to resort to the logic of the miracle to explain itself, and the ethical risk of an overweening condescension that results from an anthropological demystifying reading (a risk that other extra-anthropological demystifying accounts of the miracle would not share, due to their having a different relationship with the believers whose practices they are interrogating).

NOTE

1. It should be noted that this is not the case when discussing how miracles are conceived of in the Church of Jesus Christ of Latter-day Saints (see Bialecki 2022).

REFERENCES

Badone, E. 2013. "Reflections on Death, Religion, Identity and the Anthropology of Religion." In *A Companion to the Anthropology of Religion*, edited by J. Boddy and M. Lambek, 425–443. Hoboken, NJ: John Wiley and Sons.

Bialecki, J. 2017. *A Diagram for Fire: Miracles and Variation in an American Charismatic Movement*. Oakland: University of California Press.

——. 2018. "Anthropology and Theology in Parallax." *Anthropology of this Century* 22. http://aotcpress.com/articles/anthropology-theology-parallax/.

——. 2022. *Machines for Making Gods: Mormonism, Transhumanism, and Worlds without End*. New York: Fordham University Press.

Bielo, J. S. 2009. *Words upon the Word: An Ethnography of Evangelical Group Bible Study*. New York: New York University Press.

Candea, M. 2016. "Going Full Frontal, or the Elision of Lateral Comparison in Anthropology." *L'Homme* 218 (2): 183–218.

Coleman, S. 2000. *The Globalisation of Charismatic Christianity*. Cambridge: Cambridge University Press.

Elisha, O. 2011. *Moral Ambition: Mobilization and Social Outreach in Evangelical Megachurches*. Berkeley: University of California Press.

Engelke, M. 2002. "The Problem of Belief: Evans-Pritchard and Victor Turner on 'the Inner Life.'" *Anthropology Today* 18 (6): 3–8.

——. 2007. *A Problem of Presence: Beyond Scripture in an African Church*. Berkeley: University of California Press.

Harding, S. F. 2000. *The Book of Jerry Falwell: Fundamentalist Language and Politics*. Princeton, NJ: Princeton University Press.

Heo, A. 2018. *The Political Lives of Saints: Christian-Muslim Mediation in Egypt*. Oakland: University of California Press.

Holbraad, M. 2007. "The Power of Powder: Multiplicity and Motion in the Divinatory Cosmology of Cuban Ifá (or *Mana*, Again)." In *Thinking through Things: Theorising Artefacts Ethnographically*, edited by A. Henare, M. Holbraad, and S. Wastell, 199–235. Abingdon, UK: Routledge.

Holbraad, M., and M. A. Pedersen. 2017. *The Ontological Turn: An Anthropological Exposition*. Cambridge: Cambridge University Press.

Larsen, T. 2014. *The Slain God: Anthropologists and the Christian Faith*. Oxford: Oxford University Press.

Lemons, D., ed. 2018. *Theologically Engaged Anthropology*. Oxford: Oxford University Press.

Lewis, C. S. 1947. *Miracles: A Preliminary Study*. London: Godfrey Bles.

Luhrmann, T. M. 2012. *When God Talks Back: Understanding the American Evangelical Relationship with God*. New York: Vintage.

Marshall, R. 2014. "Christianity, Anthropology, Politics." *Current Anthropology* 55 (S10): S344–S356.

Meneses, E. 2018. "The Ontological Turn for Christians." *On Knowing Humanity* 2 (2): 28–31.

Merz, J., and S. Merz. 2017. "Occupying the Ontological Penumbra: Towards a Postsecular and Theologically Minded Anthropology." *Religions* 8 (5): 80.

Robbins, J. 2003. "What Is a Christian? Notes toward an Anthropology of Christianity." *Religion* 33 (3): 191–199.

——. 2020. *Theology and the Anthropology of Christian Life*. Oxford: Oxford University Press.

Scherz, C. 2017. "Enduring the Awkward Embrace: Ontology and Ethical Work in a Ugandan Convent." *American Anthropologist* 120 (1): 102–112.

Scott, M. W. 2013. "The Anthropology of Ontology (Religious Science?)." *Journal of the Royal Anthropological Institute* 19 (4): 859–872.

Strhan, A. 2015. *Aliens and Strangers? The Struggle for Coherence in the Everyday Lives of Evangelicals*. Oxford: Oxford University Press.

Taylor, C. 2007. *A Secular Age*. Cambridge, MA: Harvard University Press.

Vilaça, A. 2015. "Do Animists Become Naturalists When Converting to Christianity? Discussing an Ontological Turn." *Cambridge Journal of Anthropology* 33 (2): 3–19.

——. 2016. *Praying and Preying: Christianity in Indigenous Amazonia*. Oakland; University of California Press.

Willerslev, R., and C. Suhr. 2018. "Is There a Place for Faith in Anthropology? Religion, Reason, and the Ethnographer's Divine Revelation." *HAU: Journal of Ethnographic Theory* 8 (1/2): 65–78.

4

EMERGENT EXPLANATION

Matei Candea and Thomas Yarrow

What is the relationship between ethnography and explanation? Is anthropological explanation necessarily explication?

Oriented by these questions, this slightly unusual chapter takes the form of a dialogue between two old friends. Its initial prompt was an exchange of book manuscripts in 2016–2017. Matt read a draft of Tom's then-forthcoming *Architects* (2019), an ethnography of an architectural practice; Tom read a draft of Matt's then-forthcoming *Comparison in Anthropology: The Impossible Method* (2018). Both were struck by the similarities and differences between the two texts.

Both books were animated by a shared sense of the nature and purposes of anthropological knowledge production. We both felt that a set of developments— including the increasing prominence of grant-based funding for anthropological research and university auditing of "research excellence"—have inflamed an existing anthropological passion for a certain kind of "pointiness." The making of "take-home points"—preferably radically "new," "groundbreaking," and of international and interdisciplinary "significance"—is increasingly pushing out the slower, less easily transportable aspects of anthropological knowledge making.

Neither of us was surprised to find this shared ambivalence to singular, simplified argumentation. More striking was the fact that our accounts call for, and in their form exemplify, two precisely opposed explanatory orientations. While Tom's is informed by an argument for the power and importance of the *implicit* in anthropological exposition, Matt's book makes a case for the need to be more *explicit* about the purposes and limitations of our conceptual devices. These different concerns are mirrored in the form of the books themselves. Tom's book is almost entirely ethnographic, an experiment in the backgrounding of theory. Matt's book, by contrast, has no ethnography at all. In sum, the books are inside-out versions of each other.

Although neither of us took "explanation" as a key focus, the arguments just discussed bear directly on the question of what form anthropological explanation does and should take. Specifically, these relate to the ways in which anthropological explanations entail implication and explication of various kinds. Asking the question in these terms made us both wonder whether we had elaborated a shared sensibility in different directions or more profoundly disagreed. Is there an "explanation" within which both positions or strategies can sit? As we began to write this chapter, we were still not sure.

The form of the chapter tracks this emergent conversation. The first and second sections, written in our individual voices (the first by Tom and the second by Matt), outline the place where each of us started. The third section is organized as a turn-taking dialogue that sets off from these initial positions. It probes differences between our approaches, as a way to exemplify broader questions about the nature and value of anthropological explanation. The conclusion, like this introduction, is in a shared voice. Though we had not anticipated this at the outset, this dialogue led us to tease out a concept—that of "emergent explanation"—that we argue plays a particular role in anthropological thinking. Retrospectively, it became evident that the chapter is a recursive demonstration of the logic it helps to conceptualize: its form is also its finding.

Implicit Explanations

Architects is an ethnographic account of an architectural practice, focusing on the lives of ten architects and the work they undertake, mostly in the confines of a single office, based in the United Kingdom. Their comments on early drafts were not encouraging. "A bit dense," as one of them put it, "my eyes slightly glazed over." Another used architectural imagery to highlight a linked problem: "It's as though you've constructed a building and left the scaffolding on," he remarked. The "scaffolding," by which he meant conceptual reflections and theorized arguments, seemed a distraction from the descriptive passages he found most engaging. The metaphor of the scaffold is drawn from his own professional practice and is also a reflection of the sensibilities that orient it. Architects, at least in this practice, spend a lot of time discussing "precedents," drawing influences and inspiration from other designs, but in the final instance they are clear: a building cannot be explained; it has to speak for itself.

These responses made me question how and for whom I was writing, and provided the stimulus for an experiment in ethnographic form. The analogy is not precise but got me thinking: What would a description look like if conceptual engagements with other scholars were treated as "scaffolding"—enabling the construction of a descriptive object whose effectiveness depends on their ultimate removal? Perhaps the problem was not to explain their lives but to refrain from explaining them too much. In a sense there is nothing particularly new in this approach, good ethnography having long been recognized as a matter of "showing, not telling."

Rewriting the manuscript, I aimed to downplay, footnote, or excise various elements of narrative scaffolding, including some that academic readers have routinely come to expect: broadly speaking, a theorized argument of a singular kind, explicating novelty against an already-existing set of conceptual positions. Other scholars have highlighted some of the linked changes associated with the reification of this academic form of writing: the rise of interdisciplinary research relates to a proliferation of perspective so that novelty must be more explicitly stated to stand out; processes of research audit, at least in the United Kingdom, are associated with definitions of "world-leading" research, more readily recognized through novelty staged argumentatively using established professional discourse; the rise of social media as a research tool likewise leads to a proliferation of voices, and the imperative to speak loudly in order to be heard.[1] Writing is more often driven by argument, resolved as "points" with a singular focus that can be easily and quickly grasped by a readership with limited time and attention. Even as ethnography is often reified and romanticized in anthropological discussions, in practice the "showing" seems to be increasingly less valued than the "telling."

With these thoughts in mind, the first plank of academic scaffolding I sought to remove was *theory*, in the specific sense of externally derived explanatory frameworks of a singular kind. "Writing is an exercise in humility," writes Nigel Rapport: "Theory is proud in its claims at comprehension. But theory would nevertheless appear to be the principal means of *misrecognition*—not the reverse—in its making of the other into an object whose point is to prove that theory's assumptions. Academia would seem prone to theoretical pride: trafficking in coherent stories and plausible interpretations. But . . . this is to bring an artificial order to a wild world" (2015, 681).

By implication, his target is "grand theory," and its claims to what Dominic Boyer, James Faubion, and George Marcus (2015) elsewhere characterize as a "monopolizing epistemic authority," an inherent asymmetry of knower and known. Rapport advocates the antidote to this, in writing that "eschews theory for a return to the everyday." Arguably, he presents the relationship between academic theory and everyday life in overly binary terms: all descriptions must "tame" to some degree, simplifying even if only enough to bring particular forms of complexity into focus; all are oriented by more or less stated interpretive approaches, ideas drawn from other scholars or examples, that open up ways of seeing, even as they may close down others. Marilyn Strathern's (particularly 1988, 1991) insistence that "theory" and "description" occupy the same conceptual plane highlights how good descriptions arise through the comparative lens of other people and places. "Theory," from this perspective, is not a fixed set of ideas but the conceptual "remainder" of the descriptive act: how anthropological concepts are changed and extended in the act of describing particular circumstances. Still, the thrust of Rapport's argument has particular resonance in the current moment: pulled toward the assumptions and expectations of fellow professionals, anthropologists, like other academics, are routinely drawn into explanation that often seems to move away from the concerns that animate the lives of those we seek to understand. Even those approaches emphasizing the interdependence of theory and description have more often emphasized the theoretical implications of descriptions than the descriptive implications of theory.[2] My account was an attempt to move in the other direction, scaling back argument as a frame and focus of description. I hoped to amplify understanding of the complexity of architectural lived reality, to give more attention to those aspects that remain specific and inchoate, to dwell in architects' own explanations of what they do and why. Whether or not successfully, I aimed to refuse the kinds of exegesis that would render these details as epiphenomena of my own explanatory theory.

Second, and relatedly, my approach involved the deliberate attenuation of explicit *argument*. Focusing on Godfrey Lienhardt's ethnography of the Dinka, Michael Carrithers elucidates some of the elements that made the classic monographs of the middle of the twentieth century so compelling: "Lienhardt devotes his effort throughout to the knotty labor of finding the most felicitous way of characterizing the Dinka themselves, rather than adopting the established conceptual coinage of professional anthropology or engaging argumentatively with established professional opinions. He leaves us to *infer* his understanding of those other voices and how they might err" (2014, 136, emphasis added).

The vivid qualities of Lienhardt's writing were as much a function of what he said as what he did not. Literary theorist Wolfgang Iser develops this point while discussing Virginia Woolf's exposition of the role of the reader's imagination in the work of Jane Austen: "[The reader] is drawn into the events and made to supply what is meant from what is not said. What is said only appears to take on significance as a reference to what is not said; it is the implications and not the statements that give shape and weight to the meaning. But as the unsaid comes to life in the reader's imagination, so the said 'expands' to take on greater significance than might have been supposed; even trivial scenes can seem surprisingly profound" (1980, 111).

Imagination works through language as an interplay between explicit and implicit, revelation and concealment. Many good examples of this interplay exist in ethnographic writing, but the general shift to explication and argument has tended to leave less implicit.

A third and final form of textual attenuation relates to *analysis*. In her introduction to Marie Olive Reay's book *Wives and Wanderers*, Strathern explains, "In the book analysis remains very largely off stage . . . and the pride of place is given to descriptions of people's doings, as they apparently occurred, in storylike form." Comparing this to ethnographic writing of a more conventional kind, she notes, "Much ethnography is seemingly written of the moment. Yet the moment in which the ethnographer writes is also turned to the ends of exposition, and conveying a sense of immediacy has to compete with that. The trade-off between immediacy and reflection, between what is observed and what is analyzed seems inevitable." (2014, 46). If observation and analysis are inherently connected, Strathern highlights how minimization analysis has amplifying effects with respect to the capacity of observational description: without the framing post facto analysis of the observer, description captures quick changes from moment to moment, replicating the unpredictable qualities of social interactions: "An element in any 'encounter' is its unpredictability: people try to guess what will happen, watch how others behave, see how this or that person will react. The dynamic of the relationship makes everything for a moment unknown." (2014: 48) Analysis, of course, is needed, among other reasons, to spell out what is meant from what is said (or not), the contexts through which words and actions acquire significance. The aim of minimizing explanatory analysis related to a desire to amplify those forms of explanation that are emergent within the ethnographic contexts described.

I am aware of the irony that my own explanation of the limits of singular argumentation itself takes a rather argumentative and singular form. I am also conscious of the contradiction of arguing for a particular kind of exemplification that I have not in fact exemplified. I explicate these explanatory orientations and aspirations in the knowledge I have often and perhaps always fallen short of them. I hope that the book itself goes some way to demonstrating what I have here hoped to explicate. But many other and perhaps better examples of this approach exist, including a number of ethnographies whose narrative forms and sensibilities have inspired my own (particularly Crawley 2021; Luhrmann 2012; Pandian 2015; Yaneva 2009). Beyond their obvious differences of focus and approach, what I take these to have in common is the productive sense in which an explanation can be *implied* through an ethnographic description. In all these accounts, description is its own tacit explanation in ways that reach beyond a conceptual explication.

On Explaining Ourselves

Comparison in Anthropology: The Impossible Method is an account of anthropological comparison. As in a grotesque mirror image, the book consists almost entirely of what Tom's book seeks to leave out: theory, argument, and analysis. The book's prime material—what it describes—are theories and arguments. Whereas other meditations on comparison have woven their arguments and exemplified them through a range of ethnographic and historical contexts (see, for instance, Van der Veer 2016), the gambit in this book is to take anthropologists' own theories, arguments, and disagreements about comparison as the object of study and the source material. The book is, in that sense, a kind of historical ethnography of anthropology's own conceptual practices—it is, as Strathern perceptively noted, "a report from the field" (2020, 118), the field here being anthropological theory.[3] One reviewer at least was frustrated by the lack of ethnographic exemplification in the book (Gellner 2022)—but the point is precisely that the thickness of this particular style of ethnography is made out of what we normally think of as "theory."

The book is a description of these theories and arguments, but it is also self-consciously and explicitly an analysis, leading up to an argument of its own—indeed an explanation. By analyzing the recurrent patterns that emerge from anthropological writings about comparison, the book seeks to explain why, despite seemingly endless amounts of methodological reflection on the subject, anthropologists appear to have little agreement about what comparison is and how one ought to do it; it also seeks to explain why, despite a recurrent self-definition of comparison as the very heart of the discipline, anthropologists so often seem to conclude it is de jure impossible and yet carry on doing it all the same.

Its first part traces in some detail the extended and often convoluted debates anthropologists have had for around 150 years about comparative methods, paying particular attention to the recurrent ways in which they have sought to compare different modes of comparison. Over and again, these comparisons of comparatisms have tended toward dichotomies, marking out one older and misconceived vision against a newer and better alternative. These paired alternatives (historical comparison vs. functional comparison, structural vs. typological, interpretive vs. positivist, etc.) are never quite the same, but the form of the argument recurs: there always seem to be two ways of doing comparison, and one (the new one *we* are proposing) is better than the other (the old one *they* have been attempting). The result of these constant theoretical-methodological revolutions is a space of argument that undervalues continuities, shared techniques, and heuristic moves that carry over from one form of comparison to the next. There is a tendency to reinvent the wheel.

It is also a space in which differences in purpose tend to get elided. As Lawrence Fisher and Oswald Werner wrote of a different set of debates, "Any brand of anthropology can be shown to be woefully deficient if the objectives of one program of explanation are substituted for those of another explanatory program" (1978, 195). Different modes of comparison are often aiming at different ends. To ignore this is to forget the fundamental distinction between critiquing another scholar's goals and critiquing their devices. We too easily dismiss earlier visions of comparison on the grounds of what they couldn't do, or of what they systematically did wrong, without due attention to what they were trying (and not trying) to do. In so doing, we are often missing or choosing to ignore all the caveats that earlier authors set up about the necessary limits of their comparative devices. Concomitantly, in proposing bright new alternatives, or in praising those of our friends or mentors, we too easily forget what our own cherished devices can't do, or choose not to do.

Hence the book is, among other things, an argument for being explicit about the nature and crucially the limits of our conceptual devices. It is an argument for the value of explaining ourselves and our devices. The second part seeks to clarify this discussion by picking out some key formal properties of anthropological comparison, which orient the radically different uses to which comparative devices can be put. In so doing it focuses on—to borrow a central term in Tom's ethnography—"the space between" these different purposes, the methodological space in which anthropologists' comparative devices remain shared even as their purposes diverge.

This space can only be kept in view if we do away with the engrained mental habit, and scholarly convention, of taking things "with a pinch of salt." This habit gives one key to the paradoxical way in which comparison seems to be simultaneously impossibly complicated and wholly self-evident. Most of us are more or less acutely aware of the heap of objections raised at some point or other against almost every aspect of anthropological comparison—from the problem of identifying units of comparison, to the possibility of commensuration, to the politics of comparative representation . . . And yet—there's the paradox—we go on.

Thus we invoke cultural units, social groups or patterns of behavior, while all the time implying or stating that we are well aware that these are just convenient fictions and that reality is far more complex. We analogize entities while mentioning in passing that of course they are also, in other ways, profoundly different, or contrast them while gesturing to the fact that in many other ways they fade into one another. Some of us appeal to philosophically abstruse techniques for challenging the very grounds of what counts as an object or a relation, while all the while appealing to ethnographic particulars grounded in descriptions and local generalizations of the most conventional kind. At every turn, an implicit or explicit appeal to taking things "with a pinch of salt" keeps these contradictions out of view.

In one sense this is fine—such bracketing is unavoidable and productive. Comparisons can productively be imagined as bundles of heuristics that get jobs done, humble and unassuming techniques that churn away below the level of grand epistemological debates. These comparative moves, tricks, and fixes bracket extensively, they make no guarantees to absolute truth or exhaustiveness, and yet they keep the discipline going, keep it together, and produce exciting new work. It would be impossible to do any kind of intellectual work—or to live any kind of life—without bracketing. The vision of complete explicitness is a mirage.

There is a world of difference, however, between bracketing something and just forgetting about it. Heuristics are valuable primarily because we know when they fail (Wimsatt 2007). Or to put the point otherwise, in the language of politics rather than engineering, it is fine to exclude, black-box, and simplify *as long as we have a path back to and remain responsible for what is being left out* (Barad 2007).

In part because of the "pinch of salt," anthropologists have too often taken the impossibility of comparison for granted and just "gotten on with the job" under cover of some vague caveats. The resulting landscape is one in which we seem to be forever saying things we don't quite mean, to others who don't quite mean them either, but often in different ways or for different reasons. It is this habit of taking things with a pinch of salt, as much as anything else, that contributes to the sense that if we really thought about it, comparison would be impossible—so best not think about it too much.

Being more explicit about the limits and exclusions of each of our comparative heuristics, by contrast, can lead us to layer and combine them into thicker and more intricate comparative arguments. This means taking a step back from the ultimate point or aim of any given comparison, to ask what another, differently constituted comparative device might add. When your attention is hooked by a difference, ask also about similarities (and conversely); when you find yourself looking at objects, ask about the processes and relations of which these might in another sense be the effects (and conversely); and so forth. This might seem like a counterintuitive procedure. Why not simply get to the point? What it speaks to is the sense that to be animated by a purpose, to set a course for a particular horizon, is not the same as just imagining one has reached it. In that latter belief lies the risk of dwelling in platitudes and truisms. By themselves, our horizons have little power either to convince or to illuminate. After all, we can already see them from here!

This normative valuation of intricacy echoes the normative principle of "robustness." Robust combinations of heuristics are multiply redundant; they come at the same questions from different angles; they are interwoven in such a way that some can fail without sabotaging the entire enterprise. Robustness as articulated by engineering-minded philosophers of science such as William Wimsatt are implicitly wedded to one particular aim: the pursuit of the real, the objective, and the generalizable. The kind of robustness envisaged here, by contrast, could be deployed in pursuit of a broader range of aims. Indeed it would come in part from the way in which anthropologists aiming in radically different directions (toward generalization or critique, objective identifications or increasing self-doubt) work alongside one another and hold each other to account, not for their divergent aims but for their moves in the shared space of method.

Conversation
MC

In a way, the core of my argument in the previous section rejoins a claim by Fisher and Werner: "We take it to be essential and axiomatic in anthropology that one should 'explain oneself'—by making explicit one's objectives in explanation—before one advances explanatory statements" (1978, 195). Precisely because, as the introduction to this book argues, there is no single form of what might count as an "explanatory statement" in anthropology, it seems to me, intuitively, that being explicit becomes an essential component of any such statement. So is your argument for the value of the implicit an argument against explanation, or would you say there is such a thing—as your section title suggests—as an "implicit explanation"?

TY

I am not *against* explanation, nor am I opposed to explication. I want to highlight some of the routine elements of already-existing good ethnography that are elided or devalued where the emphasis is on explicated argument. This is partly a question of speed: various circumstances conspire to encourage us to write and to read quickly, to overlook subtlety, and to mistake the implicit for the absent.

I would say, by extension, that there is such a thing as an implicit explanation. This is at the heart of a lot of ethnographic writing and is both celebrated and overlooked in the disciplinary construction of ethnography as foundational. W. G. Runciman writes, "Primary understanding can itself, as always, be construed as explanation at another level. . . . [The statement], 'He is doing a rain dance,' answers, 'Why is Mr Morley stamping about on the outskirts of Bournemouth with feathers on his head?'" (1983, 168). In this instance the description (reportage, in his terms) is a fairly straightforward explanation to a straightforward, if unusual, question. The account of Mr. Morley could be further developed by adding details that might help us to understand what he was doing and why, without being explicit with respect either to the question that is being asked or to how this gives an answer. It is in the evocation of these details and the nuance with which they are evoked that the nub of good ethnography lies—hidden, in plain and obvious sight.

Though he does not put it in quite these terms, Michael Carrithers helps us to see how the craft of ethnographic description is partly in what is kept back or withheld. He sees the aim of ethnography as "creating . . . imaginative leaps to reveal the dense habits, arrangements and reasonings, and the forces of mutual entanglement and necessity that motivate human beings" (2018, 225), and he highlights the importance of apparently trivial details in opening out these "other worlds" (compare Narayan 2012, chap. 1):

> Much of the force of these minor appearances lies precisely in the resistance of these fleeting appearances to full understanding. They are somewhat explicable—this is a gourd, these are flies, this is a bird—but on the other hand their full meaning is withheld. Why are those flies there? What is that bird? How do these things have significance? This world gains its force in part through this resistance, a resistance anyone might meet when stepping into an unfamiliar scene, one which has some features that are understandable enough, but whose force of reality is amplified by those other features which are not, and which therefore challenge one's certainties. (Carrithers 2018, 226)

After *Writing Culture* (Clifford & Marcus 1986), and quite possibly before, these kinds of "vivid touches" have sedimented as part of a routine way of writing: richly evocative writing is often a rather cursory and formulaic preface to the "substance" of accounts that spell things out in more singular, more explicit terms: at one level ontologizing these details to emphasize the singular and general connecting strands (explanations of general ways of thinking and acting over and above the details); at another, elaborating how these add up to a conceptual argument (explanations of why existing theories are deficient or in need of revision).

None of this is per se an argument against explanation. At the level of contextualization, of the micro-comparisons of "this and that" (in your terms), it is indispensable. And at this level my argument is for more of it: more and richer extrapolations of what is meant from what is said; of what is happening in the silences or the gaps between the words; of how one person might say one thing in one moment and appear to contradict themselves in the next. This is not straightforwardly an argument for detail or complexity. A lot of very detailed and complex ethnographies can be very boring, which is to say that they fail, in Carrithers's (2018) terms, to "open a world," and so fail to allow readers to reimagine their own.

Returning directly to your question, my problem is not with explanation as such. I am rather voicing some disquiet that certain forms seem to be privileged at the expense of others. I am resistant to the forms of exegesis where too much emphasis seems to be on using the particulars of others' lives as illustrations of explanations of broader generalities (culture, ontology, society, and the like); I think there is a danger that we end up giving explanations that only make sense to those who are already part of a disciplinary conversation. This emphasis also leads away from the explanations that are there, complexly, more or less explicitly, in the words and deeds of those we seek to understand.

To turn this around as a question, I want to push you on your own formulation of the explicit. When you say that "the vision of complete explicitness is a mirage," to what extent is that a lamentation in relation to a goal you nonetheless think we should be aiming for? Are there, in your view, ways in which the curtailment of some forms of explication can be productive? And if so, where would these limits lie?

MC

That's a really good question—that caveat about the mirage of complete explicitness was in there precisely because I have a tendency to forget it. My weakness is the typical one of so many arguments in anthropology and beyond: one identifies a problem (in my case, "the pinch of salt") and then tugs in the opposite direction with all one's might, forgetting that one is pointing not toward an absolute good (as if it more explicitness were always better!) but toward a relative one: I think it would be nice to have a bit more explicitness, of a particular kind, in anthropology at the present time. But fundamentally, I think about explicitness what I think about comparison, or about explanation: to know how much is needed, and of what kind, one first needs to know *what for*, what the problem is. Explicitness is purpose-relative.

So to return to your question: When is the curtailment of explicitness good? My answer is, "It depends what you're trying to do," but *that* at least (what you're trying to do) needs to be made explicit. In every description, some things will need to be left out, whether that be ethnographic description or an account of "the literature," or even of one argument in one article. To say everything is to say nothing; even if it were possible, it would be boring! It might seem obvious—and a bit of a cop-out—to point out that the question of where and what to cut can only make sense in relation to an aim. What I would add is a plea for making the aim itself explicit.

And I say *that*, in turn, because my particular aim—here—is to point to the way in which anthropologists often talk (or shout) past each other because they are not being explicit about the extent to which they are just trying to do different things. But if I know roughly where they're heading, what their purposes and explanatory commitments are, it gives me a handle on what might be left implicit. It also allows me to have a conversation with these alternative accounts—maybe even to put them to use to sharpen my own—rather than just envision the encounter as a fight to the death.

I think this rejoins your earlier concern, about the way anthropologists can end up talking only to those already part of the conversation. One symptom of that, for me, is the kind of bad writing we all know (and I, for one, certainly have been guilty of), which is full of gesturing to influential authors and complex concepts—whether it be to praise or to trash them—without explicating them. It's another "pinch of salt" gesture—it's the "you know what I mean when I say X" tone. The stuff that you don't need to spell out is what you have to assume your reader already knows. The more of that stuff there is, the smaller your implied readership. Hence why I so love the advice Annemarie Mol once gave me: "Write for your students, not for your teachers." I always took that advice to mean spelling things out (and in the process—no small benefit!—realizing whether you yourself understood them properly). But I realize in reading your text that one could also take it the other way, toward less framing—not allowing the account of the actual subject matter to be overshadowed by endless theory or meta-meta-meta-reflexivity.[4]

So from a similar concern, we're stressing different things. You're suggesting—I think—that a text is more open, less narrowly targeted, if it is more focused on the object than on the framework. I'm suggesting that a text is more open if it comes with a clear, accessible account of what it's for and what it is not trying to do. I don't think those are incompatible—indeed they might be mutually strengthening.[5]

That's my answer to your question. But your previous answer interestingly throws a spanner in the works by introducing or perhaps implying the idea—which I intuitively really like—of explanation as a kind of emergent property of the relation between a text and its reader. If you describe something well enough, I might find an explanation in there of something that was a puzzle to me but that you weren't particularly intending to explain. That's how I understand the idea that "the account . . . could be further developed by adding details that might help us to understand what [X] was doing and why, without being explicit with respect either to the question that is being asked or to how this gives an answer." This isn't so much an implicit explanation, however (which suggests you already know where you're trying to get to and have somehow produced that effect by cutting something out), and more like a "by-product explanation." The richer your account, the more likely that it will spark something off in someone (or rather, hopefully, lots of different things in lots of different people) that you could not have predicted or intentionally engineered. That space between the author and the readers is where a certain kind of understanding emerges. And it's true, fundamentally: good ethnography is supposed to give more than what you put in.

The idea of a by-product or, better perhaps, an "emergent" explanation does make my insistence on stating one's purposes seem a bit clunky—who cares what the author intended if the text works? And yet, I still think that would be letting the author off the hook a bit too easily. I still want to know what they were aiming for, even if in the end their account takes me elsewhere. "The author is dead" is convincing as a sort of abstract perspective on literature in general, but it's no way to live an academic life.

My questions to you: Have we cracked—some? all?—of anthropological "explanation" if we say that it happens, not within a single text, but somehow between an author and a reader (see Reed, this volume)? And a crucial reader here, as your own example illustrates, would be those whom in an older language one thought of as the "informants" themselves.[6] And if there's value in that thought, what, if any, are its limits?

TY

I agree this is an important aspect of anthropological explanation, though, for the kinds of reasons you so well set out in your book, I would be resistant to any sense that anthropological explanation could ever really be "cracked."

Your answer prompts the reflection that there are two ways in which an explanation can be clear: either in showing your "workings," allowing the reader to trace the steps you have taken; or through focusing on what those workings lead you to—in this case the descriptive object. I would agree that both of these can be effective (or ineffective) strategies, and the question of effectiveness is relative both to the writer's aims and to the readers'. Knowing how a painting was made (using what techniques, during what period, by what kind of painter, under what kind of influences) might help to explain the meaning of that painting, though it may also undermine the capacity of the painting to "speak for itself." Hence a lot of artists' resistance to these kinds of contextualizing moves.[7] I take it that this is the distinction you highlight between the object and the framework. I am not saying anthropologists should concern themselves with the object instead of the framework but rather, to reprise an earlier point, that the current political economy of higher education seems to lead to a distorting preoccupation with the framework.

I agree that a lot of ethnographies have the "by-product" explanatory function you describe. The reader gets more than the writer intends and the more so, the richer and more multistranded the description. From the writer's perspective, this quality might be amplified by a kind of underdetermination, dwelling in the specifics in a manner that allows the generalities, comparisons, and lessons to be drawn in different directions. The less the analogy is made in one explanatory direction, the more the reader is free to make it in their own. Perhaps this by-product explanatory function also explains why Bronislaw Malinowski's ethnography continues to speak to us, even as his theories are now of mostly historical interest. We can return to those circumstances and elaborate them in endlessly new directions. And perhaps there is also something in these classic ethnographies that we have lost, or at least abridged. The details of the case far exceeded the explanation they were intended to support. A lot of more recent ethnographic writing is more centrally oriented to illustrate argument.

Ethnography can also work as an implicit explanation, in the sense of a concept or idea that is there without being explicit. Most ethnographic writing does this to some degree, making a description a demonstration of an idea that is less than fully spelled out. Maybe this is more like ethnography as allegory: there is a message, which is more powerful because the reader finds it themselves. I would see these as two distinct ways of "saying more" by, in certain respects, "saying less" in others. In both instances the conceptual framework disappears in order to foreground the descriptive object. A world is opened for a reader more directly and immediately, because the descriptive language is transparent—not in the sense of revealing itself, but rather to the extent the reader sees through it.

Your discussion of comparison helpfully highlights how these are routinely invoked, in clarifying the forms these comparisons can take, and in reminding us how frequently we are drawn back to the same heuristic devices. I am in full agreement with your diagnosis that valorizations of "frontal comparison" (how understanding "them" helps us to understand "us") have tended to elide or devalue the central role of "lateral comparison"—the way in which we understand the "here" of a particular case in relation to the "there" of others. Am I right to infer from your account that you are saying that comparisons help us to explain, and the more, and more explicit, the better? Or could you imagine such a thing as an "implicit comparison"? This is really an extension of my thinking laid out earlier in this chapter, and the argument that there can be a virtue to not fully articulating the comparative relations through which a text is built. For instance, "here and now" comparisons are intensified by curtailing "there and then" comparisons. Might ethnography open a world more effectively, or anyway differently, without the constant deferral and relation to others? Even to the extent that ethnographic understanding is pieced together through these various comparative understandings, might there, on the foregoing logic, be a narrative rationale for reining them in? Of many good examples, Kath Weston's *Traveling Light* (2008) illustrates the amplification and intensification that occurs when the focus is squarely on the ethnographic "here and now."

MC

Before answering your question, I just wanted to mention that one thing you wrote in your previous answer clears up for me how we end up in different positions while aiming at the same thing—the point where, as it were, our sensibilities go out of synch. You write, "There are two ways in which an explanation can be clear: either in showing your 'workings,' allowing the reader to trace the steps you have taken; or through focusing on what those workings lead you to—in this case the descriptive object."

That formulation made me realize that we share a contrast between object and framework, but we apply it differently. In your contrast, the "object" is the description (or the reality behind it, perhaps?) and the framework is the additional layer of explicit commentary on the object or description.

By contrast, in my usage, ethnography (thick description, profusely lateral comparison, etc.) is the framework, the device, and the setup, and the "object"—what this is all leading toward—is the "point," the argument, the conclusion, the end, or the purpose of the description. This is why, in arguing for essentially the same thing—the value of "staying with" slow ethnographic and descriptive richness—you call for less framing, and I call for more.

But to come back to your question. The short answer is, yes, I agree that simply outlining one case and letting the reader compare with other cases they already know can be productive. The text itself is not explicitly comparative, but it becomes or rather "affords" a comparison in a relational way, like the "emergent explanations" introduced earlier. Indeed this could be a classic instance of what might be meant by a relational or emergent explanation: your case makes me think of a comparison that explains something to me about something else. We could apply our (emergent!) distinction between "implicit" and "by-product" here: an implicit comparison would be one in which the author already has a further point of application in mind that he or she artfully conceals, hoping that the reader will tease it out for themselves. By-product comparisons would be all of the possible other ways in which readers could build comparisons out of the one case presented. And since we never know what our readers already know—indeed, that's the beauty of it—the range of by-product comparisons or explanations could be limitless, and surprising.

Let me take one example, to try to tease out this "implicit" versus "by-product" distinction further. It starts from Alexei Yurchak's argument in *Everything Was Forever* (2006), about semantic shift in late Soviet socialism—the way official language came to operate as a pure form, dissociated from its earlier meaning. Yurchak's account was and continues to be an incredibly rich source of by-product comparisons for me, and I will come to one of those in a minute. But Yurchak and Boyer later explicitly drew out one key comparison, between the hollowing out of late socialist discourse and the hollowing out of "late capitalist" or "neoliberal" discourse (see, for instance, Boyer 2013; Boyer and Howe 2015; Boyer and Yurchak 2010). This explains interesting echoes in terms of parodic humor, for instance. That's a very interesting analogy (although it might be intriguing to excavate further some of its limits).

By contrast, the by-product comparison that struck me most directly upon reading Yurchak's book was grounded in his description of the way the emptying out of official language affords the formation of an "us" (*svoi*) community: a majority of people who bond around the knowledge that they say things without quite meaning them. To be *svoi* is to plot a course between two ways of taking Soviet language seriously: *svoi* are neither true believers (extremists, apparatchiks) nor committed or outspoken critics (dissidents). They are "normal people," living in the middle, in a space characterized by a particular kind of pragmatism, humor, and everyday ethics. Many believe in the original ideals of socialism, the onetime reference of a now-empty language, while recognizing that the systemic way of pursuing them is broken—they thus do their best to act well in an untenable situation. And they also make some occasionally unsavory compromises. Indeed it is precisely the refusal of such compromises that marks out dissidents, from the *svoi* perspective, as unsympathetic characters who refuse to accept a kind of moral community of compromise and in the process make waves for their *svoi* counterparts. To paraphrase an archetypal joke told by Yurchak, everyone is standing in a pool of shit up to their necks, but the dissidents are making it worse by waving their arms about in indignation.

Now as it happens—and I have no reason to think Yurchak specifically intended this—that description made me think (on a completely different scale of seriousness, of course, but that is how comparisons often work) of the particular ambivalence created among (some) academics today by the managerial language increasingly imposed on our practice by university administrations. I'm picking this example precisely because it nicely takes us back to the common gripe from which we both started. Excellence indicators, feedback forms, and quality assurances have devolved into meaningless formalities associated with direct power. That situation has fostered explicit critique, certainly, but it has also led to the constitution of more ambivalent everyday intimations of community among working academics, *svoi*, "normal people" as it were, who neither believe in the meaning and value of these forms nor stand up against them explicitly (which would make waves and trouble for everyone else). Like *svoi* in Yurchak's account, many of us hold dear the actual ideals that this managerial language is purportedly trying to point to. Indeed many of us struggle to make space for *actually* good teaching and *actually* rigorous and thought-provoking research, often against the grain of these managerial requirements themselves.

Whatever the value of this rough-and-ready comparison, it exemplifies the sort of dynamic we've been talking about: through the comparison that I drew out of it, Yurchak's account *explained* things about a situation familiar to me, without ever explicitly setting out to do so. And I mean "explained" in a number of different senses here, which range across the epistemological spectrum of visions of explanation. Reading Yurchak with my own academic life in mind outlined a structure, linking discursive, affective, practical considerations into a pattern; it suggested some complex bundles of causal or quasi-causal relations (the emptiness of language, added to a clear power structure, can lead to a particular set of moral and relational options); it helped me get an interpretive handle on why self-proclaimed "dissidents" against academic managerialism might occasionally seem unlovable even to those who might fundamentally agree with them—and so forth.

Is that a by-product comparison or explanation, or was that implicitly "there" in Yurchak's account? I don't know, but if it was the latter—that is, if Yurchak had intended it but then kept it hidden or held it back—I don't see what the added value of that move would have been. Conversely, this by-product comparison or explanation sprang to my mind without being hampered by the fact that Yurchak himself has a very clear and explicit set of arguments in that book—the book is, among other things, an explanation of how state socialism could seem unshakable and yet, as soon as it had fallen away, could seem so obviously to have been teetering. Nor was this hampered, either, by the fact that I encountered the text in relation to specific further comparisons by Yurchak and Boyer, which made it seem like the key comparative point of relevance was to a particular genre of political comedy or political performance. In other words, I don't think that the author's telling me what they intended is likely to limit me or throw me off the scent of other potential comparisons. Being told what lessons (the author thinks) are to be drawn doesn't limit my own ability to draw other lessons.

That being said, I agree that a text in which the description is crowded out by theoretical apparatus will be less effective at doing that elicitative work. Equally, I don't think it is productive or necessary to *actively erase or submerge* one's explanations, arguments, or comparisons. When you say, "Most ethnographic writing does this to some degree, making a description a demonstration of an idea that is less than fully spelled out," I agree—but I would add that this is because it can't be fully spelled out, not because of a careful decision to withhold full exposition. There is always more than one point to any good description. That's why you can't reduce a description to a point. To give the point *and not the description* is a radical loss, including of the potential for further (unexpected) comparisons or by-product explanations. But to give one point—to add it, rather than substitute it to the description—doesn't curtail further ones. To come back to your metaphor, I don't think that knowing the techniques of painting, or the intentions or historical context of the painter, dulls the effect of any given painting—not in the way in which, for instance, knowing how a magic trick is done destroys the magic trick, or being explicit about how much a meal cost destroys the hospitable effect of inviting someone to partake of it.

Where I think we're in full agreement—and here we're back to these values of thickness and slowness—is that the author's point or purpose can't ever replace the actual description. This is true whether this is a description of one case or a description of lots of lateral comparisons of this and this and this and that. Indeed one key argument of my work on comparison is that those reduce to each other: if you zoom into the texture of ethnography, what it is actually made of, then you see that every "single-case" ethnography is already built out of lateral comparisons of moments, instances, individual people, particular statements, and so on. The thickness and richness of the description is already—in my terms—a matter of the multiplication of lateral comparisons. And it's true that, by contrast, frontal comparisons (comparisons not of "this and that" but of "us and them") are often used as ways of drawing things to a point. They are very good at marking out, explicitly, what matters, where the key contrast or similarity lies. As you noted earlier, frontal comparisons are a classic device for making "pointy" theoretical value out of thick ethnographic description ("Here, *precisely*, is how their conceptual world transforms ours!"). My concern—that the excitement of frontal comparison can tend to crowd out the value of lateral comparison—thus maps very closely onto yours. And of course, just as you're not suggesting that we do away with theory, I'm not suggesting that we do away with frontal comparison—just that we replace it within its proper role as one among other anthropological heuristics.

On Emergent Explanations

This conversation doesn't have a natural endpoint. For the purposes of this chapter, however, one might round things off here by pointing to one central concept that has come together in the foregoing pages of the chapter—namely, the concept of an "emergent explanation." Retrospectively we might define this in general terms as the ways in which an explanation emerges between and across different explanatory contexts that relate without being commensurate. Our account has foregrounded the productive ways in which such explanatory differences may be reconciled without resolving into a singular frame. Emergent explanations keep different explanatory aims and assumptions productively in view and actively related.

We offer the concept of emergent explanation as a critical alternative to those explanatory forms that seek to collapse or resolve difference, most obviously in the form of singularizing arguments, monocausal explanations, and those that generalize—for instance in ontological, cultural, or sociological terms—as truths over and above the contexts they relate. We hope this formulation adds conceptual precision to the more instinctive explanatory orientations that framed our account: emergent explanations necessarily work in slow and concrete ways that do not lend themselves to totalization or generalization. They are not incompatible with summary but remind us that the sum is always productively more and less than the parts.

Our shared investments in this concept are located in relation to specific aims and assumptions, which the dialogue has helped us to understand and formulate. In hindsight, we might recognize how our dialogue was framed by a normative question, which can now be recast more descriptively as two distinctive versions of how best to encourage explanatory emergence. Each of these anticipates and frames two specific kinds of readerly response.

Through Tom's contributions, the idea of an *implicit explanation* foregrounds the explanatory potential of description: how descriptions of specific ethnographic contexts open explanatory possibilities, conceptual affordances, and imaginative possibilities in ways that are unanticipated and open-ended. In these cases, it was suggested that description involves tacit explanation that is distinct from the straightforward absence of explanation. The reader infers or imagines concepts in a way that depends on the absence of explication.

Matt's discussion, by contrast, foregrounds the productive effect of being explicit about what particular accounts and analytical devices (such as particular forms of comparison) were intended to do, and what they were not intended to do, in order to leave the reader free to go somewhere else with the material, to do something else with the analytical devices, beyond the horizon and interests of the author. Here explanatory emergence is facilitated by the way in which the author's explanatory frameworks are laid out explicitly, so that they can be bypassed or borrowed and put to work in other contexts.

In specific ways, our contributions have highlighted distinctive forms of explanatory emergence through which anthropological texts are routinely built. Matt has made explicit how explanations are built intertextually as relationships between concepts and contexts that are in some sense analytically reconciled. Tom foregrounds how ethnographic writing has an emergent quality involving the juxtaposition and comparison of explanatory difference within a given field. In both these senses, the explanatory work of anthropology often has an interstitial quality, residing between and across other explanatory concepts and contexts. Comparisons juxtapose contexts that help to explain each other. "This" illuminates "that" and vice versa. However, the insights that emerge from these ethnographic and analytic relations cannot be subsumed in positions over or beyond these elements.

Our dialogue led to a concept that neither had anticipated (emergent explanation) and is therefore an instance of what this concept purports to explain: through our chapter, explanation emerges as an unfolding relation between positions. At least for the authors, the result is not a collapsing or resolution of those differences but a better and more reconciled sense of where those differences lie. From both of our perspectives, the chapter helps to explain something that we hadn't understood as we set out to write it. Our explanation is emergent in the dialogue, in the sense of being led toward an unanticipated understanding through a process. It remains epistemologically emergent in the sense that it relates our differences of orientation without resolving these. We hope this ultimate irresolution creates a space in which readers can draw their own conclusions.

NOTES

1. This point has been made by a number of commentators from various disciplinary perspectives, including anthropologist Marilyn Strathern (2000), sociologist Frank Furedi (2004), science studies scholar Isabelle Stengers (2018), and literary critic Stefan Collini (2016).

2. Godfrey Lienhardt's approach to ethnography has some resonances with recent accounts, in their insistence on starting from understandings of the ontological basis of others' categorical distinctions (I am thinking particularly of Viveiros de Castro's "Perspectival Anthropology and the Method of Controlled Equivocation" [2004] and Holbraad's *Truth in Motion* [2012]). My own account draws inspiration from these approaches: in their insistence that "theory" and "description" occupy a single plane of explanaton; and in the methodological orientation that engenders commitment to the effort to understand others' lives, as the necessary corollary to a skepticism toward anthropology's own concepts and theories. Description of the particularities of others' lives requires that we—professional anthropologists—reconfigure our categories in the act of bending them

to circumstances for which no encompassing explanation exists. By the same token, ethnographic description is the means by which new concepts are generated, as old ones are extended or found to be wanting. The rationale is compelling (Englund and Yarrow 2013), and many of the resulting descriptions are insightful. However, asymmetries are reintroduced where the point of this equivocation is less the production of faithful descriptions than the novel conceptual points that derive from these. Despite a number of notable examples to the contrary, proponents of this approach seem more often oriented by the aim of unfolding theory (ethnographically derived concepts) from description (the circumstances of other people's lives) than to the production of accounts in which description *is* the point. In this respect Lienhardt exemplifies a distinct approach, from which I draw inspiration.

3. In respect of that strategy, the book has a far more distinguished precursor in Strathern's own *Partial Connections* (1991; updated 2005). As one reviewer just as perceptively noted, this is the sort of book a former journal editor would write "in recovery mode" (Shryock 2019, 414).

4. I have some sympathy with Latour (1988) when he sarcastically points at the towering layers of reflexivity piled on in some postmodern accounts: here is me thinking about me thinking about me thinking about me writing this thing about me thinking that . . . It's as if we thought our readers were too naïve, he says, and so we had to diminish the power of our writing, by stepping outside the text to caveat it. Equally, though, I am no longer convinced by Latour's converse proposal, that we should just live with the fact that all we do is tell stories (even when they are stories about us telling stories . . .), and so that instead of caveating and diminishing their power to convince, we just try to make our stories as convincing as possible, using every rhetorical and stylistic trick in the book. That's in essence his argument against explanation too—a description that needs an explanation is not a good enough description—and I no longer find that convincing.

5. It's no surprise, perhaps, that Mol's own *The Body Multiple* (2002) is written in two layers—I wonder if you're arguing for the top layer and I'm arguing for the bottom layer?

6. This idea gets us close to the vision of explanation that, as we note in the introduction, philosophers of science have described as "pragmatic"—a vision of explanation as relative to the interests and perspectives of those who receive it.

7. See also Rapport (this volume).

REFERENCES

Barad, K. M. 2007. *Meeting the Universe Halfway: Quantum Physics and the Entanglement of Matter and Meaning*. Durham: Duke University Press.

Boyer, D. 2013. "Simply the Best: Parody and Political Sincerity in Iceland." *American Ethnologist* 40:276–287.

Boyer, D., J. D. Faubion, and G. E. Marcus, eds. 2015. *Theory Can Be More than It Used to Be: Learning Anthropology's Method in a Time of Transition*. Ithaca, NY: Cornell University Press.

Boyer, D., and C. Howe. 2015. "Portable Analytics and Lateral Theory." In *Theory Can Be More than It Used to Be: Learning Anthropology's Method in a Time of Transition*, edited by D. Boyer, J. D. Faubion, and G. E. Marcus, 15–38. Ithaca, NY: Cornell University Press.

Boyer, D., and A. Yurchak. 2010. "American Stiob: Or, What Late-Socialist Aesthetics of Parody Reveal about Contemporary Political Culture in the West." *Cultural Anthropology* 25:179–221.

Candea, M. 2018. *Comparison in Anthropology: The Impossible Method*. Cambridge: Cambridge University Press.

Carrithers, M. 2014. "Anthropology as Irony and Philosophy, or the Knots in Simple Ethnographic Projects." *HAU: Journal of Ethnographic Theory* 4:117–142.

——. 2018. "How to Open a World 1: Humanism as Method." In *Anthropology as Hom-
age: Festschrift for Ivo Strecker*, edited by F. Girke, S. Thubauville, and W. Smidt,
225–250. Cologne: Rudiger Koppe Verlag.

Clifford, J., and G. Marcus, eds. 1986. *Writing Culture: The Poetics and Politics of Ethnography*. Berkeley: University of California Press.

Collini, S. 2016. "Who Are the Spongers Now?" *London Review of Books* 38:33–37.

Crawley, M. 2021. *Out of Thin Air: Running Wisdom and Magic from above the Clouds
in Ethiopia*. London: Bloomsbury.

Englund, H., and T. Yarrow. 2013. "The Place of Theory: Rights, Networks and Ethnographic Comparison." *Social Analysis* 57(2): 132–159.

Fisher, L. E., and O. Werner. 1978. "Explaining Explanation: Tension in American Anthropology." *Journal of Anthropological Research* 34:194–218.

Furedi, F. 2004. *Where Have All the Intellectuals Gone?* London: Continuum.

Gellner, D. 2022. Review of *Comparison in Anthropology: The Impossible Method*, by M.
Candea. *Journal of the Royal Anthropological Institute* 28:378–379.

Holbraad, M. 2012. *Truth in Motion: The Recursive Anthropology of Cuban Divination*.
Chicago: University of Chicago Press.

Iser, W. 1980. "Interaction between Text and Reader." In *The Reader in the Text: Essays
on Audience and Interpretation*, edited by S. Suleiman, 106–119 Princeton, NJ:
Princeton University Press.

Latour, B. 1988. "The Politics of Explanation: An Alternative." In *Knowledge and Reflexivity: New Frontiers in the Sociology of Knowledge*, edited by S. Woolgar, 155–176.
London: Sage.

Luhrmann, T. M. 2012. *When God Talks Back: Understanding the American Evangelical
Relationship with God*. New York: Vintage.

Mol, A. 2002. *The Body Multiple: Ontology in Medical Practice*. Durham, NC: Duke University Press.

Narayan, K. 2012. *Alive in the Writing: Crafting Ethnography in the Company of Chek-
hov*. Chicago: University of Chicago Press.

Pandian, A. 2015. *Reel World: An Anthropology of Creation*. Durham, NC: Duke University Press.

Rapport, N. 2015. "The Consequences of Anthropological Writing." *Journal of the Royal
Anthropological Institute* 21:680–683.

Runciman, W. G. 1983. *A Treatise on Social Theory*. Vol. 1, *The Methodology of Social
Theory*. Cambridge: Cambridge University Press.

Shryock, A. 2019. "The New Basics: Pushing 'Refresh' on the Comparative Method." Review of *Comparison in Anthropology: The Impossible Method*, by M. Candea. *History and Anthropology* 31 (3): 410–416.

Stengers, I. 2018. *Another Science Is Possible: A Manifesto for Slow Science*, translated by
Stephen Muecke. London: Wiley.

Strathern, M. 1988. *The Gender of the Gift: Problems with Women and Problems with Society in Melanesia*. Berkeley: University of California Press.

——. 1991. *Partial Connections*. Savage, MD: Rowman and Littlefield.

——. 2014. "Introduction." In *Wives and Wanderers in a New Guinea Highlands Society:
Women's Lives in the Wahgi Valley*, edited by Marie Olive Reay, 43–56. Acton, Australia: ANU Press.

——, ed. 2000. *Audit Cultures: Anthropological Studies of Accountability, Ethics and the
Academy*. London: Routledge.

——. 2020. *Relations: An Anthropological Account*. Durham, NC: Duke University Press.

Van der Veer, P. 2016. *The Value of Comparison*. Durham, NC: Duke University Press.

Viveiros de Castro, E. 2004. "Perspectival Anthropology and the Method of Controlled Equivocation." *Tipiti* 2:3–22.

Weston, K. 2008. *Traveling Light: On the Road with America's Poor*. Boston: Beacon.

Wimsatt, W. C. 2007. *Re-engineering Philosophy for Limited Beings: Piecewise Approximations to Reality*. Cambridge, MA: Harvard University Press.

Yaneva, A. 2009. *Made by the Office of Metropolitan Architecture: An Ethnography of Design*. Rotterdam: 010 Publishers.

Yarrow, T. 2019. *Architects: Portraits of a Practice*. Ithaca, NY: Cornell University Press.

Yurchak, A. 2006. *Everything Was Forever, Until It Was No More: The Last Soviet Generation*. Princeton, NJ: Princeton University Press.

BOURDIEU, THE DEMYSTIFYING POWER OF INDIVIDUALISM, AND THE CRISIS OF ANTHROPOLOGY

Gildas Salmon
Translated by Nicolas Carter

There was a time when anthropologists used to apologize for not sufficiently explaining the behaviors, institutions, or ways of thinking that they studied. Their discipline was still young, they said; for the time being, all they could do was offer a description, which would serve as material for the day when the human sciences finally reached maturity. Well, no one is holding their breath any more. And the claim to explain is now (and has been for some time) met with pervasive skepticism. If it were just a healthy skepticism about the prospect—always just around the corner—of a nomological synthesis in line with the natural sciences, it might be seen as a sign of the confidence acquired by a professional group with enough self-assurance to define its own standards endogenously. But in reality this sentiment hides much more than a desire to escape the injunctions of an epistemology based on a faulty template: it is, above all, the forms of explanation specific to anthropology, which in its "golden age" defined its very identity, that are now rejected wholesale; a rejection all the more total in that it is beyond debate and simply goes without saying in practice.

Modern anthropology's crisis of explanation is an autoimmune disease. It is symptomatic of a constantly renewed protest against the program that presided over the birth of the discipline in the late nineteenth and early twentieth centuries. Explaining, back then, was about taking a practice and associating it with a social form of organization by means of rules or collective norms. Whether we stop at identifying shared values or endeavor to see in these the expression of a particular division of labor or mode of production—the long-standing quarrel between the "understanding" approaches and those that claim to be more rigorously explanatory—is less important here than the fact that we subsume individual action into a collective form.[1] This operation is not, of course, limited to anthropology: it underpins all the social sciences and is particularly strongly shared with sociology. And yet it continues to elicit a special sense of unease among anthropologists. Which is not to say that this should be viewed as a local phenomenon; on the contrary, the self-loathing that dogs anthropology should be seen as the expression of a crisis that has gripped the apparatus of the social sciences as a whole.

The social sciences are political sciences: they seek not only to describe but also to orient action.[2] Their birth in nineteenth-century Europe reflected an attempt to acquire, through new tools of inquiry, an intellectual and practical hold over the accelerating political, economic, technical, and ethical transformations we have bundled together under the term *modernization.* At the heart of this process, which classical sociology set out to elucidate and regulate, lies the rise of individualism, understood as an emphasis on the individual as endowed with rights and as an autonomous agent, particularly (but not exclusively) in the economic field (Karsenti 2006). At the theoretical level, this movement found an echo in the doctrine of natural law and political economy. Placing the individual at the pinnacle of the social order, measuring the rationality of that order by its ability to satisfy the interests of the individuals within it, freeing them from the straightjacket of the collective norms that stifle their capacity for economic initiative—such forms of reasoning do not merely express the individualization of modern societies: they strive to intensify and accelerate it, dismissing all that stands in their way as vestiges or obstacles.

Compared with these individualizing forms of knowledge, sociology ranks as a countermovement: its founding act—whether we ascribe it to Émile Durkheim, Max Weber, or even Karl Marx—was not to deny the process of individualization at work in European societies but rather to describe it as a product of nonindividual factors, be they morphological transformations, the displacement of religious norms, or the history of modes of production. From this angle, sociological explanation is about reframing the way modern societies spontaneously look at themselves, by asserting that only a holistic viewpoint is able to grasp the conditions under which the individual is produced, and in so doing cure the pathologies engendered by individualistic forms of economic, legal, or psychological reflexivity.

The crisis afflicting anthropology since the last third of the twentieth century stems from the central but uncomfortable position it occupies in this system. On the one hand, it is the condition sine qua non for the triumph of the holistic viewpoint. The study of nonindividualistic societies (nonindividualistic in the sense that they do not systematically understand actions in terms of economic calculations, subjective rights, or even individual human responsibility) serves to isolate, in a more legible form, types of collective determination of practices that can then be traced through into modern societies. But this first impetus is indissociable from a second one—couched in privative terms that designate these societies as "nonmodern," "nonindividualistic," or worse, "primitive"—that consists in asking anthropology what it is that modern societies are breaking away from when they individualize.

This second movement, which was treated as a given in classical sociology, fell into crisis after 1945, bringing the first down with it. An unprecedented pessimism about the trajectory taken by modern societies, combined with the shock wave of decolonization, challenged the idea that anthropological knowledge of the "nonmoderns" (though people were suddenly hesitant to use such labels) was in any way subordinate to the self-understanding of the "moderns." The rejection of evolutionism, decried as an intolerable form of eurocentrism, exposed an asymmetry between sociological holism and anthropological holism. In sociology, individual actions are embedded in collective determinations as a way of taking a sideways look at the process of individualization, the existence of which is recognized as a core social fact about modern societies; in anthropology, however, the same approach seems destined to confirm the absence of any concept of the individual as such.

It is clearly impossible to strip this conclusion of its normative implications: as individual autonomy is the cardinal value of modern societies, any holistic explanation is automatically complicit in denying recognition to those who, as a result, find themselves reduced to the status of mere executors of collective norms; in other words, to heteronomy. Starting in the 1970s, under the dual pressure of the common accusation leveled at anthropologists—namely, that they were reifying an immutable social order that ruled out any prospect of emancipation for the citizens of postcolonial nations—and the new surge of individualism that had taken hold of Western societies, anthropology regrouped around the epistemic and political imperative of demonstrating that individual action could not be reduced to norms, to rules, or to the wider group, even in the seemingly least individualistic societies. This paradoxical program makes anthropology a social counterscience destined to relentlessly undermine its own legacy: a conceptual infrastructure suspected of confining agents inside rigid, essentializing frameworks.

The sudden disaffection for structuralism and the exoneration of ethnography from any anthropological ambitions, limiting it to a celebration of singularity or a postmodern collage of heterogeneous voices, are symptoms of the deliberately counterexplanatory nature of some of the most important trends in anthropology in recent decades. While acknowledging the salutary effects—

making us wary of the easy appeal of a holistic approach that might be exercised to the detriment of those to whom it is applied—we are entitled to ask, after four decades, whether this program of self-demystification is not a victim of the law of diminishing returns. For the answer to this question, and for new ideas to put anthropology back on its feet without once again subordinating it to sociological evolutionism, we can of course only look to the anthropologists. The aim, in this chapter, is therefore simply to offer a description of this sea change in the economy of anthropological knowledge, of which the ripples are still very much being felt today. Because it is one of the earliest expressions of this transformation, and because it explicitly challenges the classical paradigm, Pierre Bourdieu's *Outline of a Theory of Practice* (1972) offers a special insight into this crisis of holism. The question it poses is nothing less than this: What place can anthropology occupy, and what place does it seek to occupy—other than rejecting the one originally assigned to it—in (or perhaps outside) the space of the social sciences? It is therefore from this work, rather than from the radical forms of deconstruction that emerged in the wake of postmodernism, that we start out.

In Praise of Strategy

The founding act of Bourdieu's program is a critique of ethnology, aimed primarily at its dominant form in the France of the 1960s and 1970s: the structural anthropology of Claude Lévi-Strauss. For Bourdieu, however—himself an ethnographer of Kabylia—structuralism is only the most extreme form of the objectivist illusion inherent in the ethnologist's position of exteriority relative to the society under study. This problem is, admittedly, common to all the social sciences: under the label of the "scholastic illusion," Bourdieu was constantly highlighting the difficulties raised by the position of the researcher within the division of labor. As an agent "kept in reserve" away from production tasks, the intellectual tends spontaneously to project his or her disconnection from the world—the *skholè*, which suspends all sense of practical urgency—onto agents who seek not to interpret their environment but to act on it (Bourdieu 1972, 226; 1997). With ethnology, however, this exteriority is doubled, as the familiarity that sociologists always have with the members of their own society, to a greater or lesser degree depending on their class differential, is no longer present. The holism that comes so spontaneously to anthropologists, that of the model and the rule, owes much more to the nature of the ethnographic relationship than it does (as the evolutionists maintained) to the type of society studied. To believe that there are societies where the behaviors of agents really do *obey* rules—as opposed to modern societies where the rise of individualism means that we have to take account of interests—is to equate the ethnographer's intellectual approach to activities whose practical grammar is unfamiliar with the determining principle of action (Bourdieu 1972, 227–239). That being the case, we cannot arrive at the "praxeological" knowledge that Bourdieu calls for unless we forever abandon the forms of explanation preferred by ethnologists.

Logically enough, it is in the field of kinship—the flagship of comparative anthropology ever since the *Elementary Structures of Kinship* (Lévi-Strauss 1949)—that Bourdieu sets up his stall. "La parenté comme représentation et comme volonté" (Kinship as representation and intention), outwardly an account of an exception that runs counter to the exchange theory of marriage—"Arab"-style marriage between parallel cousins—in fact uses this example to challenge the very foundations of the structuralist approach, which reasons in terms of kinship systems. The ethnologist, being "outside of practice," and having no interest in the forms of marriage observed, takes a purely theoretical view of them (Bourdieu 1972, 108). This reduction of practice to theory, which Bourdieu calls "objectivism" because it ignores the viewpoint of the actors, is reflected in the primacy given to the legal language of the rule. Only someone who is not looking to get married can afford to overlook the obvious fact that the name of the game is not to marry by the rules but rather to marry well, and that, far from blindly following a rule that assigns them a preferential spouse, those involved adopt matrimonial strategies aimed at accumulating symbolic and economic capital. One must understand the violence of the struggles that lie behind the order of the rule: the supposed reciprocity of matrimonial exchanges masks a power play in which family trees are manipulated to present, in the most favorable light, alliances that could never be deduced from the logic of genealogy alone (122–125). Even names are usurped. Far from being a faithful reflection of genealogy, such marriages reflect a constant struggle for position: to name one's son after a famous ancestor is to claim the prestige of the bloodline, to the detriment of other branches of the family (101).

This form of demystification is so well attuned to our critical common sense that it can be hard for us to perceive its paradoxical side. With a little effort of historicization, however, we can uncover a surprising turnaround in the economy of anthropological knowledge. The generations of anthropologists of the late nineteenth and first half of the twentieth centuries, such as Franz Boas, Marcel Mauss, and indeed Lévi-Strauss, fought to gain recognition for the idea that those who had hitherto been dismissed as savages in fact followed elaborate systems of norms. To pursue the theme of kinship, Lévi-Strauss's theory of reciprocity showed that complex and seemingly irrational sets of rules could be reduced to a small number of perfectly coherent social integration mechanisms (Lévi-Strauss 1949). In other words, in the classical phase of anthropology, the collective norm is what elevates individual action. It is worth looking back at *The Gift* here. Mauss can hardly be accused of naïveté: the agonistic logic he sees at work in the potlatch proves that there is no such thing as a "free gift." And yet, unlike Bourdieu's, the thrust of his argument is not about unmasking the self-interested calculations that lie behind ostentatious shows of generosity. No, Mauss seeks to demonstrate that the economics of modern European societies cannot simply be reduced to utilitarian calculations, and that one cannot entirely ignore the archaic—in the sense of fundamental (Mauss would say "eternal")—principle of the creation of reciprocity and obligation through exchange. The "archaic," in other words, contains the truth about modernity, and it should lead us to identify and reactivate, in the modern world, forms of solidarity that cannot be reduced to purely mercantile logic, specifically in the form of social insurance mechanisms (Mauss [1923] 1950, 260). Bourdieu, on the other hand, uses modern economics as the yardstick of truth for a set of practices that the Kabyles (Algerian Berbers) themselves insist on presenting as disinterested: in his case, it is about demystifying the gift by comparing it to mercantile exchange, bringing to the surface forms of self-regarding calculation that such societies—in which the economy is not disembedded—refuse to acknowledge.

That this operation was presented as a way of enriching our conception of the agent in nonmodern societies says more about us, perhaps, than it does about the people under discussion. Its success shows that this type of demystification satisfied a key requirement in Western societies where, from the 1970s onward, strategic action became the only authentic form of action, while obedience to collective norms was relegated to the level of "mechanical" execution. In answer to Lévi-Strauss, who argued that the rules put in place by Australian societies to ensure harmonious social integration could only be understood by means of high-level formalization techniques, Bourdieu countered that structural anthropology reduced the individual to a puppet, governed by rigid rules, whereas individuals were in fact capable of cheating and of manipulating the norms to their own advantage (Bourdieu 1980, 167). This criticism is founded on the axiom that to respect social agents, one must accord them the status of *homo economicus*. Under the cover of a critique of narrow economism, the concept of symbolic capital allows individual optimizing rationality to be extended to behaviors that cannot be explained by the search for profit in an immediately material form. If we accept, with Durkheim, that the cult of the individual is the normative underpinning of modern societies (Durkheim 1893), then anthropology's current crisis of explanation must be seen as a consequence of transformations in this curious religion: when the irreducibility of the individual to the group is held up as a core value in their own societies, anthropologists can no longer put forward holistic arguments without appearing to deny their informants the status of full-fledged subjects.

Conversely, revealing individualistic strategies of material or symbolic capital accumulation among Kabyle peasants now passes as a kind of rehabilitation.

Rekindling Criticism

Denouncing the illusion inherent in the ethnologist's position of exteriority is only the first step in Bourdieu's critique. The real problem is that the ethnologist is the objective accomplice of the dominant class. By adopting the viewpoint of the rule, the ethnologist is a half-consenting victim of the official image that the group wants to present of itself. All too happy to find good informants who can supply systems of rules that correspond to the epistemological canons, the ethnologist generally holds back from pushing the questioning too far. In so doing he or she enshrines, as objective truth, the vision of the social order that the dominant succeed in imposing, to their advantage (Bourdieu 1972, 108, 148). As a result of this reversal of perspective, the so-called view from afar is requalified as an unquestioning adherence to the viewpoint of those in power: the ethnologist is the one who does not even have the bare minimum of critical distance shared by the dominating and the dominated, all of whom more or less know, often in rather obscure ways, just how much self-interested calculation goes into fabricating the social order. Although Bourdieu often couches it in epistemological terms, his critique of structural anthropology is above all a political one. The radicality of his stance goes well beyond the opposition between objectivism and subjectivism: Bourdieu's sociology is not structuralism with a bit of phenomenology added on. It is the knowledge that there is no external viewpoint on society. From this perspective, ethnology, seen as a fundamentally conservative discourse, is reduced to an exaltation of the established order.

This devaluation of ethnology in favor of a sociology of domination is linked to the rekindling of a form of demystification that had been banned from anthropology decades earlier (Bourdieu 1980, 246). Anthropology had managed to obtain scientific legitimacy during the twentieth century only by suspending all criticism of the societies it studied. The critique of non-Western societies was, of course, central to the discourse of the colonial powers, a discourse embodied by the twin figures of the missionary and the administrator. Assertions that the Brahmans or the Marabouts were no more than crafty profiteers taking advantage of popular superstition to maintain their prestige, that local elites were corrupt and purely self-serving when they pretended to set out collective norms, or that the colonized societies forced women into abject submission were commonplace in the colonial literature of the nineteenth century.

The obligatory suspension of criticism by which ethnologists sought to free themselves from such value judgments does not of course imply that they adhered unreservedly to the norms and practices of the societies they described. Lévi-Strauss formulated a canonical version of this new professional ethic in a chapter of *Tristes Tropiques* in which he affirms that the degree of injustice is roughly the same in every society (1955, chap. 38). Every society is therefore a legitimate target of criticism. But the ethnologists' position demands that they refrain from denouncing injustice in the societies they study. It is only in their own society that they have any right to push for political reform, as criticism can only come from within. In an asymmetrical power situation where the ethnologist belongs to a society that is richer and more powerful than the one studied, any criticism from the outside is automatically taken as a scientific justification for the domination exerted on these societies by states of European origin.

There is indisputably something transgressive about Bourdieu's stance, but it can only be understood in the light of a broader history of criticism in the social sciences. We should therefore begin by taking a step back in time. With its suspension of criticism of the "Other," while at the same time maintaining the possibility—even the requirement—of criticism "at home," anthropology in the first half of the twentieth century triggered a general crisis in the type of criticism that had been introduced by classical sociology. The sociological critique, as defined by Durkheim and, with some variants, by the other founding fathers of the field, relied crucially on anthropology as it sought to find a balance between the modern and nonmodern elements within contemporary societies.

All true sociology is based on a duality of some sort. Unless they shut themselves away inside a static vision of the social order, sociologists and anthropologists cannot simply be content with describing its internal coherence. They must strive to reveal a tension between (at least) two heterogeneous principles of social organization. The most developed form of this model is found in Durkheim, in the form of the tension between mechanical solidarity, based on resemblance, and organic solidarity, based on the functional integration of difference (Durkheim 1893). But the opposition between status and contract in Henry Maine, between *Gemeinschaft* and *Gesellschaft* in Ferdinand Tönnies, or between hierarchy and equality in Louis Dumont plays a similar role. Although these concepts do not map onto each other perfectly, it is obvious in each case that one of the principles is more modern, and is defined by reference to political economy and contract law, while the other is more nonmodern, and that it is through anthropology that we can grasp this other mode of social cohesion in its purest form. That being the case, the core problem of classical sociology is how to strike the right balance between these two elements. And as a general rule, the critical formula adopted by sociology is not to oppose the moderniza-tion of society but to show that this modernization needs to be held in check by ensuring that we never forget the nonmodern principle, which prevents mod-ern society from dissolving into a disparate scattering of economic agents or legal subjects.[3]

This model, which underpinned the politics of the social sciences, was mor-tally wounded by the critique of evolutionism. Boas was probably one of the first to dispel the idea of a unitary scale of social evolution, arguing instead that socie-ties are the fruit of histories that cannot be reduced to each other (Salmon 2013a). More widely, anthropology's journey toward autonomy, as it gradually emancipated itself from its status as an auxiliary science to sociology, favored the conviction that "primitives" could not be plotted onto earlier stages of a his-torical timeline that the Europeans had covered more quickly than the rest, and that could somehow be identified from the progressive transition from one mode of solidarity to another. By the same token, the idea of using anthropology to avoid and rectify the excessive individualization of modern societies became in-operative: the rejection of evolutionism precluded the whole idea of slowing down modernization by reactivating nonmodern elements, since *nonmodern* was now defined as an imaginary retroprojection dreamed up by the moderns.

Incorporating Structuralism

What kind of explanation, what kind of critique, can anthropology bring to bear if its role is no longer to identify some sort of counterweight to modern indi-vidualism? This question, which loomed large over the last third of the twenti-eth century, continues to trouble us today, and the identification of optimizing strategies among the peasants of Kabylia offers a provocative answer: anthro-pology serves to demystify the belief in rules. Its task now is to give the social sciences a good lesson in individualism, and to cure them of their fictitious be-lief in a unified and harmonious social order. What makes this turnaround even more spectacular is that just a few years earlier, Bourdieu's analysis of the same society in *Le Déracinement* remained within the orbit of the classical paradigm. In it, he described the trauma caused by the brutal entry into the market econ-omy of peasants for whom utilitarian calculations remained an alien concept. The main thrust of his criticism is a denunciation of a forced march toward mod-ernization: because it does not give Kabyle society the time it needs to adapt and reconfigure its traditional forms of solidarity, the regrouping of the popu-lation imposed by the French Army is presented as nothing less than a break-down of society. Reading the description offered ten years later in *Outline of a*

Theory of Practice, it is hard to believe that the Kabyle peasants, now portrayed as deft optimizers of symbolic and material capital—albeit while never openly admitting to it—could have been destabilized by the introduction into their working arrangements of a form of accounting.

Does this turnaround mean that the duality between mechanical integration, based on uniformity and rule, and organic integration, which leaves room for individual initiative and the interplay of interests, is now a thing of the past? And that anthropology, as penance for having long underestimated the individualization of nonmodern societies, must now reorganize itself around a strict methodological individualism? Bourdieu's answer is actually more complex than that. It is not so much about eliminating the dualism inherited from the Durkheimian tradition as about rearticulating it in the form of a dialectic between the official and unofficial, of which his sociology represents, in some ways, a mirror image. The paradox, in other words, is that while anthropology is adopting individualistic instruments to reveal the mechanisms of domination in supposedly nonmodern societies, sociology is at the same time adopting—for domestic use—a set of holistic analytics with the aim of subverting the individualistic-meritocratic ideology that justifies the domination of one class over another.

To understand this curious dual-action mechanism, we need to consider the tense relationship that Bourdieu entertains with structural anthropology. His critique of the legalism of the *Elementary Structures* must not be allowed to mask the importance of the structuralist legacy for Bourdieu, in particular its "transformational" analysis, which he incorporates into his sociology while at the same time detaching it from the comparative ambitions it served in Lévi-Strauss.

The reproach often leveled at structural anthropology—that it immobilizes the social order in a rigid framework—is based on a profound misunderstanding. The concept of transformation, which Lévi-Strauss forged in the analysis of myths, in fact involves uncovering a dynamic that refers not to the evolutionary hierarchization of societies but to their horizontal articulation with each other. The basic principle of structural analysis is that every society is crisscrossed by lateral possibilities that are actuated by other societies. A myth, for example, can never be understood in isolation. It does not exist for its own sake; it is a transformation of stories told by neighboring societies. The only way to "explain" a myth is to retrace the process by which it is simultaneously translated and altered through a set of systematic operations (metaphorical transposition, inversion, etc.) when it crosses a cultural, linguistic, or ecological barrier. In this sense, a culture is not a self-enclosed totality but a point at which an unstable equilibrium is negotiated within a network of variants (Salmon 2013b). Structuralism is indisputably a form of holism inasmuch as its positioning theory of identity supposes the primacy of the system over the elements, but the system in question is located in the relations between societies, which define themselves and each other by the ways in which they differ. It thereby avoids the trap of defining its object of study privatively: whereas classical sociology defined the nonmoderns in opposition to Europe, at the risk of neglecting the differences between them, structural anthropology sets out from the networks of relations they maintain *with each other* in order to explain how differentiated identities are produced.

Bourdieu is not interested in the comparative problem. His critique of the *Elementary Structures* makes that perfectly clear. Whereas Lévi-Strauss set out primarily to account for the diversity of matrimonial systems, Bourdieu repatriates the whole question of kinship back within a single society. His aim is not to explain the diversity of social orders but to reveal the domination effects involved in keeping the Social Order as it is. As a result, the two approaches intersect more than they actually contradict each other. Lévi-Strauss himself, who never really saw Bourdieu's work as a genuine objection, emphasized that people undeniably adopt strategies, but the rules they play by—whether they follow them or break them—are not the same everywhere (Lévi-Strauss [1988] 2001, 145).

This side-lining of the comparative problem obeys the principle that there is no outside—that is, no fence to sit on in the primordial division between the dominant and the dominated. Like it or not, ethnologists belong to the situation they describe, and from this viewpoint, by suspending their criticism of the forms of domination they observe—in the name of their respect for a society to which they do not belong—they can only be siding with the dominant.[4] Though it explains why Bourdieu feels entitled to break free from cultural relativism, this principle seems destined to render obsolete the structural analysis techniques that Lévi-Strauss developed to describe the operations by which a myth passes from one society to another and is systematically inverted by those who borrow it. And yet . . . from the text on the Kabyle house in the early 1960s through to *Distinction* (Bourdieu 1979), transformational analysis lies at the heart of the Bourdieusian program. With this key difference: he gives it a twist that might be described as a "folding" operation. Instead of using structural analysis to grasp the mental operations involved in passing from one culture to another, he employs it as a technique for revealing how the public face of the social articulates with its hidden side.

This displacement is visible in "The Kabyle House or the World Reversed," a text that can be read as the generative formula of his sociology. The principle behind the analysis is to show that the layout of the Kabyle house plays on a set of oppositions between light and dark, up and down, dry and wet, raw and cooked, masculine and feminine, which are disposed in such a way that the house appears as a microcosm, reflecting the outside world by means of a general inversion of its coordinates (Bourdieu 1972, 71). The house is the dark, feminine side of the public world, which is a masculine world:

If we now go back to the internal organization of the house, we can see that its orientation is exactly the reverse of that of the external space, as if it had been obtained by a half-rotation on the axis of the front wall or the threshold. . . . The importance and symbolic value of the threshold within the system cannot be fully understood unless it is seen that it owes its function as a magical boundary to the fact that it is the site of a meeting of contraries as well as of a logical inversion and that, as the necessary meeting-point and crossing-point between the two spaces, defined in terms of socially qualified body movements, it is the place where the world is reversed. (Bourdieu 1972; Nice [trans.] 1990, 281–282)

This demonstration allows us to measure Bourdieu's debt to structuralism and to identify the principles by which he would divert transformational analysis from its initial purposes in order to set up a new regime of sociological criticism. In keeping with the model defined in *Mythologiques*, the crossing of a barrier—in this case the threshold of the house—produces a reversal of all coordinates. But beyond the apparent fidelity to Lévi-Strauss, Bourdieu subjects this structural analysis to three correlative displacements. The first reflects the absence of exteriority: Bourdieu does not study the circulation of symbolic systems between villages; he is interested in the ability of a social order to self-replicate from the inside, to turn in on itself by developing a dark side that is nonetheless structurally linked to the official world. The second displacement is to do with the importance given to the body. In Lévi-Strauss, transformations are mental operations. In this text, by contrast, the transformation is made tangible by a bodily operation: the half rotation performed on the threshold of the house, a gesture that conditions the transition from the public world of men to the secret world of women. The third displacement lies in the hierarchical nature of the transformation described. Lévi-Strauss was analyzing transformations between the myths of neighboring societies, and thus between formally equivalent entities, even if the balance of power between neighboring groups can vary considerably. The same is not true of Bourdieu's analysis of the Kabyle house. The transformation is intrinsically hierarchical; it does not take place between variants from different locations, but between a structurally unequal front side and reverse side (82).

The Twofold Truth of the Social

With these three displacements—the folding inward of the social order, the primacy of the body, and the hierarchical nature of the transformations between a dominant space and a dominated space—we have all the ingredients we need to understand the double-sided mechanism by which Bourdieu articulates holism and individualism, and the inverse positions that anthropology and sociology occupy within it.

The first point, the social order's ability to engender a mirror-image duplicate of itself—we can call this the schismogenesis of the official and the unofficial—clearly evokes Marx and his characterization of ideology as the imaginary inversion of a reality constituted by the relations of production. However, this comparison runs the risk of overlooking a key element: even if the discovery of a hidden inverted variant of the official version has a demystifying effect, as with the revelation of the strategies that govern the choice of a spouse, Bourdieu insists on the fact that the official level nonetheless possesses a reality that has to be taken into account in the analysis: "The official definition of reality is part of a full definition of social reality and . . . this imaginary anthropology has very real effects" (Bourdieu 1980; Nice [trans.] 1990, 108).[5] Unlike Marx, Bourdieu does not only confront the ideological illusion with the economic reality: he contrasts two different modes of social cohesion, which bear more than a passing resemblance to Durkheim's two modes of solidarity. The level that Bourdieu describes as being that of rules corresponds to the mechanical solidarity that underpins the representations shared by the group, while the level of interests can be compared to organic solidarity, since a form of group integration is produced through these matrimonial strategies or gift exchanges, even if it does lead to domination effects. But where Durkheim saw an authentic form of solidarity, Bourdieu sees only the interplay of individual egoisms, thus rejecting the founding act by which Durkheim separated his sociology from political economy. This sought to maintain a holistic viewpoint at the very core of modern economics by asserting that the division of labor was itself a source of solidarity. With Bourdieu, however, we are back to a head-to-head confrontation between a type of mechanical social integration that is illusory (but nonetheless real inasmuch as agents have to pretend to conform) and a maximization of interests consistent with the most orthodox economic rationality.

The principle underlying this mechanism is that a society is incapable of unifying in conformity with the values it claims to hold, and that it therefore relies—unavowedly—on a mode of integration that it refuses to acknowledge. On this point Bourdieu is faithful to classical sociology, for which every society plays on two heterogeneous principles of solidarity. But where Durkheim saw these two principles as dovetailing together, with organic solidarity gradually taking precedence as societies evolve toward modernity, Bourdieu folds them together to show that one is hidden beneath the other. It is this figure of the fold that allows the sociological duality of the principles of integration to function as a demystification device. Whence the importance of the concept of "twofold truth" (Bourdieu 1972, 368), which sets the sociologist the task of seeing, in every situation, the two contradictory—but nonetheless both very real—forces of social unification. Here Bourdieu is rekindling the ambition, typical of the Durkheimian school, of diagnosing the maladjustments of a society by reference to itself (Boltanski 2009, 29–30), except that these maladjustments no longer take the form of discrepancies in the process of historical evolution (such as where the law lags behind public morality or the actual division of labor) but rather assume that of an insoluble contradiction between two principles that can interrelate only in denial mode. This makes it possible to criticize a society entirely from the inside, without reactivating the old evolutionist instincts that had been disbarred by anthropology.

The second displacement that Bourdieu makes relative to Lévi-Straussian structuralism lies, as we saw, in the role he assigns to the body. In his analysis of the Kabyle house, the inverted symmetry that unites macrocosm and microcosm is linked to the half turn performed on the threshold, and therefore to the body as potential for action, as capacity for movement. If we are to hold this text up as the general matrix of Bourdieusian sociology—as I am seeking to do—then we should qualify this point. In "The Kabyle House or the World Reversed," the body acts as the operator of the transition between an outside world and an inside world, both of which correspond to distinct physical spaces. But if we ask what plays the role of the house in Bourdieu's sociology—the role of the mirror image of the public world—the answer would have to be that it is generally the body itself, in the form of the habitus. The body as a set of rule-governed gestures is the operator of the fold that bends the social space in on itself.

The concept of habitus can be seen as a paradoxical inversion of Noam Chomsky's concept of competence. The founding argument of generative grammar, and indeed of the dominant research program in the cognitive sciences, is the thesis of the underdetermination of the stimulus, which Chomsky used to refute behaviorism: the input (i.e., the phrases that the child hears during the language-learning phase) is infinitely poorer than the output (i.e., the ability of any speaker of a language to produce an infinity of well-formed utterances). Since the disproportion between the ultimately very limited number of phrases heard and the infinity of phrases that can be produced is so vast, Chomsky asserts that language learning is not a social process (Chomsky 1959, 1965). For him, linguistic (especially grammatical) competence is a biological given, and the learning process simply sets the parameters of certain secondary characteristics of this innate capacity. Bourdieu takes this model and inverts it: the habitus is indeed supposed to act as the generative formula for the diversity of an individual's practices, but for Bourdieu, contrary to Chomsky, the stimulus is *over*determined. One of the axioms of his sociology resides in the disproportionate weight given to a small number of social experiences acquired in early education: these shape the child's schemes of perception and action so deeply that they also determine all future situations in which the individual is involved.

What this means is that any ordinary sociological situation (any situation outside of the infant learning process) is *overdetermined* in the meaning of the word as used by Sigmund Freud, who uses it to refer to the way features of dreams can be involved simultaneously in several different associative series. The official reading of the situation is superimposed by the secret reading, to which habitus provides the key. The school examination, for example, which in its official definition neutralizes all social affiliations in order to judge candidates solely on the technical competencies they have acquired, is covertly overdetermined by the varying distance between the class habitus of the examiner and that of the student. This is the core of Bourdieu's critique of education: unmasking the subtle interplay of affinities or divergences of habitus that lies beneath the surface of the supposedly meritocratic universality of the school system. Bourgeois students, whose habitus is spontaneously adjusted to that of their examiners, always enjoy an unjustified and unjustifiable advantage over students from the "lower" classes, whose habitus is maladjusted relative to the institution and its agents (Bourdieu and Passeron 1970). The world reversed, then, is the body itself, which, through its attitudes and gestures, undermines the official definition of every situation. Bourdieu's sociology is very much a "sociology of tests" or "sociology of trials" (*sociologie des épreuves*)—to use an expression that later gained currency (Boltanski and Laurent 1991; Latour 1984)—but it quickly leads into a sociology of domination, because tests, and especially school exams, are structurally biased.

This takes us to the third displacement relative to structural anthropology: the hierarchical nature of the transformations. Where Lévi-Strauss studied the relationships between variants separated in space, Bourdieu uses structural inversion as an operator for the transition between two hierarchical levels, the official and the unofficial. And one of the more singular features of the Bourdieusian critique is the reversibility of this hierarchy. Of course, in every society, the official represents the dominant, public pole, while the unofficial embodies its secret, shameful flipside. When we look at the content of these two levels, however, we find a strict inversion between Kabyle society—which for Bourdieu fulfills the role of embodying traditional societies, alongside other examples closer to home such as the Béarn—and the France of the 1960s to 1980s, whose role is to embody modern societies.[6] At the risk of laboring the point, in Kabyle society, it is mechanical solidarity—the rule—that occupies the official pole, while the language of self-interest is its unspoken underside. In France, on the other hand, where the economy is disembedded, the interplay of interests is much more readily acknowledged, and so the unmasking of individual strategies does not have the same demystifying impact. Indeed, the school example shows that in our modern societies, the official language is that of organic solidarity, while mechanical solidarity is cast in the role of the darker reality behind the shared ideals.

In his work on education, Bourdieu always takes as his standard the model of an education system tailored to the needs of the economy, devoted exclusively to producing specialists endowed with differentiated technical competencies that correspond to the current state of the division of labor (Bourdieu and Passeron 1970, 202–206). The reason why he refers to this yardstick is that it relates to one of the key justifications for education: as an agent of organic integration in modern societies. It would be more accurate to say that the education system in modern societies acts as an exchange mechanism between the mechanical and the organic. It functions as a mechanical integrator in that by dispensing the same education to all, it is the locus for the inculcation of shared values. But at the same time as schools dispense this common education, the examination system produces an organic distribution in that individuals are assigned, on the basis of their talents, to occupations that will enable each of them to play their own role in the division of labor. The education system is therefore a mechanical institution with an organic vocation. It is this that makes it the focal point for the integration of modern societies.

The critical gesture tirelessly repeated in *The Inheritors*, *Reproduction*, and *State Nobility* seeks to demonstrate that the allegedly organic logic of the education system is constantly being undermined by latent forms of mechanical solidarity that, of course, no longer correspond to forms of integration of the group as a whole, but to partial mechanical solidarities, restricted to a single class. The vector of explanation and criticism in ideologically individualistic societies is therefore not economic calculation, as it was in the Kabyle ethnographies, but the lurking presence of class solidarity behind what outwardly appears to be a strictly functional selection process. This means that the hierarchy between the official and the unofficial is not a universal constant; it is a characteristic specific to every society that values one form of social integration at the expense of the other. Though Bourdieu never says so in as many words, his theoretical model assumes that every society needs both mechanical and organic solidarity, but that they can be articulated only by refusing to openly acknowledge one of the two forms. We should enter a caveat, however, as regards the symmetry between the principles of intelligibility in modern and nonmodern societies: "mechanical" and "organic" do not have the same meaning in each case. In the case of Kabylia, the mechanical takes the Durkheimian form of the shared rule, while the organic is reduced to the interplay of economic interests. In 1960s and 1970s France, on the other hand, the organic is valued as a principle of functional solidarity. Here, we are talking about organic solidarity in its fullest sense, not merely the logic of economic maximization. But this official organic solidarity is undermined by a mechanical solidarity that, in this case, is nothing more than class solidarity. So while the mechanical may act as a catalyst for demystification in modern societies, it does not unite them; it divides them irreducibly in the form of class antagonisms.

This chiasmus that governs the economy of sociological knowledge when it moves from nonmodern to modern societies gives rise to a counterintuitive principle: namely that the body takes on greater significance in the framework of a critical sociology of modern societies. Of course, the body plays a cardinal role everywhere in the production of the social order: every society is constructed primarily through the education of the body (Bourdieu 1972, 296). The difference is that in nonmodern societies, differentiated and hierarchical habitus are explicitly encoded in the body. The prototype is found in the construction of masculine domination: while the whole education of Kabyle boys teaches them to strike a self-confident pose, staring frankly upward and outward, the women are expected to lower their gaze, walk with small steps, and make themselves as inconspicuous as possible (292). Because it is accepted for what it is, this differential qualification of the body cannot act as a demystifying principle. It is not the body that is denied, but self-interest. In modern societies, by contrast, the logic of self-interest is more widely accepted; what is unavowable is the way officially egalitarian situations, and in particular school or professional examination situations, are subverted by the subtle inculcation of hierarchical dispositions into the members of different classes. In organic-ideology societies, habitus is therefore the structural equivalent of self-interest in mechanical-ideology societies.

As we saw from the reading of the *Outline of a Theory of Practice*, Bourdieu employs the modern—in the shape of capital accumulation strategies—as the truth of the nonmodern. In a further twist, this formula is reversed, because it is equally true that the nonmodern—this time in the form of the shaping of differentiated habitus—is the truth of the modern. This reversibility of demystification ultimately imbues anthropology with a more complex role than is suggested in Bourdieu's purely ethnographic works. If individualism is, after all, the primary tool for the study of traditional societies, such studies nonetheless serve to provide sociology with holistic instruments for unmasking the hidden face of officially individualistic societies.

Anthropology Left to Its Own Devices

The model employed by Bourdieu offers a uniquely illuminating illustration of the paradoxical position anthropology has been left in by the disintegration of the classical model. In antagonistic mode, its mission is to protest against an exaggerated holism that refuses to see the members of extra-European societies as autonomous individuals in their own right. But there has to be more to it than this salutary demystification, important though that is; otherwise anthropology would slide into a kind of pure individualism that, by losing sight of the issue of individuals' social production, would take it outside the remit of the social sciences.

Individualism, in anthropology, is of protest value only. That is why it only very rarely leads to individualistic modes of explanation. Bourdieu is one of the few to venture down this path, when he introduces economic optimization into the social practices of Kabyle peasants. But he does so as part of a two-stage mechanism, by leveraging anthropology's ascetic influence on sociology to dispel any romantic belief in obedience to rules and in the virtues of harmonious social integration, and then—beyond this initial demystifying phase—by revealing habitus-forming practices that are then redeployed to challenge the ideology of individualistic-meritocratic societies. In this sense, even if he gives a significant twist to the classical model, Bourdieu preserves some of its most fundamental characteristics, in particular the subordination of anthropology to sociology. Anthropology can afford to be individualistic if it is destined to serve as a critical tool for sociology, which is not. *Distinction* illustrates this paradox perfectly: in ideologically individualistic societies, Bourdieu's aim is to show that the development of taste—and thus the accumulation of symbolic capital—does not obey an individualistic logic; instead, it conforms to collective mechanisms of distinction, for which he borrows the model from the structural anthropology of Lévi-Strauss (individual strategies exist—there is no reason to deny it—but they take place inside a space whose coordinates they do not define).

The question to be asked is this: Does antiholism offer anthropology a real purpose, or does it limit its horizon to an indefinite protest against a classical model from which we will never really break free? For those who, unlike Bourdieu, do not want to use anthropology *inside* what is basically a sociological program, but rather to produce anthropological knowledge, it just makes life more difficult. The success enjoyed in the discipline by postmodernism owes at least something to this discomfort: the joy of deconstruction is that it allows anthropologists to be antiholistic without having to embrace any kind of economism, which they might have to do if they adopted any serious methodological individualism. That being the case, the renunciation of any attempt at explanation—not only the causal determination of behaviors but also, far more importantly for the social sciences, the conceptual determination of what practices are—seems less like a price to be paid and more like an escape route to avoid the burden of having to construct new ways of making collective practices intelligible, ways that go beyond criticism.

Those who refuse to take the easy way out expose themselves to a potentially paralyzing tension. The case of Jeanne Favret-Saada is probably the clearest illustration. The huge popularity of *Les Mots, la mort, les sorts* (*Deadly Words*) (1977) stems from the way it suspends explanation in favor of a subjective synthesis of supposedly archaic practices: rather than explain belief in witchcraft, the purpose of the inquiry is to show how an anthropologist from the French National Center for Scientific Research—that bastion of modern rationalist individualism—could also become caught up in these practices (not actually witchcraft as such, but at least the removal of spells). However, despite the success encountered by this kind of rehabilitation via an ethnography of *firsthand subjective experience*, we should not forget that for the author, it was merely the first step toward revealing a "system of places (or positions)" that would make accusations of witchcraft—and the rituals employed to counter it—intelligible. The inability to fulfill this promise, for more than thirty years, is probably at least as telling as the ultimately very classical form taken by her return to the explanatory regime, in which she links the use of spell-breaking rituals to the fragilities inherent in the organization of family farms in Normandy in the 1960s (Favret-Saada 2009; Salmon 2014).

It would be instructive to retrace the way in which anthropologists have tried to escape the dead end of protest-driven individualism by constructing new forms of holism that are above all suspicion of asymmetry between moderns and nonmoderns (of which the concept of ontology can be seen, at least for the time being, as one of the culminating points: Salmon 2016). But that lies outside the scope of this chapter. It is certain, however, that if we embark down the path of individualistic symmetrization (more individualism for the Others, be they non-Westerners or, equally well, the dominated, to put them on an even keel with the individualism of the dominant) instead of holistic symmetrization (more holism at home, especially when analyzing the dominant, for better holism elsewhere), we run the risk of neglecting the crucial question of whether, and how, other collective forms of existence and practice might affect us collectively.

NOTES

1. Contrary to popular belief, the question of formal causality is much more important for the epistemology of the social sciences than that of efficient causality.

2. To illustrate this point, which has become obscured by an erroneous interpretation of the Weberian imperative of axiological neutrality (Kalinowski 2005), one could cite most of the classic works of sociology. Mannheim's refocusing in *Ideologie und Utopie* (1929) has the advantage of clarity. For a reading of Durkheim along these lines, see Callegaro 2015.

3. One of the most consequential formulations of this idea that the onward march of modernization needs to be slowed in order to make it bearable for society is found in Polanyi's *The Great Transformation* (1944).

4. The rejection of the position of exteriority that anthropologists generally used to claim is one of the major trends in the ethnography of the 1970s and 1980s: variants can be found, for example, in Jeanne Favret-Saada or in the postmodernism of James Clifford. What sets Bourdieu apart is that this rejection is directly bound up with the problem of domination: the fact that he did his fieldwork in Algeria during its independence struggle was doubtless a decisive factor in the primacy he gives to questions of power. Bourdieu does not insist on this point, but there is no doubt that the colonial authorities frequently enshrined the viewpoint of local elites whose cooperation they courted as the "official version." In this respect, the principle of "no exteriority" is a valuable tool for the purposes of a sociology of colonialism.

5. While acknowledging that the level of values is irreducible to that of interests, Bourdieu nonetheless tries to articulate the two by means of the concept of interest: "One is right to refuse to credit the rule with the efficacy that legalism ascribes to it, but it must not be forgotten that there is an interest in 'toeing the line' which can be the basis of strategies aimed at regularizing the agent's situation, putting him in the right, in a sense beating the group at its own game by presenting his interests in the misrecognizable guise of the values recognized by the group" (Bourdieu 1980, Nice [trans.] 1990, 108–109). This attempt—which reflects the ascendancy accorded to explanations of an individualistic order—has something contradictory about it. If the strategy of passing one's own interests off as values recognized by the group is to make any sense, the group must first recognize these values: the logical grammar of the simulacrum dictates that it can exist only by reference to a reality that it respects and at same time circumvents.

6. Although Bourdieu rejects the evolutionism of classical sociology, he maintains the contrast between cases that embody "modernity" and those that embody "tradition"—cases that always need to be demystified.

REFERENCES

Boltanski, L. 2009. *De la critique*. Paris: Gallimard.
Boltanski, L., and T. Laurent. 1991. *De la justification*. Paris: Gallimard.
Bourdieu, P. 1972. *Esquisse d'une théorie de la pratique*. Geneva: Droz. ("The Kabyle House or the World Reversed" is also appearing in translation in *The Logic of Practice*, trans. R. Nice, Stanford, CA: Stanford University Press, 1990).
——. 1979. *La Distinction*. Paris: Éditions de Minuit.
——. 1980. *Le Sens pratique*. Paris: Éditions de Minuit. (Also appearing in translation in *The Logic of Practice*, trans. R. Nice. Stanford, CA: Stanford University Press, 1990.)
——. 1997. *Méditations pascaliennes*. Paris: Éditions du Seuil.
Bourdieu, P., and J.-C. Passeron. 1970. *La Reproduction*. Paris: Éditions de Minuit.
Callegaro, F. 2015. *La Science politique des modernes*. Paris: Éditions Economica.
Chomsky, N. 1959. Review of *Verbal Behavior*, by B. F. Skinner. *Language* 35 (1): 26–58.
——. 1965. *Aspects of the Theory of Syntax*. Cambridge, MA: MIT Press.
Durkheim, É. 1893. *De la division du travail social*. Paris: Félix Alcan.
Favret-Saada, J. 1977. *Les Mots, la mort, les sorts*. Paris: Gallimard.
——. 2009. *Désorceler*. Paris: Éditions de l'Olivier.
Kalinowski, I. 2005. "Leçons wébériennes sur la science et la propagande." In *La Science, profession et vocation*, by M. Weber, 65–273. Paris: Éditions Agone.
Karsenti, B. 2006. *La Société en personnes*. Paris: Éditions Economica.
Latour, B. 1984. *Les Microbes: Guerre et paix*. Paris: Métaillé.
Lévi-Strauss, C. 1949. *Les Structures élémentaires de la parenté*. Paris: Presses universitaires de France.

———. 1955. *Tristes tropiques*. Paris: Plon.

———. (1988) 2001. *De près et de loin: Entretiens avec Didier Eribon*. Paris: Éditions Odile Jacob.

Mannheim, K. 1929. *Ideologie und Utopie*. Bonn: Friedrich Cohen Verlag.

Mauss, M. (1923) 1950. *Essai sur le don*. In *Sociologie et anthrropologie*, 143–279. Paris: Presses universitaires de France.

Polanyi, K. 1944. *The Great Transformation*. New York: Farrar and Rinehart.

Salmon, G. 2013a. "Forme et variante, Franz Boas dans l'histoire du comparatisme." In *Franz Boas, le travail du regard*, edited by M. Espagne and I. Kalinowski, 191–220. Paris: Armand Colin.

———. 2013b. *Les Structures de l'esprit: Lévi-Strauss et les mythes*. Paris: Presses universitaires de France.

———. 2014. "De la critique de l'objectivité à la cartographie des positions impossibles: Relire Jeanne Favret-Saada après *Désorceler*." *Sociologies*. https://doi.org/10.4000/sociologies.4786.

———. 2016. "On Ontological Delegation: The Birth of Neoclassical Anthropology." In *Comparative Metaphysics: Ontology after Anthropology*, edited by P. Charbonnier, G. Salmon, and P. Skafish, 41–60. London: Rowman and Littlefield.

6

THE ECONOMIC EXPLANATION

Richard Staley

Two things motivate my interest in the role of economic explanations in anthropology. In his eloquent 2017 Marilyn Strathern Lecture at the University of Cambridge, Tim Ingold offered an account of the university and a vision of anthropology that sought to combat the marketization of the former.[1] Similarly, in the Universities and Colleges Union strike over pensions that roiled British education shortly before we workshopped our papers in March 2018, the immediate dispute concerned diverging views about the financial security of the pension scheme, but many saw the primary issue to lie in the ways that universities are becoming businesses rather than educational institutions: "You say marketize, we say organize!" went a chant that was reprised when the union went back on strike over pensions and conditions in November 2019. I want to address the pervasive sense that the economy provides a fundamental explanation for many aspects of social life, but also that this is, or often should be, contested, making discussions about the nature and role of economic considerations particularly important politically. So one aim of this chapter is to raise questions about the roles that economic concerns have in anthropological investigations and explanations.[2]

A second motivation is to explore aspects of the early history of "economic anthropology," with its critical relations to the economics discipline. Christopher Gregory has called on scholars to rehabilitate the 1920s and 1930s thought of Bronislaw Malinowski and John Maynard Keynes on uncertainty and risk (countering recent recourse to the contemporaneous work of the economist Frank Knight on those topics), in light of the implications this might have "for our understanding of the market mechanism today" (Gregory 2017, 1).[3] In the first edition of *Gifts and Commodities*, published in 1982, Gregory had sought to escape the "old ideas" ushered into mainstream economics by the marginal revolution of the 1870s. He achieved this by combining economic anthropology with the tradition of political economy to which Adam Smith and Karl Marx had contributed (with its extensive study of commodity production), before Stanley Jevons and Leon Walras made economy rest on the marginal utility of consumption. Gregory focused on developing an anthropology of value, establishing the relations between gift and kinship as the reproduction of commodities and people. More recently, he notes, anthropologists following the work of Arjun Appadurai and Michel Callon have in turn sought to escape the old ideas of pre-1980s economic anthropology by moving into the economists' domain to mount a critique of their theory of goods. Gregory thinks future scholars will have to escape the old ideas of both traditions, but this will require a multifaceted study of the past combining intellectual, political, and economic history with comparative ethnography. His argument helps orient this chapter, in which I focus on Malinowski rather than Keynes. Callon and other anthropologists developing cultural approaches to economics have typically examined the formation of new markets and marketization in the late twentieth century, offering persuasive examples of the "performativity" of economic concepts—the sense in which such concepts may help create the objects they purport to describe. My study of the period from the 1870s will bring together historical and ethnographic perspectives to offer a better treatment of the performativity of broad concepts framing common understandings of the economy, economic activities, and economic life (see especially Callon 1998; Mitchell 2007). Our work will involve reaching historical understandings of epistemologically economic approaches—to the ontology of economies. I first examine the movement of diverse concepts of explanation and economy between physics, economics, and anthropology, showing that the explanatory economies of Ernst Mach in particular combined a relational precision with arguments against hierarchies of explanation. Tracing changing understandings of "the economy" and "mechanism" will then indicate the importance of tracking both core concepts and the framing concepts that bridge disciplines and build links to social mores.

Explanatory Economies

My contribution begins at an apparent historical and disciplinary distance, at least twice removed from this book's concern with the role of ethnographic explanation in current anthropology. In the late nineteenth century the Austrian physicist Ernst Mach helped initiate critiques of the mechanical worldview with its reductionist, atomistic approaches to physics, which he described in 1871 as being so widely held that standing against them risked putting oneself out of step with modern culture (Mach [1872] 1911, 38–39).[4] Mach advanced specific critiques while articulating an extremely general stance against what had proved a highly successful intellectual program (which was also based strongly on the material advances of steam engines, thermodynamics, and power generation). It will be helpful to think briefly about his work now, both because, like several authors in this book, Mach was arguing against a form of explanatory foundationalism and because his strategies became important outside physics, even in some cases for anthropology.

Mach was certainly not arguing against all elements of the mechanical worldview. He had begun his work as an atomist and initially accepted common hierarchical treatments that depicted physics as applied mechanics and biology as applied physics: an explanatory hierarchy of the sciences. Celebrating the social physics of Adolphe Quetelet for its statistical regularities, he also sought an exact psychology in research stimulated by Gustav Fechner's studies of psychophysics, aiming to bridge the cleft between inner and outer (Mach 1863; Staley 2021). But by 1871 Mach pursued the limits of mechanics from two sides. On the one hand, he argued that insights often described as the fruit of the mechanical account of heat actually had a much broader foundation in understandings of causality. They were more general than mechanics. Revealingly, Mach thought the idea that a cause determines the effect may have been known in full clearness "at a very low stage in human culture." He argued a higher stage of knowledge is distinguished not by a difference in the conception of causality but by the manner in which it is applied (Mach [1872] 1911, 63–64).

Mach's view that the form of thought underlying scientific work was shared in other realms was important to his understanding of the relations between different disciplines. He argued the concept of soul is an abstraction of the same kind as the concept of matter. Considering the fields most relevant to his own early research on visual, aural, and bodily perception and motion, Mach regarded physics, physiology, and psychology as approaching the same phenomena from different perspectives. He thought mechanical approaches were considered more fundamental and intelligible than others largely because the history of mechanics was older and richer than other fields, but over time thermal or electrical approaches might come to have this status. Thus what appeared to be more fundamental depended on custom and history. In 1883 Mach took this historical, "anthropological" approach to the status of current science to the extent of critiquing the medieval basis for Isaac Newton's discussions of absolutes, citing E. B. Tylor in arguing that traces of fetishism were retained in current conceptions of forces (Mach 1883, 435; [1883] 1960, 558; Tylor 1873, 160, 183).

Apart from arguing all scientific thought rests on abstraction and analogy, Mach also argued science chiefly concerns the convenience and saving of thought: it is *economical*. In 1871, for example, he described the value of the law of fall as lying in the convenience of its use, its economic value as a synoptical aggregate of individual facts. A second scientific problem of an economic nature was the question of resolving complicated facts into as few and as simple facts as possible. This was what counted as an explanation. In a striking formulation, he described the process as one of tracing uncommon unintelligibilities back to common unintelligibilities—facts that are not further resolvable, such as the acceleration of one mass toward another. Thus what counts as fundamental is on the one hand an economical question and on the other hand a matter of taste. Mach noted he had maintained this view since he began teaching in 1861 but had also met it through the Viennese political economist Emanuel Herrmann (Mach [1872] 1911, 55, 88). It went along with his understanding that causal phenomena expressed simply the functional dependence of one phenomenon on another. Later Mach elaborated this account in an 1882 public lecture on the economy of science and a concluding section of his major 1883 study of mechanics, maintaining that the goal of physical science was the simplest and most economical description of appearances, and arguing further that with the knowledge of its economic character, all mysticism disappeared from science (Mach [1882] 1898; 1883, 452–453). Described as descriptionism, the approach has been regarded as characteristic of fin de siècle physics (see Heilbron 1982; Porter 1994; Staley 2008).

Mach's economies insisted on new precision about particulars such as mass, time, and space but were deflationary about general aims. His arguments against the foundational status of physics and mechanics were advanced in both *The Science of Mechanics* and his *Contributions to the Analysis of the Sensations* in 1886 (Mach 1883, 1886, [1890] 1897). Collectively these books were influential in shaping perspectives on the position of psychology as a science (in contrast, the leading exponent of laboratory-based experimental psychology, Wilhelm Wundt, had argued for the preeminence of motion in the causal structure of the sciences), as well as in arguments for the social sciences that stressed the significance of scientific method in the United States (Boring 1957, chap. 18; Danziger 1979; Porter 1994). And Mach's views were also central in shaping the early work of Bronislaw Malinowski.

Trained in mathematics and physics, the young Polish scientist finished his doctoral dissertation on the principle of economy in science in 1906. Malinowski followed Mach in regarding the concept of function as the primary scientific tool, expressing the interrelations and mutual interdependence of phenomena (Malinowski [1906] 1993, 94; Young 2004). Mach had also offered the most satisfactory formulation of the principle of economy, on the borderland between scientific methodology and cognitive theory, but Malinowski drew on Richard Avenarius in pointing to a tension between psychological and sociological approaches he thought Mach had not addressed fully (Malinowski [1906] 1993, 104, 112–113). Arguing science was a collective social process that did not depend on the psychological insight of the typical, normal man, or a plebiscite of mankind, Malinowski (like Mach) regarded the economy of science to express an adaptation of thoughts to facts, but pressed still more insistently that it could be justified objectively: "If we treat science from the standpoint of its practical, as it were, biological significance to the individual, and not from a theoretical-comparative standpoint, we are able to assume the physical definition of its laws" (Malinowski [1906] 1993, 112).

Robert Thornton and Peter Skalník's extensive introduction to *The Early Writings of Bronislaw Malinowski* argues persuasively for Mach's significance to Malinowski (with Friedrich Nietzsche), but this phase of his work is rarely considered closely in discussing Malinowski's treatment of economic issues in the Trobriands—usually regarded as the founding moments of economic anthropology (Thornton and Skalník 1993; see also Firth 1957, 212–214).[5] But my study will have suggested two important points. First, Malinowski's functionalism and treatments of economics elaborated on concepts he had first encountered as a student. Admittedly they were transformed radically in the different contexts of anthropological explanations of behavior and social institutions, or accounts of gift exchange and trade, but this was also in accord with Mach's refusal to see major distinctions between different kinds of thought. Malinowski showed a similar readiness to move across disciplines. Having finished his dissertation in Krakow, Malinowski traveled first to Leipzig, studying with the psychologist Wilhelm Wundt and economic historian Karl Bücher, and then to the London School of Economics, where he began studies in sociology and anthropology. Malinowski's early works bear clear traces of these moves, and often arc back to his earliest interests with continual references to the physicist in *Argonauts of the Western Pacific*, for example. As well as noting the long-standing nature of his concern with function and economy, my second major point about Malinowski's dissertation is that these concepts were strongly associated with epistemology, and the borders between method and cognitive theory.

Both these features are evident in the gradual development of his treatments of economic issues. In 1913 Malinowski published an account of economic aspects of the *intichiuma* ceremonies of central Australia, which he knew from the work of Baldwin Spencer, F. J. Gillen, and Carl Strehlow, and addressed in order to combat the views of Sir James Frazer (Malinowski [1912] 1993). Focusing on the division of labor expressed in totemic systems, Frazer had argued that being engaged in magic had rendered barren what might otherwise have flowed from an inevitably fruitful economic principle. Malinowski's counter was to explore relations between magic, religion, and economics in the social organization of the ceremonies, the collective effort they involved, and the practical aim they expressed of increasing numbers of a species. He also offered an account of the aims of theoretical ethnography, which he explicitly stated were like those of theoretical physics and chemistry. Each involved the exact description of the results of field research and observation, and "the province of theory . . . is to afford exact concepts, discuss and analyze observed connections of facts, and foresee new ones" (Malinowski [1912] 1993, 224).[6] Accordingly Malinowski engaged in a careful analysis of concepts of economy and magic (which he treated as a form of primitive technique), in order to propose new interrelations between them. While eschewing any universal evolutionary system, Malinowski did suggest that the mix of magical and rational elements in the mutual engagement of magic and economic concerns was a pathway to increasingly rational approaches, significant for the evolution of economics.[7] A year later he took up related concerns with property rights, division of labor, and the relations between family household and economic organization in his sociological study *The Family among the Australian Aborigines* (Malinowski 1913).

Economic Anthropology, the Economic Theorist, and "the Prevalent Mores of Social Discussion"

Malinowski's next major work on economic issues was published in the *Economical Journal* in 1921, drawing on the extensive fieldwork in the Trobriands that also formed the basis for *Argonauts of the Western Pacific* in 1922. Malinowski saw little precedent for his anthropological study of economic issues and critiqued Bücher's work in particular, arguing deficient materials had led Bücher to conclude savages were in a pre-economic stage. Among Trobriand Islanders, in contrast, Malinowski discerned distinct forms of economic organization. His study of land tenure showed Trobriand concepts of ownership involved several distinct legal and economic relationships different from Western ones, with the chief and garden magician each holding overrights to land belonging to individuals, and diverse stages in preparation and growing being marked by magical ceremonies controlling the forces of nature and the work of man. If economic *production* showed such rich interrelations, Malinowski was also now far more concerned to disabuse readers of the thought that natives required outside pressure to offer sustained and efficient *labor*—either individually or working communally on different scales from household to village. A similarly complex social organization was evident in canoe and house building and fishing, and Malinowski showed that what could be called the "financialization" of tribal life was bound up with chiefly power and displays of wealth, and governed by gift and countergift organized by kin and in-law relationships, as well as by dues and tributes to the chief. Malinowski thus argued that economic concerns thoroughly pervaded social life: wherever a native moved, whether to a feast, in expedition, or in warfare, they would deal with the problems of gift and countergift. But in his short article Malinowski refrained from going into the kind of detail he did in *Argonauts*, in order to focus more clearly on the public economy of the tribe, with some major tribal events offering examples and an extended discussion of exchange (and brief reference to the Kula ring) showing that, despite the prevalence of trade, nothing like money existed in the Trobriands.

In conclusion, Malinowski stated that the new conception he had outlined needed a new term and chose one (that had occasionally been used earlier): "Tribal Economy." He developed the term in clear contrast to common understandings of both primitive and Western economics, and it is worth quoting his discussion at some length, partly to display the contracted form in which Malinowski deployed these contrasts, with their several, specific elements. Malinowski wrote,

> In savage societies national economy certainly does not exist, if we mean by the term a system of free competitive exchange of goods and services, with the interplay of supply and demand determining value and regulating all economic life. But there is a long step between this and Buecher's assumption that the only alternative is a pre-economic stage, where an individual person or a single household satisfy their primary wants as best they can, without any more elaborate mechanism than division of labour according to sex, and an occasional spasmodic bit of barter. Instead, we find a state of affairs where production, exchange and consumption are socially organized and regulated by custom, and where a special system of traditional values governs their activities and spurs them on to efforts. (1921, 15)

In this paper, addressed to economists, Malinowski called for further economic research into native conceptions, in the spirit of wide comparison and sharp contrast. Refusing to generalize from one sample, Malinowski thought further comparative work might offer interesting results capable of refreshing and fertilizing theory, writing, "We might be able to grasp the nature of the economic mechanism of savage life, and incidentally we might be able to answer many questions referring to the origins and development of economic institutions" (12).

We should note both the novelty of Malinowski's conceptual strategy and his incidental conservativism. The significance of his extension of the meaning of economics can be highlighted by noting that in a study of risk and uncertainty in the same year, the Iowa (later University of Chicago) economist Frank Knight *defined* economics in terms of free enterprise, writing, "Economics is the study of a particular form of organization of human want-satisfying activity which has become prevalent in Western nations and spread over the greater part of the field of conduct. It is called free enterprise or the competitive system. It is obviously not at all completely or perfectly competitive, but just as indisputably its general principles are those of free competition" ([1921] 1933, 9).

Like Malinowski, Knight used a comparison with physics—but specifically with theoretical mechanics—to develop an understanding of theoretical economics. He emphasized the importance of general principles to economics and, as Mach may have (but to different effect), stressed the need to recognize the assumptions underlying their application to complex facts. Neglecting this had hampered economic theorists making untenable deductions, often of vicious character, which naturally harmed the credibility of theory. Knight thought it imperative that "the contrast between these simplified assumptions and the complex facts of life be made as conspicuous and as familiar as has been done in mechanics" ([1921] 1933, 9).[8]

Malinowski's argument for a different kind of economics was novel. More conservatively, he assumed a continuity of institutions oriented toward explaining the origins and development of Western economic life, and wrote of refreshing theory rather than critiquing Western understandings of its own economic activities. Nevertheless, addressing an anthropological readership in *Argonauts of the Western Pacific*, Malinowski sharpened his perspective on Western economics by criticizing the assumption of "Primitive Economic Man," a "fanciful, dummy creature" he thought featured in current economic textbooks, ran through its popular and semipopular literature, and also haunted the work of anthropologists. Attempting to explode the notion once and for all, Malinowski contrasted the assumed rationalistic self-interest of this imaginary savage with the complex aims and motives of Trobriand gardeners, with their ostentatious displays of produce that fed their sisters' families, not their own, and their pride in good work (Malinowski [1922] 1961, 60–62, 96; see also Firth 1957, 217). This provided a foil for an extended treatment of complex social systems, and Malinowski offered a nuanced portrait of the imagined savage as a didactic device used to illustrate deductions actually based on work in developed economics.[9] But his discussion has been interpreted as a problematic legacy, encouraging other anthropologists to work as he is thought to have, deriving their knowledge from sociology and general reading rather than close engagement with current economic thought. At least, this is the perspective Edward LeClair and Harold Schneider present looking back in 1968 (drawing also on aspects of Raymond Firth's much more comprehensive appreciation) (LeClair and Schneider 1968, 3–5; Firth 1957, 211–212). In his 1940 book *The Economic Life of Primitive Peoples*, Melville Herskovits (37–38) offered a more sympathetic perspective, suggesting that Malinowski and other pioneers had not presented economics as an economist would, because of their emphasis on the cultural setting of economic data.

Like Malinowski, Herskovits lamented earlier neglect of economic subtlety, working to establish economic anthropology as a distinct subfield by drawing together the detailed but dispersed anthropological studies of Malinowski, Firth on Maori economics in 1929, Audrey Richards's 1932 study of food in a South African tribe, and others (Herskovits 1940, 37–38). Yet Herskovits himself was savaged for precisely the same fault of economic naïveté by Knight—who nevertheless admitted "the errors and prejudices of this book are an integral part of the prevalent mores of social discussion" (Knight 1941, 268). This highlights an important point central to the aims of this chapter. Despite the justified concern of the specialist anthropologist or economist to argue against caricature, for the social commentator of the day (or the historian looking back), responding to prevalent mores or what counts as a discipline may be just as important as fidelity to more sophisticated disciplinary knowledge. The charges of disciplinary naïveté that have followed Malinowski and the authors of other early works in economic anthropology are in part surely costs of their originality of endeavor. Yet they have been brought from both sides often and long enough to have become a consistent trope. Notably, they run through the debates between "formalists" accepting conventional economic thought and "substantivists" who followed the work of Karl Polanyi in regarding premarket economies to reflect socially embedded relationships of reciprocity and communal redistribution, and who have often been attacked as Malinowski and Herskovits were. The naïveté charge therefore reflects at the same time arguments in the consolidation of particular fields of expertise and interpretive approaches, and significant perspectives on the relations between specialist and lay knowledge. "You say marketize, we say organize!" went protest chants outside Great St. Mary's Church, and that is surely a slogan—but students from the Department of Social Anthropology at Cambridge also held up placards featuring Meyer Fortes, Polanyi, and Appadurai and reading, "Standing together against pension cut is one of our FORTES," "POLANYI cut pension NOT a GREAT TRANSFORMATION," "PROVOKED BY YOUR ECONOMISIN'," and "CUSAS SOLIDARITY APPA-DO-RIGHT BY OUR STAFF."

Mechanisms and the Economy

A second reason for paying close attention to Malinowski's condensed discussion of tribal and developed economics is the assumptions it reveals about national economy, and its use of the metaphor of mechanism—both features that may point to particularities of the period in which he wrote, and which will help us approach Gregory's interest in the historical foundations for our understanding of the market mechanism. Before considering their interrelations, it will be helpful to note that Gregory himself had paid close attention to the period in the nineteenth century in which concepts of political economy had been followed by the marginal revolution, without examining the period in the 1920s and 1930s.[10] The work of Timothy Mitchell suggests some avenues through which this might be approached. Mitchell has argued that while terms like *national economy* and models of the economy had been advanced since the work of Adam Smith at least, it is distinctive that through the course of the nineteenth century these had always been regarded as political economies of management and public administration. Otherwise the primary reference of economy was to household stewardship. In his view it was only in the course of the 1920s and 1930s and especially after the Great Depression that it became possible to think in the English language of the general concept of *the economy*, or as Malinowski puts it here, of "national economy" as a bounded and comprehensive entity in which critically *all* economic life is regulated by supply and demand.

Mitchell argues that this possibility came from the work of Keynes and others managing the circulation of money in the bounded geographical space of colonial India, which he argues led them to refer to the economy as "a self-contained mechanism whose internal parts are imagined to move in a dynamic and regular interaction, separate from the irregular interaction of the mechanism as a whole with what could now be called its exterior" (Mitchell 2002, 82; 2005). Linguistically, Mitchell draws support from the way Georg Simmel described markets and money in his turn-of-the-century account of the city. Simmel consistently wrote in the qualified plural of *metropolitan* markets and the particular singular of *a* money economy. It was only in 1950 that his English-language translators Hans Gerth and C. Wright Mills rendered the latter more general as *the* money economy (Mitchell 2002, 81–82). Simmel thought that, under primitive conditions, production had been bound in intimate personal relations, but modern cities were supplied by production for the market, and this enhanced the intellectualistic and abstract mentality characteristic of natural science (Simmel [1903] 2007, 184–185). But there is also support for Mitchell's argument closer to home in Daniel Hirschman's (2016) account of the rise of national statistics and gross domestic product in the 1930s, quantifying the economic sphere; and from Jon

Agar's (2003, chap. 6) historical work on early computing, which shows that mechanism was the governing metaphor for British government, and that in the 1920s and 1930s in particular a movement of expert "mechanizers" helped secure Treasury control over the Civil Service through what they described as the mechanization of the treatment of records, tasks, and files.

This was a period in which concepts of the machine, mechanism, and mechanization proliferated to run through social and intellectual life, as well as the reservoirs, gears, and armatures of heat engines and electricity generators, and extended to encompass the city as well as the factory (Staley 2018). Both Knight and Malinowski referred to mechanics and mechanism, but we should note that while Malinowski took care to outline why he called garden magic a "system," he refers to the division of labor as a "mechanism" and to the "economic mechanism" of savage life without particular comment.[11] In the essay on the gift Marcel Mauss published in 1923–24, he argued it was only recently that Western societies had made man an "economic animal," noting that many in the West are still not members of the genus and writing, "*Homo oeconomicus* is not behind us but lies ahead, as does the man of morality and duty, the man of science and reason. For a very long time man was different, and he has not been a machine for very long, made complicated by a calculating machine" ([1950] 2000, 76). Writing in 1940, Herskovits preceded his comparative discussions of specific aspects of economic activity with an introductory chapter on life "before the machine," making the point that most of the world's population still lived without machines and outlining the varied effects of industrial processes in a machine society. Yet outlining the specific terms in which the economist Friedrich Hayek articulated his concept of the free-market economy will indicate that considerable conceptual work was involved in achieving a form of persuasive generality about the economy—and this depended critically on a very particular use of a concept of mechanism.

It is important to note first that historians have shown that in the postwar period, debates about economic planning and freedom stimulated by the significant national management of wartime resources had involved considerable common ground for most of their participants. Neoliberals like Hayek (working first in Vienna and from 1931 at the London School of Economics) and the Chicago-trained Herbert Simon were suspicious of the moral failures of nineteenth-century capitalism and liberalism, endorsed significant government regulation, and shared values with socialists, while many economists used models of socialism and of markets hand in hand methodologically (Bockman 2011; Jackson 2010). In a 1937 article, Hayek shifted from thinking about markets in terms of the flow of goods to the question of information, and identified the critical problem that equilibrium theories of the perfect market had to encompass the markets of all the individual commodities. As Hayek put a point to which

Malinowski had gestured, "The whole economic system must be assumed to be one perfect market in which everybody knows everything" (and we might note that although Malinowski thought his informants often showed the insight of a scientist, antiquarian, or sociologist, he insisted only the anthropologist fully understood the Kula trade ring) (von Hayek 1937, 44–45; Malinowski [1925] 1974, 34–35). Hayek now began to describe the division of knowledge as the central problem of economics as a science, perhaps even more significant than the division of labor, and questioned how individuals would acquire the knowledge required of the perfect market (having, himself, little faith in expert planning).

Hayek found his solution in "the price system" only in 1945, a year after he had made his intellectual and propagandistic break with socialism thoroughly complete in *The Road to Serfdom*, where his arguments against socialism within the West were now fueled by the conviction that socialism led inevitably to totalitarianism. Having long argued that planners should never be thought to be in a better position to make value judgments than individuals in the market, Hayek now described how consumers react to the changing price of tin to save and direct resources elsewhere even without knowing why the metal was scarce. He argued limited individual fields of vision overlapped enough to pass on the information, allowing the economy to operate as one system, with the whole acting as one market, writing, "It is more than a metaphor to describe the price system as a kind of machinery for registering change, or a system of telecommunications which enables individual producers to watch merely the movement of a few pointers, as an engineer might watch the hands of a few dials, in order to adjust their activities to changes of which they may never know more than is reflected in the price movement" (1945, 521).

The terms in which Hayek expresses his confidence in prices as the market mechanism illustrate some of the limitations of his solution. Historians have stressed that Hayek naturalized the market from this point, while critics might doubt whether it really is more than a metaphor (Caldwell 2004; Mirowski 2007). But these terms also highlight significant features of economics in this period. First, Hayek's initial caution and later confidence confirm the pertinence and historical specificity of Mitchell's argument about the gradual rise of the general concept of the economy only from the 1920s. In the similar grounds but clear contrasts between Knight's general but theoretical principles of economics, Malinowski's careful introduction of a new kind of economy, and Hayek's insistence that the whole economic system must function as a perfect market, we can see that quite subtle distinctions were highly important to technical treatments of concepts of the economy in this period, and these were changing.

Yet a distinctly different use of concepts is evident in Hayek's reference to machinery, another term that featured in the discussions of both anthropologists and economists, who shifted its metaphorical weight in diverse invocations. In particular, while Knight used a tight analogy with theoretical mechanics as an explanatory strategy, Malinowski and Hayek both paired their careful thought on the economy with more allusive references to mechanisms and machinery. Other scholars have emphasized that anthropologists and economists sought to clarify or gain disciplinary ground in their articulation of strong perspectives on *Homo economicus* or the primitive. Yet at the same time each also drew on less clearly articulated, shared assumptions about the rise of machine society and social mechanisms. I suggest that these functioned performatively, borrowing on what Knight called "prevalent mores of social discussion" to help shape a more general conception of economics—which over time has in turn helped provide space for new institutions and new markets (as Callon and others have documented). That process has often been accompanied by both persuasion and sharp critique, as our strikes show; and the cultural mores I have identified, the powerful voice of lay perspectives must surely be appreciated historically alongside the explicitly anthropological or economic treatment of value and recent forms of marketization that have gained scholarly attention. We must explain the core concepts, rendered newly explicit, but also framing concepts that are much less fully analyzed but bridge different fields, such as economy and mechanism.

This chapter has brought elements of the histories of physics, anthropology, and economics into common perspective by examining diverse accounts of explanation, and examples of explanation in practice, that each engaged concepts of economy: as an explanatory strategy, in the work of Mach and Malinowski, or as subject matter for Malinowski, Knight, and Hayek. In particular, I have illustrated some of the possibilities of beginning to tell the histories of economics and anthropology at the same time, exploring interrelations between them that might ultimately allow us to set both disciplines in motion. Analysts such as Heath Pearson and Gregory have insisted that the primary methods of anthropology and neoclassical economics diverged in this period, with the latter taking an individualistically psychological and deductive approach. Nevertheless, they shared a common culture of discourse and many terms of reference as a result of their mutual examination of organization, social systems, and values. Here I have touched on common tropes, whether closely examined like primitive economical man or comparatively unnoticed like mechanism, in order to suggest points of contact— sometimes contested—in each discipline's work to establish links between lay and specialist knowledge, often at the expense of the other discipline. Such tropes are particularly powerful because they use social mores to gain disciplinary ground.

A further way of pursuing similar aims would address the relations between economic perspectives and anthropological research in the dimensions of ethnographic practice and publication rather than discourse. I have in mind work establishing the economies of the anthropologist at work—such as Malinowski or Franz Boas paying to elicit stories or written accounts from informants, collaborators, or colleagues like Ibena, who was the chief of Kasana'i village in the Trobriands, and George Hunt of the Tlingit on the Pacific Northwest Coast of North America—and the possibility of setting these thoroughly in conversation with the way they helped build up an anthropological understanding of the Kula ring and potlatch. This would incorporate the question of how the anthropologist gained their knowledge into our studies of primitive economies, as Gregory often does in discussing the unfolding stages of Malinowski's, Mauss's, and his own treatments of gifts. For example—to build on Isaiah Wilner's (2015, 2013) study of the role of the Kwakwaka'wakw people in the development of Boas's thought—accounting for the mutual demands that Boas and Hunt placed on their relationship might now allow us to bring a further productive term into the brilliant account of the potlatch that Marshall Sahlins used to argue that "the world system is the rational expression of relative cultural logics, that is in the terms of exchange-value" (Sahlins 1988, 8).

But there is one final, more direct implication I would urge on the basis of this study. Recognizing the merely discursive reality of the general concept of the economy, we should unmake it creatively, adopting the lesson of Mach's economical precision to parse economic activities only through the more specific ways that they have actually found value, whether monetary, measured, or social. We might then speak of GDP and Trobriand gardens but should recognize that the economy does not exist as one thing, but many, differently valued.[12] Indeed, a brilliant exemplification of the conceptual clarity that can be achieved through a renewed, epistemologically economical focus on the elements of economic life has been provided by Anthony Pickles's (2020) study of "transfers" as the basis for what are normally parsed as the transactional exchanges of gift or market economies.

NOTES

1. The lecture is unpublished, but see also Ingold 2017.

2. For a lively and learned overview of the history of economic anthropology that explores the rich anthropological literature pertinent to this general aim, see Hart 2007.

3. For a brief overview, see Gregory 2000.

4. For excellent studies, see Banks 2003, 180–192; Wegener 2010.

5. For a treatment of Malinowski's work on the Trobriands as foundational if flawed (from the perspective of formal rather than substantivist approaches to economic anthropology), see LeClair and Schneider 1968, 3–5.

6. The rhetorical strategy helped position him as leading a new approach, but it was already familiar in the Victorian period.

7. Malinowski's earliest discussions of the relations between magic and the economy prefigure the 1925 account of magic and science that Gregory points to as an alternative to Knight's account of uncertainty. There Malinowski notes the difference between fish-

ing in the lagoon, where the activity is merely practical and magic is not needed, and fishing on the open sea, fraught with its dangers and calling forth magic. In general, in the same way that Mach had emphasized a similar conception of causation even in low stages of culture, Malinowski regarded "primitive" science as broadly the same as any other science yet also essentially pragmatic and oriented to convenient ends (Gregory 2017, xlix; Malinowski 1974, 31).

8. He drew on perpetual motion in outlining his comparison and emphasized equilibrium phenomena (as Mach did) in both physics and economics: see also Knight (1921) 1933, 11.

9. Heath Pearson has provided an amplified account of *Homo economicus*, exploring different registers in anthropologists' and economists' depictions of the relations between the psychology of economic man and primitive man. His focus on psychology and neglect of the more extended arguments of the anthropologists involved prevents him from giving a reliable understanding of the period; see also the critiques of Ferguson and Gregory: Pearson 2000; Ferguson 2000; Gregory 2000.

10. It is also worth noting that despite his attack on mechanism and physicalist approaches, the historian of economics Philip Mirowski has similarly neglected this period in favor of the 1870s and the post–World War II period; Mirowski 1988, 1989, 2002.

11. See Malinowski (1922) 1961, 59, for the discussion of system.

12. I would like to thank workshop participants, Simon Schaffer, Efram Sera-Shriar, and members of the Consortium for History of Science, Technology and Medicine working group Sciences of the Senses, for their careful reading, and the latter for pushing me to this point.

REFERENCES

Agar, J. 2003. *The Government Machine: A Revolutionary History of the Computer, History of Computing.* Cambridge, MA: MIT Press.

Banks, E. C. 2003. *Ernst Mach's World Elements: A Study in Natural Philosophy.* Dordrecht: Kluwer.

Bockman, J. 2011. *Markets in the Name of Socialism: The Left-Wing Origins of Neoliberalism.* Stanford, CA: Stanford University Press.

Boring, E. G. 1957. *A History of Experimental Psychology.* 2nd ed. Century Psychology. New York: Appleton-Century-Crofts.

Caldwell, B. 2004. *Hayek's Challenge: An Intellectual Biography of F. A. Hayek.* Chicago: University of Chicago Press.

Callon, M. 1998. "Introduction: The Embeddedness of Economic Markets in Economics." In *The Laws of the Markets,* edited by M. Callon, 1–57. Oxford: Blackwell.

Danziger, K. 1979. "The Positivist Repudiation of Wundt." *Journal of the History of the Behavioral Sciences* 15:205–230.

Ferguson, J. 2000. "Economics and Barbarism: An Anthropological Comment on Pearson's 'Homo Economicus.'" *History of Political Economy* 32 (4): 991–998.

Firth, R. 1957. "The Place of Malinowski in Economic Anthropology." In *Man and Culture: An Evaluation of the Work of Bronislaw Malinowski,* edited by R. Firth, 209–227. London: Routledge and Kegan Paul.

Gregory, C. A. 2000. "Anthropology, Economics, and Political Economy: A Critique of Pearson." *History of Political Economy* 32 (4): 999–1010.

———. 2017. *Gifts and Commodities.* 2nd ed. Chicago: HAU Books.

Hart, K. 2007. "A Short History of Economic Anthropology." Memory Bank, November 9, 2007. https://thememorybank.co.uk/a-short-history-of-economic-anthropology/.

Hayek, F. A. 1945. "The Use of Knowledge in Society." *American Economic Review* 35:519–530.

Heilbron, J. L. 1982. "*Fin-de-Siècle* Physics." In *Science, Technology and Society in the Time of Alfred Nobel*, edited by C. G. Bernhard, E. Crawford, and P. Sörbom, 51–73. Oxford: Nobel Foundation.

Herskovits, M. J. 1940. *The Economic Life of Primitive Peoples*. New York: A. A. Knopf.

Hirschman, D. A. 2016. "Inventing the Economy; Or: How We Learned to Stop Worrying and Love the GDP." PhD diss., University of Michigan.

Ingold, T. 2017. *Anthropology and/as Education*. Abingdon, UK: Routledge.

Jackson, B. 2010. "At the Origins of Neo-liberalism: The Free Economy and the Strong State, 1930–1947." *Historical Journal of Film, Radio and Television* 53:129–151.

Knight, F. H. (1921) 1933. *Risk, Uncertainty and Profit*. Reprints of Scarce Tracts in Economic and Political Science. London: London School of Economics and Political Science.

———. 1941. "Anthropology and Economics." *Journal of Political Economy* 49 (2): 247–268.

LeClair, E. E., and H. K. Schneider, eds. 1968. *Economic Anthropology: Readings in Theory and Analysis*. New York: Holt, Rinehart and Winston.

Mach, E. 1863. "Vorträge über Psychophysik." *Oesterreichische Zeitschrift für praktische Heilkunde* 9:146–148, 167–170, 202–204, 225–228, 242–245, 260–261, 277–279, 294–298, 316–318, 335–338, 352–354, 362–366.

———. (1872) 1911. *History and Root of the Principle of the Conservation of Energy*. Translated by P. E. B. Jourdain. Chicago: Open Court; London: Kegan Paul, Trench, Trübner.

———. (1882) 1898. "On the Economical Nature of Physical Inquiry." In *Popular Scientific Lectures*, 186–213. Chicago: Open Court; London: Kegan Paul, Trench, Trübner.

———. 1883. *Die Mechanik in ihrer Entwickelung historisch-kritisch dargestellt*. Leipzig: F. A. Brockhaus.

———. (1883) 1960. *The Science of Mechanics: A Critical and Historical Account of Its Development*. Translated by T. J. McCormack. 6th ed., with additions through the 9th German ed. LaSalle, IL: Open Court. Originally published as *Die Mechanik in ihrer Entwicklung*.

———. 1886. *Beiträge zur Analyse der Empfindungen*. Jena: Fischer.

———. (1890) 1897. *Contributions to the Analysis of the Sensations*. Translated by C. M. Williams. Chicago: Open Court.

Malinowski, B. (1906) 1993. "On the Principle of the Economy of Thought." In *The Early Writings of Bronislaw Malinowski*, edited by R. J. Thornton and P. Skalník, 89–115. Cambridge: Cambridge University Press.

———. (1912) 1993. "On the Economic Aspects of the *Intichiuma* Ceremonies." In *The Early Writings of Bronislaw Malinowski*, edited by R. J. Thornton and P. Skalník, 209–227. Cambridge: Cambridge University Press.

———. 1913. *The Family among the Australian Aborigines: A Sociological Study*. University of London Monographs on Sociology. London: University of London.

———. 1921. "The Primitive Economics of the Trobriand Islanders." *Economic Journal* 31 (121): 1–16.

———. (1922) 1961. *Argonauts of the Western Pacific: An Account of Native Enterprise and Adventure in the Archipelagoes of Melanesian New Guinea*. New York: Dutton.

———. (1925) 1974. "Magic, Science, and Religion." In *Magic, Science, and Religion, and Other Essays*, 17–92. London: Souvenir Press.

———. 1974. *Magic, Science, and Religion, and Other Essays*. London: Souvenir Press.

Mauss, M. (1950) 2000. *The Gift: The Form and Reason for Exchange in Archaic Societies*. Translated by W. D. Halls. New York: W. W. Norton.

Mirowski, P. 1988. *Against Mechanism: Protecting Economics from Science*. Totowa, NJ: Rowman and Littlefield.

——. 1989. *More Heat than Light: Economics as Social Physics, Physics as Nature's Economics*. Historical Perspectives on Modern Economics. Cambridge: Cambridge University Press.

——. 2002. *Machine Dreams: Economics Becomes a Cyborg Science*. Cambridge: Cambridge University Press.

——. 2007. "Naturalizing the Market on the Road to Revisionism: Caldwell on Hayek's Challenge." *Journal of Institutional Economics* 3:351–372.

Mitchell, T. 2002. *Rule of Experts—Egypt, Techno-politics, Modernity*. Berkeley: University of California Press.

——. 2005. "Economics: Economists and the Economy in the Twentieth Century." In *The Politics of Method in the Human Sciences: Positivism and Its Others in the Social Sciences*, edited by G. Steinmetz, 126–141. Durham, NC: Duke University Press.

——. 2007. "The Properties of Markets." In *Do Economists Make Markets? On the Performativity of Economics*, edited by D. MacKenzie, F. Munieza, and L. Siu, 244–275. Princeton, NJ: Princeton University Press.

Pearson, H. 2000. "Homo Economicus Goes Native, 1859–1945: The Rise and Fall of Primitive Economics." *History of Political Economy* 32 (4): 933–990.

Pickles, A. J. 2020. "Transfers: A Deductive Approach to Gifts, Gambles, and Economy at Large." *Current Anthropology* 61 (1): 11–29.

Porter, T. M. 1994. "The Death of the Object: *Fin de Siècle* Philosophy of Physics." In *Modernist Impulses in the Human Sciences, 1870–1930*, edited by D. Ross, 128–151. Baltimore: Johns Hopkins University Press.

Sahlins, M. 1988. "Cosmologies of Capitalism: The Trans-Pacific Sector of 'The World System.'" *Proceedings of the British Academy* 74:1–51.

Simmel, G. (1903) 2007. "Extract from 'The Metropolis and Mental Life.'" In *Modernism*, edited by M. H. Whitworth, 182–189. Malden, MA: Blackwell. Originally published in *The Sociology of Georg Simmel*, translated and edited by K. H. Wolff (1950; New York: Free Press of Glencoe, 1964), 409–417.

Staley, R. 2008. "The Fin de Siècle Thesis." *Berichte zur Wissenschaftsgeschichte* 31:311–330.

——. 2018. "The Interwar Period as a Machine Age: Mechanics, the Machine, Mechanisms and the Market in Discourse." *Science in Context* 31 (3): 263–292.

——. 2021. "Sensory Studies, or When Physics Was Psychophysics: Ernst Mach and Physics between Physiology and Psychology, 1860–71." *History of Science* 59 (1): 93–118.

Thornton, R. J., and P. Skalník. 1993. "Introduction: Malinowski's Reading, Writing, 1904–1914." In *The Early Writings of Bronislaw Malinowski*, edited by R. J. Thornton and P. Skalník, 1–64. Cambridge: Cambridge University Press.

Tylor, E. B. 1873. *Primitive Culture: Researches into the Development of Mythology, Philosophy, Religion, Art, and Custom*. Vol. 2 of 2. London: J. Murray.

von Hayek, F. A. 1937. "Economics and Knowledge." *Economica* 4 (13): 33–54.

Wegener, D. 2010. "De-anthropomorphizing Energy and Energy Conservation: The Case of Max Planck and Ernst Mach." *Studies in History and Philosophy of Modern Physics* 41:146–159.

Wilner, I. L. 2013. "A Global Potlatch: Identifying the Indigenous Influence on Western Thought." *American Indian Culture and Research Journal* 37 (2): 87–114.

——. 2015. "Friends in This World: The Relationship of George Hunt and Franz Boas." In *The Franz Boas Papers*, edited by R. Darnell, 163–189. Lincoln: University of Nebraska Press.

Young, M. W. 2004. *Malinowski: Odyssey of an Anthropologist, 1884–1920*. New Haven, CT: Yale University Press.

Part 2

ETHNOGRAPHIES OF EXPLANATION

ANTHROPOLOGICAL EXPLANATION BY VIRTUE OF INDIVIDUAL WORLDVIEWS AND THE CASE OF STANLEY SPENCER

Nigel Rapport

Why did the renowned British painter Stanley Spencer (1891–1959) determine to distort the shape and scale of the human figure in those "visionary" paintings of "beloved" social relations that he felt were his most significant: his "message" and "gift" to humankind? The distortions were not always appreciated at the time or conducive to his public reputation. Indeed, campaigns of editorials and letters in the national press decried Spencer's "repulsive" figures that passed the bounds of good taste. The "peculiar mannerisms and distortions," wrote the *Sunday Times*, "recall the experience of a nightmare" (quoted in Hyman 2001, 31). Did not Spencer's "warped art" and refusal to paint the normal appearance of nature evince both blasphemy and a "world of madness" beyond "the frontier of reason" (*Continental Daily Mail* 1935)? Surely the art stimulated "the universal condemnation of normal persons" and called into question Spencer's moral healthiness? This chapter will argue that Spencer was led to distort not by way of an affectation of "modern art," nor due to a lack of skill in draftsmanship—his nudes, landscapes, and still lifes can be brutal in their honesty and photographic in their accuracy—but because of the metaphysic of love that he developed: his "loving vision" of worldly truth.

The case of Spencer, an iconic figure in twentieth-century art, is used in this chapter as a means to illustrate the significance of explanation in terms of an individual's worldviews. Human beings act on the basis of their worldviews and their life-projects. Given the privacy of personal consciousness—the opacity of one person to another—and given the ambiguity of the means by which human beings endeavor to communicate among themselves, worldviews and life-projects are inherently individual and personal phenomena. In understanding the distortion in Spencer's art in terms of how he interpreted the world around him and determined to act within it, the chapter argues that to explain in social anthropology is to do justice to individual and personal senses of being-in-the-world. This, in turn, entails two moments of analysis. First is to provide an account of an individual's worldviews: those constructions of self, world, and other, those notions of ontology, cause, and value, that each individual human being will furnish themselves with in order to make sense of themselves and their environments. At any one time, there will be a set of personal constructs that an individual maintains and that is regularly evoked by perceived or remembered stimuli. The second moment of analysis is to provide an account of what transpires when individuals interact socially and their different worldviews indirectly come into contact: "indirectly" because it is never personal consciousnesses that meet in social interaction—it is never possible to know how another human being is experiencing the world—but rather the expression of consciousness in symbolic forms (words, gestures, displays, and so on) that are intrinsically ambiguous. Social interaction is always a translation between different individuals' different worldviews (Rapport 2001). Social anthropological "explanation" may thus encompass the social world—of structure and culture—that is made by the interaction of different personal worlds of meaning: the worlds that each individual inhabits and the effects when these worlds collide. To "explain" social interaction is to understand symbolic exchange in terms of the different individual worldviews from which the meaning and purpose of the words, gestures, and displays (and so on) derive. To explain social interaction and social life is to understand how individual members of a social milieu are inhabiting, animating, their shared symbolic forms with meanings and identities that they have personally construed.

Moreover, it need not be the case that individuals construct only one worldview for themselves; they may inhabit any number at the same time, each responsible for a particular outlook and ethos, and affording a particular set of identities to the environing world, including the identity of the individuals themselves. As much as the social milieu, each individual may comprise a diverse assemblage of ideas, personae, and behavioral intentions: individuals experientially located in a diversity of distinct, self-contained worlds of people, events, values, norms, and constraints (Rapport 1993).

Social life exists as a messy complexity—multiple, contradictory, even chaotic: a muddling through. A social milieu is a place where a diversity of individual worldviews intersect and overlap, collide and diverge, influence and oppose one another. Explanation of social life is not best served by neat, mechanical models, by claims of overarching systems of structure and function, of synthesis and consensus (Rapport 2017). The diversity does not yield an orderly singularity since individual constructions of experience are inexorably perspectival, endlessly creative, and inevitably imbued with "the secrecy of subjectivity" (Levinas 1985, 78).

The argument may be illustrated, appropriately enough, through the distortions wrought by the painting of Spencer: his departure from a conventionally "accurate" portrayal of human beings in order to present the vision of true identity and true relationality that was granted him. To "explain" why Spencer distorted the human figure is to understand the place that love held in his worldviews and what that love meant. To "explain" the effect of Spencer's distortions on the world of art and beyond—on the Royal Academy, on Winston Churchill—is to enter into the worldviews of his audience.

Spencer died in 1959, so this cannot be a face-to-face relation with a research subject. However, Spencer was an obsessive writer, leaving an archive of millions of words—notebooks, diaries, love letters, correspondence with his agent, lengthy analyses, lists and descriptions of his paintings—now housed at the Tate Gallery in London and the Stanley Spencer Gallery in Cookham. Words were as important to him as paint, Spencer claimed, and he wished the titles of his paintings to be as "full" as the images, such was their role in explicating his composition. As his biographer, Kitty Hauser, writes, "Perhaps more than any other artist, [Spencer] expended almost as much energy in describing his paintings as he did in creating them. Even after his works had been made, exhibited and sold. Spencer would return again and again to them in his writings, analysing their hidden meanings, and their place in his oeuvre as a whole. . . . These esoteric and personal meanings are far from self-evident from the images alone, leaving the critic unavoidably in the dark" (2001, 12).

Spencer also felt a special ownership of, and affinity to, his writing, wanting his words to be respected as his personal language alone: "Don't try to make a boiled-down simplified version of anything I say . . . : the second-hand examples I have seen of myself I could not recognise" (quoted in Robinson 1976, 7).

To respect these words is to "converse" with Spencer, I shall say, even to the extent that his personal, private being-in-the-world may become visible (Rapport 2016).

Worldview, Society, Culture

"Worldview" is the common English translation of the German word *Weltanschauung*, meaning overarching philosophy or outlook. *Worldview* describes fundamental conceptions of the world, conceptions that ramify into thought and feeling, and conceptions that give rise to how individuals behave in the world. William James spoke of "the mind's conversations with itself" (1890, 239). Not necessarily fixed or jointed or coherent, possibly rambling, whimsical, elastic, fluid—hence a "stream of thought, of consciousness, or of subjective life"—there was nonetheless a singularity to the inner voice of consciousness: it was an emanation from one creative source, however refracted into different moments, moods, and situations, even different personae or selves. Worldview comprises the sum of expressions in the mind's conversation with itself. It includes will and intentionality; rational and irrational engagements with the world; emotional reactions and aspirations; sensations of pain, touch, and smell; discernments of worth; moral choices; loves and hates.

Worldview can also be defined as that being-in-the-world that *precedes* expression. The word implies a theorizing of causation and of sequence such that behavior is not seen as automatic or meaningless—unintentioned, purely reactive—nor as necessarily explicit, a "face" value. Rather, behavior is the translation of worldview into expressive forms, such that, as the Latin adage has it, "Si bis faciunt idem, non est idem" (If two people do the same thing, it is not the same thing) (Devereux 1978, 125–127). Individuals might meet in interaction while at the same time executing moves, achieving positions, proclaiming successes, and so on, in private and possibly very different game plans. Indeed, the worldviews of each individual—the "ideoverse" (Schwartz 1978, 429) of thought and affect, values, plans, techniques, people, and things—will likely be unique. Each individual is likely to possess a complex cognitive system of interrelated objects that amounts to a private world, rarely if ever achieving "cognitive communality" with another. Rather, human beings organize themselves, integrating their behaviors into reliable and joint systems—social structures—not by possessing uniform cognitive maps or even having equivalent motives but by learning that under certain circumstances others' behavior is predictable and can be confidently interrelated with certain actions of their own. A social system comprises sets of "equivalent behavioral expectancies," as Anthony Wallace termed it (1970, 24–33), individuals regularly engaging in routine interactions with one another because they have developed a capacity for mutual prediction. The "members" of these interactions will not be found "threaded like beads on a string of common motives" (24). They will likely interact in a stable and mutually rewarding fashion—maintaining institutions and social structures—and they organize themselves culturally into communities and traditions in spite of having radically different interests, habits, personalities, and customs, and despite there being no one cognitive or emotional or evaluational map that members share.

The synthesizing processes by which the individuals come together and engage in interaction entail the habitual exchange of sets of shared symbols. These "habituses" perdure to the extent that individuals agree to go on recognizing the symbols' existence and how, conventionally, they might expect to see them exchanged. Beyond this, however, social systems have no life. Society and culture may not be construed as things-in-themselves, possessing their own interests, needs, functions, or agency, for the symbolic forms (words, things, rituals, institutions) are empty and inert when not animated by individual intentionalities. At best the symbolic forms of social systems come to "enjoy" inertia; they are the remnants of past practice (dictionaries, roads, interactional routines) from whose bricolage individuals mine the resources—physical, emotional, political—to express new meanings and promote new life-projects. Societies may exist without consisting of replications of cognitive uniformity, and cultures need not represent standards, norms, practices, rules, views, or beliefs that are shared alike by their members.

This is not an argument for solipsism, or for sociocultural milieux being understood as idealistic manifestations of individual desires. Law and institutionalism, discrimination and violence, exploitation and enslavement are components of real experience, but one does not misconstrue how these *become* real. An exchange of symbolic forms between individuals gives rise to sociocultural normativities, continually and routinely, but not as things-in-themselves. Law and institutionalism, discrimination and violence, exploitation and enslavement continue to depend on their being inhabited by individual actors and animated by their meaning and purpose. This is not an argument in denial of pattern or structure in social life. Rather it is to say that while traditions of cultural symbology that come to characterize particular sociocultural milieux may formally synthesize individuals into societal "members," *living in alignment with others does not translate as living with, through, or by virtue of others.* Social milieux remain sites where distinct individual interpretations, worldviews, and life-projects— the aims, plans, and end points to which individuals would have their actions lead—aggregate and abut against one another in complex, even chaotic, ways (Rapport 2003).

Stanley Spencer and Distortion

> *The Beatitudes of Love* strikes me as a pathological series of pictures, hideous of subject and flatly painted. Yet when I look at them one after another, I cannot help laughing at their preposterous solemnity. . . . These sex fancies floating above any possible reality in the end provoke merriment rather than disgust. But I am now safe from him. That makes all the difference.

This is Patricia Preece (quoted in Collis 1972, 109), dictating an account of her time in the 1930s as Spencer's second wife. Preece went on:

> I thought the figures caricatures, willfully distorted and made ugly for the fun of it. Many other critics agreed with my opinion. Such stuff couldn't be taken seriously, they said. It was too grotesque. (105)

Also:

> It was to be many years before the public would readily accept his figure compositions. They were generally considered willfully distorted, caricatures and hideous. No one understood their significance vis-à-vis his private life. Indeed, they were so frank an expression of his perverse joy in the degraded and humiliating that their meaning could hardly have been made plain. (64)

Preece's marriage to Spencer was not an enduring one. But nor was her dismissive opinion of Spencer's "distorted" compositions particular to her, as indicated by the reactions in the newspapers of the day cited earlier. The president of the Royal Academy in London, Alfred Munnings, urged a police prosecution of Spencer on grounds of obscenity and pornography. Winston Churchill deplored the "incorrect articulation" of the bodies: "If Mr Spencer's work represents enlightenment, then we should be grateful for our present obscurity"; rather than "resurrection" in a Spencerian world, he, for one, would prefer "eternal sleep" (quoted in Rothenstein 1970, 133–134).

My main concern, notwithstanding (in the expanse of this chapter), is with how Spencer himself understood his paintings, and the place of distortion in them in particular. "I shall never forget Eddie Marsh confronted with them. It fogged his monocle; he had to keep wiping it and having another go. 'Oh Stanley, are people really like that?' I said: 'What's the matter with them? They're all right aren't they?' 'Terrible, terrible, Stanley!' Poor Eddie." This is Spencer recalling with some amusement the reaction of one of his early supporters and patrons to being shown *The Beatitudes of Love* (quoted in M. Collis 1962, 144). "Poor Eddie" nicely captures something of Spencer's self-belief, his confidence in what he was doing. This is not to say, however, that Spencer set out to depart from natural appearances and proportions. This "was not intended or deliberate or wished for," Spencer explained to another acquaintance; indeed, it "caused consternation in me when after I had done it I realized 'the mistake'" (quoted in Bell 2001, 153). But nor was correcting the "mistake" to be undertaken either, for this would be to "ruin the design." Furthermore, Spencer considered, was it not the case that if you took the average person and you stripped them of their surface coverings, and how convention and politeness deemed that the human figure ought to look, their true forms would resemble those in *The Beatitudes of Love*? These are serious and authentic portrayals, Spencer insisted: he was neither "poking fun" nor "being Rabelaisian" or "horrible." To the contrary: "I clearly say in my pictures that I think these people are nice" (Tate Gallery Archive Microfiche 16B).

Spencer returned repeatedly to the matter of his distortions in his writings. But it was also the case that he came to no single or even consistent conclusion as to why he distorted the human figure and why he retained this distortion as a final effect. Rather, four very different perspectives on the matter can be identified. They might be named "distortion from design," "from emotion," "from spirit," and "from divinity," and I outline each in turn.

Distortion from Design

Spencer wrote, "I should say that my pictures are uncannily coherent, that that is what is so interesting about them" (quoted in Glew 2001, 144–145). The reason distortion occurred was that the things represented in these "remarkable" compositions were present not only for their own sake but for the sake of a larger design of which they are part: "Everything has a number of jobs to do in a picture and often a distortion occurs when something happens to have so much to express" (Spencer quoted in MacCarthy 1997, 136). Each picture consisted of an extraordinary number of different kinds of relationships existing between its parts, each of which, Spencer was happy to say, had been perfectly conceived and clearly expressed:

> My pictures consist of a number of shapes but the whole picture is a shape—the whole picture makes one form, one being. A human being consists of a number of different shapes and altogether they constitute one shape, one form—a human being. Therefore a figure in a picture has also to be a part of the being that the picture is: it has got to be, so to speak, not just itself but itself as part of the being or form of something it belongs to, and it has got to show how it belongs and to what part it belongs. There is a sort of spiritual articulation throughout composition. (Tate Gallery Archive Microfiche 16B)

In short, a design is a thing-in-itself. In an extended example, Spencer imagines designing a monogram:

> The reason for distortion occurring in my figure paintings is, as far as I can see, as follows: Suppose you were to take the letter A and tried to

make it as clear as possible to a child or someone who'd never seen it. You would choose the most "A-like" example of that letter you could find. But if you were told to make a monogram of the letters A, B and C, you would have to conceal the likeness of the A in order to make it subservient to what you were actually making. What is it you are making? Is it only the letter A, or is it A, B and C? No: you are making something out of the three letters: you are making a monogram or a design and, as a design should be, it is a new thing. Now, in making something that has the distinction of being a thing in itself—that will, if analyzed, prove to be the three letters yet something else besides—it will be a thing itself considered independently of what it is made; in other words, it will be a design. (Tate Gallery Archive Microfiche 16B)

And if one were to replace the monogram analogy with something more painterly: "Well then, if instead of a letter you take a human being, and there are three of them, you cannot think of one in particular, and its shape, but only that there are three, and each belongs to the other, and is contributing a solution to the whole" (Spencer quoted in Sorrell 1954, 34).

Artistry is a natural process, and painting a human body is equivalent to the formation of the body itself in the womb. There is a natural coziness, then, Spencer suggested, to the way that the couple in *The Beatitudes of Love: Knowing* (figure 1) appear as two parts of one body, insinuating themselves against each other: "They seem to find their place of rest where they can best serve each other in the same way as a liver will adapt itself to the shape of a stomach and so on." Each human being "belongs" to the other "members" of the composition, part of a "solution" to a supervening issue of design: "A thing in a picture may be one thing but, in view of what it is doing as part of the composition, it is a hundred things" (Tate Gallery Archive Microfiche 16B).

Distortion from Emotion

A second and different way that Spencer explained his having distorted the contents of his paintings concerned their subject matter. In the pictures that mattered to him—the visionary figure paintings—the subject matter was "all feeling." Spencer was painting an emotional *insight* rather than a physical sight: "I have tried to express ... all my spiritual love—the love of my happy home, my happy childhood, all the people I have loved. If I could marry those emotions of love with the normal forms of human beings, I should have a perfect picture. But the shapes that mean those emotions to me do not happen to be the shapes of ordinary humans"

FIGURE 1. *The Beatitudes of Love: Knowing,* by Stanley Spencer, 1938 (oil on canvas 66 × 56 cm). Source: Private Collection. © Estate of Stanley Spencer. All rights reserved, Bridgeman Images.

(quoted in *Daily Express* 1950). Achieving a near likeness was not the issue uppermost in his mind (or body) so much as being in the right "spiritual atmosphere" for painting and conceiving of a composition when "ripe to do so" (quoted in Glew 2001:144–145).

In 1937–1938, at the time of *The Beatitudes of Love* series, Spencer wrote a long essay to himself entitled "Distortion," referring again to the "deformation" of how the husband and wife are represented in *The Beatitudes of Love: Knowing.* Here is an extract from the essay:

> What really happens is this—your emotion of pleasure tells you there are *some* letters or *some* things in your mind, and you also know that the emotion is a kind of structure that can hold, support and assist in the process of becoming expressed, without in any way distorting or destroying what finally proves to be the letters or things which have gone to make it. The sense of desire and anticipation of something good

is the same as with a midwife who knows what to do without knowing any more than that something is going to be born.

The only thing that will guarantee this most complex image of my mind being finally landed, so to speak, in the form of a picture in its purest, most undestroyed, and most "untampered with" form is this very "remote-from-being-born-as-a-picture" emotion which I experience in the earliest stages of a picture's production. So you can see that, in this early stage, there is very little apparently to go on—in fact one wonders if there is anything there at all. One therefore has to carry this impression across a vast region where endless doubts arise. Why? Because, during this whole period, the image in the mind is only very dimly perceived and one must make no mistake as to its identity; in my case, the least flicker of distrust in the first outset of the thing would completely destroy the meaning. . . .

Well now, suppose I see that one of these bits of structure has made some miscalculation as to the space needed for some such item as a girl's arm, the miscalculation arises in this way: the girl is the wife, say, of a very broadly shaped man and she has passed her arm across to her husband's waistcoat-buttons and rests her hand there. When I look, I see that the gesture is absolutely right: the design and the design relationship are right. I can also see that the arm is too long. That being the case, I can only come to the conclusion that the strength of my emotion and wish has not been quite strong or pure enough to be able to project the image sufficiently far into the earlier stage of "cage" making where it would have been possible to make the fact conform to the shape of the carrier and vice versa. The arm is part of the entire form of the picture and is perfectly placed and an integral part of the whole composition. It is not a question of altering the arm and making it the right length; it is a question of the degree of feeling in the first instance. . . . Then what *can* be done? One might attempt to get back to those realms of thought and feeling in which the picture was first conceived and try to re-awaken the emotions one felt—a difficult matter. Then once again you start to formulate the picture and, this time when you look at the result, you find that you have not rectified the faulty arm-length too successfully and, on the other hand, you may have lost other important points of character or made further distortions. (Tate Gallery Archive Microfiche 16B)

This is a complex and revealing piece of writing: Spencer coming to terms with his own creative process. Different parts of his mind or body are involved at different stages in an embodied process. An emotion must find a form. Distortion occurred when the emotion was not "strong" or "pure" enough to "project" a perfect image into the framework or "cage" that carried the design: the emotion and the framework do not conform perfectly to each other.

Spencer was quite exercised by the idea that he might be confused with "modern painters"—Pablo Picasso and the cubists in Paris or George Grosz and Otto Dix of the German Neue Sachlichkeit. His distortions were not a deliberate stylistic ploy, an affectation or satirical conceit, but something that emerged as a result of the emotion of creation. If he were to make an arm, say, "miles longer than an actual human being's arm," then—completely different from the "Continentals"—he had made a mistake. But it nevertheless represented him operating at the "fullest extent of my inspirational powers at the time of the conception," immersed in the emotions that inspired (quoted in Bell 2001, 153).

Distortion from Spirit

A third way that Spencer construed distortion in his figure pictures arose through his painting a heavenly "love-scheme." His pictures were a perfect representation of things' identity and of their proper ("beloved") relations in God's Creation: "I think it is wonderful how men are a part of the spirit, the same as the corner in the wall or the slope of the land is part of it" (quoted in Carline 1978, 91).

The desire and love that he felt identified the world and its contents and revealed their essential harmony—and this was what Spencer painted. "Every thing every item is looking to be unified into one special thing which thing will give to it & reveal, its essential meaning. Until then things are things without their daddys and mummies" (Tate Gallery Archive 8419.2.4). Love and desire moved the artist nearer to the true identification of objects seen as naturally belonging to the single body of Creation.

It was also the case, however, that even while he aimed at normal appearance, his realizing of this heavenly love-scheme would commonly take Spencer beyond the "normal." His paintings, he explained, were the product of a powerful inner need "that is not covered by any immediate object I see"; the existence of the need or "longing" was "proof of the existence of what I long for"—that there was something out there to be longed for and made into a representation—but finding it would take Spencer beyond the apparent objectivity of the world. That was why his visionary figure paintings were "something akin to what it would be like to perform a miracle" (Spencer quoted in Bell 2001, 153). In other words, his visionary conceptions must be understood as miraculous transformations of the world, miraculous communings with the world that overcame all barriers of convention:

> There is no question of barriers. . . . One has not only got to perceive the identity of a person or a bush, but the identity of the person and bush considered together, joined together to make some new identity, just as if an arm and a leg had been found and the finder was one who did not know of the existence of arms and legs joined to a body and could only therefore arrive at any further identification of their nature by approaching nearer to essential harmony when through love and desire it might discover the further identifying factors of its nature in their both belong[ing] to one body. (Spencer quoted in Nesbitt 1992, 16)

The most whole, true, or "religious" enjoyment of nature took one beyond what one thought one knew and who one thought one was to a new knowledge of the world: to God's heavenly Creation. However "amazing and wonderful" his figurations would ever be unacceptable. Second, even for Spencer—for any human being—straining toward God's true composition of the world was necessarily going to result in imperfection: "With me the strain of trying to affect a recovery of this spiritual eyesight has been so great that it has necessitated my temporarily neglecting the physical eyesight: not deliberately doing so, but finding it to be the case where & when one of these two experiences had overtaken the other where the spiritual eyesight has distorted normal appearance it has been meaningful & where the physical eye has claimed too much ascendency it has been meaningless" (quoted in Glew 2001, 229).

The difficulty was an absolute one. Unlike God, a human being had the disadvantage of being trapped in one body and positioned always in one physical space, whereas, in order to see "lovingly," truly, as one Creation, the artist should ideally incorporate the world, as God does, join with it, and have all the world become his self.

His (Spencerian) "love-scheme" was the scheming—the training, the habitual practice, the freeing himself to see—by virtue of which the artist puts himself in a position to know the world for what it truly is and comes to a realization of what God's scheme for Creation was: the essential and meaningful harmony of the world and all its contents. The design of a painting should ideally reflect and make manifest the design of Creation; the different parts in a painting "consort" with one another for the purpose of "praising" God's Creation, "all fused and all one" (quoted in Glew 2001:230). Instinctively Spencer knew that "fusion"—between himself and the world, and between one thing in the world and everything else—was necessary, was fulfilling, and was true. He knew of his own covetousness—his envy concerning every thing, every relationship, and every person who was not (yet) himself—and he knew of the strength of his love, strong enough to absorb anything into its scheme: "The design element in my pictures is the shape of my love. I am wanting & hoping for a time when I can have my jaws reticulated so that I can swallow a human being whole without it having to be mis-shaped in order to fit into my design, fit into my love scheme" (Tate Gallery Archive 733.2.422). In his pictorial designs, Spencer tried to make this fusion manifest so that the "shape of [his] love" reflected the shape of God's Creation. Inevitably there was distortion, however, because even the artist was not God.

To bring separate things together through love fulfilled each thing's identity and proved each thing's existence. The effort to bring about fusion between what was you and what was outside you was worth any effort because of the ecstasy of meaningfulness and joy that might result. To effect a fusion and reveal what all the parts together meant was to walk with God. Spencer did his best to avoid an arm being too long, say, because this was an indication of fusion not having been perfectly effected, but then it was the human condition ultimately to fall short.

Distortion from Divinity

The final reason that Spencer found for distortion occurring in his paintings concerned the divine nature of art as a phenomenon: "Art is one of the many things God made besides trees, tigers, human beings etc. Art is a thing which has its identity established in every bit the same way & to the same degree as has the tree or the egg. Art is not the expression of something else. Art does not express nature. They are two separate things. . . . Art is not an illustration. An illustration throws light on something not itself. . . . Art is created by God and revealed to us either by our own power of perception or some other" (Tate Gallery Archive 825.22).

While the "birth" of his artworks was something he came to anticipate—and to rejoice in in the anticipation—their "conception" remained "secret & imperceptible" (Tate Gallery Archive 825.22). This imperceptibility, Spencer reckoned, showed how art itself was a phenomenon—part of the natural world, part of divine Creation—since the ultimate conceptions of nature (the birth of the universe and so on) were similarly secret. When he painted, Spencer was not so much representing or displaying Creation as immersing himself in it. To paint was to examine the identity of Art, as he might a tree or egg. Art was a thing-in-itself: it had its own nature, distinct from everything else. To practice art was to perceive a given part of the universe.

The occurrence of seeming distortion, therefore, was simply the natural shape of artfulness. It might seem as if the artwork was "about" human beings whose forms and proportions had been distorted, but actually the artwork was manifesting another part of God's Creation: "art-beings." Hence, "good art" was "just saying 'ta' to God," the miraculous, blessed, joyful act of being able to give perfect praise through divine practice (Spencer quoted in Rothenstein 1970, 50).

Stanley Spencer's Worldviews

Spencer reached no single conclusion about the appearance of distortion in his painting of the human figure. Instead he constructed four different perspectives on the matter (at least), amounting, I would say, to reason from within four different worldviews. His foregoing reflections represent four very different constructions of the world, and the place of art, human beings, the artist, and the divine and heavenly within it, including the design of his own artistic compositions and Spencer himself. Nor is there consistency among these perspectives. Reasoning from design to emotion to spirit to divinity does not give on to a coherent version of the nature of distortion, nor of its origin. When Spencer reasons from design, then, it leads him to a conception of the painting as a thing-in-itself, its composition having its own aesthetic and amounting to a relational whole. When he reasons from emotion, he focuses on the process of inspiration as its own thing, natural yet opaque: feelings give on to forms that may or may not embody a perfect ratio between the physical and the emotional. When he reasons from spirit, he accepts the figuration to be a phenomenon emerging from the practice of loving the world so as to incorporate God's harmonious whole, his scheme, possibly in transfiguration of the merely superficial appearance of reality. But then reasoning from divinity, Spencer recognizes that the practicing of art is a distinct thing that God has created, with its own phenomenology; art cannot be expected to resemble or recall anything else.

Nor did Spencer reach consistent conclusions concerning how distortion in his paintings was to be evaluated. Distortion was sometimes something to welcome and sometimes to regret. When reasoning from design or emotion, Spencer reckons distortion as something for which he was responsible, even culpable, while reasoning from spirit or divinity causes distortion to seem inevitable, a worldly condition. Distortion is something Spencer can anticipate occurring in his artworks when reasoning from spirit or design; while it is unanticipated and its occurrence a surprise when reasoning from divinity or emotion. From one perspective, the possible imperfection of his painting is not to be denied, Spencer's inability always to achieve a perfect ratio between physicality and spirituality:

> People who are not painters never see how complicated nature is, a
> group of moving people, for example. I want to express certain ideas,

certain feelings I have about people, or about places. If I could express myself clearly and forcefully without any distortion of nature I would do so, but to do that I have to draw as well as Michelangelo. It's too bad that I don't draw as well as Michelangelo, because it means that in order to say what I want I have sometimes to pull and push nature this way and that. (Spencer quoted in Rothenstein 1984, 117)

From another perspective, however, distortion is a nonissue: this was how people actually looked and how they were lovable. He did not distort the world; he painted the true heavenly nature of God's Creation.

It is striking, too, that these distinct perspectives and reasonings are not related to particular aspects of his biography according to Spencer. It is not that he reckons distortion to pertain to one part of his life—such as the 1930s when *The Beatitudes of Love* series was painted—or one set of circumstances more than another. Spencer continually wrote, read, and rewrote his thoughts, cataloged and recataloged his notes, and the foregoing perspectives perdured: distinct lifelong constructions of his environment and his places within it. In no expression, moreover, no worldview, does Spencer deny the authenticity or integrity of his vision—disown, specifically, the seriousness and importance of *The Beatitudes of Love*. To paint is simply to express different varieties of love: "Let me point out that the love I have for [the people in my pictures] is not to be confused with the special love I feel towards a picture in seeing how each item takes its place. This latter love is a delight one feels in being able to express an idea eloquently through several items in the picture. . . . But both these loves are very near each other nevertheless" (Tate Gallery Archive Microfiche 16B).

Conclusion

It is through Spencer's words, I have argued, that an audience might hope to approach as closely as possible an explanation of distortion in his visionary depictions: what distortion was, why it occurred, what it meant, why it was retained. Even if it were asserted that individuals' own creative processes are ultimately beyond their ability to verbalize or even ratiocinate—being embodied practices—I would want to say that it is from within individual worldviews that such creativity emerges. The form of expression and the meaning contained in Spencer's distortions—the desire, the intentionality, the embodying—owe their nature to the personal worldviews from which they derived.

Interiority—an individual's stream of consciousness, the continual conversation had with the self—remains something of a terra incognita in social anthropology. Literary fiction has been less circumspect in this regard, with the likes of E. M. Forster claiming such fiction to be therefore "truer" than social science in portraying how consciousness felt and was socially lived and displaying "the hidden life at its source" (1984, 55–56). Notwithstanding, it is in terms of individual interiority that I would urge an *anthropological* explanation of social interaction (Rapport 2008). More specifically, my argument is that by virtue of personal worldviews, individuals construct, populate, and anticipate the worlds around them and enter into them. Their worldviews furnish them with expectations before interacting with others, with their perspectives during such meetings, and with their conclusions afterward. To "explain" social interaction is to have recourse to the worlds that individual members are inhabiting, sensorially, the life-projects on which they understand themselves to be entrained. It may be objected that this form of explanation precludes sociocultural context. Did not Spencer, for instance, operate in the contexts of "modern art," newspapers, art galleries, agents, wives, prime ministers, courts of law, discourses of beauty, God, and love, as a white, British, aspirant, upper-working-class, artistic male? Through an appreciation of worldviews, however, another understanding of context is foregrounded. Here, context originates before social situations. It is something that individuals bring to social interactions and deploy within them. Context concerns the situational way in which individuals interpret symbolic forms—relating them to others so as to accrue personal "association nets" of meaning—according to the interior worlds of a personal phenomenology. It is thus that the same personal context may be inhabited in any number of externally different settings, and vice versa: the "same" interactional setting might be personally contextualized in any number of different ways. The foundational determination of context is individual and possibly private (Rapport 1999).

Focusing on worldviews as the primary contexts that individuals inhabit in sociocultural milieux means that the anthropologist is not led to procuring a singular or even coherent account of either social interaction or cultural belonging. Not only do worldviews fail to translate into a set of common-denominational, community-wide perspectives, but this individual diversity refuses to be tied to externally defined or classificatory situations; the logic behind these personal contexts is subjective and particular, embodied and sensory. To explain anthropologically by way of worldviews is not to "corrupt" the ethnographic truth of individuality: not to impose a social or cultural collectivity in the name of structure and system, tradition and belonging. "The will to a system is a lack of integrity," as Friedrich Nietzsche wrote ([1889] 1979, 25). To attempt an honest account of the human experience is to embrace contrariety and inconsistency—distortion; one respects the integrity of personal worldviews over against the assumption of homogeneous, coherent, mechanistic social or cultural wholes (Rapport 1997). In spite of the distorted picture that may result, it is to the diversity of individual orderings of the world that the anthropologist aspires to do justice.

Plainly put, anthropological explanation entails aligning the worldviews and life-projects of those individuals involved in a milieu at a particular time and place as these worldviews and life-projects find expression in the cultural symbologies and the social structures that are current. It is worldviews and life-projects that inhabit and animate the otherwise-inert symbols and structures with individual will, meaning, and intentionality. It is the inherent ambiguity of the same symbolic and structural forms that enables a diversity of individualities to come together, in alignment, as "a" society, "a" community; it is that ambiguity that enables diversity—within and between individuals—to disguise itself, superficially, as sociocultural pattern. Social structure and cultural tradition—the habitualities of symbolic exchange, the institutionalism of social process—are recast as moments in which an assemblage of individual meanings and motivations find expression, connecting tangentially with one another, colliding and coevolving.

A diversity of worldviews in a social milieu amounts to a possibly chaotic coming-together, a moment-by-moment muddling-through from which the fate and development of societies and cultures ultimately derive.

REFERENCES

Bell, K. 2001. *Stanley Spencer*. London: Phaidon.
Carline, R. 1978. *Stanley Spencer at War*. London: Faber and Faber.
Collis, L. 1972. *A Private View of Stanley Spencer*. London: Heinemann.
Collis, M. 1962. *Stanley Spencer*. London: Harvill.
Continental Daily Mail. 1935. "Royal Academy Controversy." April 27, 1935.
Daily Express. 1950. "Royal Academy's Prodigal Son," April 29, 1950.
Daily Telegraph. 1950. "Resurrection" (a Letter from Lady Dorothy Paterson). July 17, 1950.
Devereux, G. 1978. *Ethnopsychoanalysis*. Berkeley: University of California Press.
Forster, E. M. 1984. *Aspects of the Novel*. Harmondsworth, UK: Penguin.
Glew, A. 2001. *Stanley Spencer: Letters and Writing*. London: Tate.
Hauser, K. 2001. *Stanley Spencer*. London: Tate.
Hyman, T. 2001. "Stanley Spencer: Angles and Dirt." In *Stanley Spencer*, edited by T. Hyman and P. Wright, 10–41. London: Tate.
James, W. 1890. *Principles of Psychology*. New York: Holt.
Levinas, E. 1985. *Ethics and Infinity*. Translated by R. Cohen. Pittsburgh: Duquesne University Press.
MacCarthy, F. 1997. *Stanley Spencer*. New Haven, CT: Yale University Press.
Nesbitt, J. 1992. *Stanley Spencer*. Liverpool: Tate Gallery Liverpool.
Nietzsche, F. (1889) 1979. *Twilight of the Idols*. Harmondsworth, UK: Penguin.
Rapport, N. 1993. *Diverse World-Views in an English Village*. Edinburgh: Edinburgh University Press.
——. 1997. "The 'Contrarieties' of Israel: An Essay on the Cognitive Importance and the Creative Promise of Both/And." *Journal of the Royal Anthropological Institute* 3 (4): 653–672.

——. 1999. "Context as an Act of Personal Externalization: Gregory Bateson and the Harvey Family in the English Village of Wanet." In *The Problem of Context*, edited by R. Dilley, 187–211. Oxford: Berghahn.

——. 2001. "Communicational Distortion and the Constitution of Society: Indirection as a Form of Life." In *An Anthropology of Indirect Communication*, edited by W. Watson and J. Hendry, 19–33. London: Routledge.

——. 2003. *I Am Dynamite: An Alternative Anthropology of Power*. London: Routledge.

——. 2008. "Gratuitousness: Notes towards an Anthropology of Interiority." *Australian Journal of Anthropology* 19 (3): 331–349.

——. 2016. *Distortion and Love: An Anthropological Reading of the Art and Life of Stanley Spencer*. London: Ashgate.

——, ed. 2017. *Distortion: Social Processes beyond the Structured and Systemic*. London: Routledge.

Robinson, D. 1976. Introduction to *Stanley Spencer, 1891–1959*, edited by D. Robinson, 5–7. Glasgow: Arts Council of Great Britain.

Rothenstein, J. 1970. *Stanley Spencer*. London: Paul Elec.

——. 1984. *Modern English Painters*. London: Macdonald.

Schwartz, T. 1978. "Where Is the Culture? Personality as the Distributive Locus of Culture." In *The Making of Psychological Anthropology*, edited by G. Spindler, 419–441. Berkeley: University of California Press.

Sorrell, M. 1954. "The Loved World of Stanley Spencer." *Studio* 147 (731): 33–39.

Tate Gallery Archive 733.2.422–4. "Stanley Spencer, three documents, Sept 1948, written by Stanley Spencer consisting of notes about his writings, landscape painting, especially his early ones and notes on Roger Fry's article in 'The Nation and Athenaeum,' 12 March 1927 and a note headed 'Accentuate the Positive, Eliminate the Negative.'" [1948].

Tate Gallery Archive 825.22. "Richard Carline, extracts from lectures by Stanley Spencer in the 1920s, lent by Spencer to Richard Carline who was writing the brochure about Spencer's work at Burghclere." [1920s].

Tate Gallery Archive 8419.2.4. "John Rothenstein, manuscript explaining Stanley Spencer's view on the Resurrection." n.d.

Tate Gallery Archive Microfiche 16B. "Stanley Spencer's notes, typed, edited and indexed by Dudley Tooth 1942–1946."

Wallace, A. 1970. *Culture and Personality*. New York: Random House.

EXPLAINING POST-TRUTH

Jonathan Mair

In this chapter, I will be concerned with Vox Day's influential 2015 book *SJWs Always Lie*, which was largely responsible for introducing the term *social justice warrior* (SJW) to public discourse in the United States and elsewhere. Underlying Day's first-order claims about science, race, Donald Trump, Brexit, and so on is a systematic second-order account of the nature of information and of consumers of information. In what follows, I argue that we ought to pay closer attention to this second-order content, rather than focusing exclusively on the first-order content, as analysts of post-truth have so far done. I propose that we adapt a concept from psychology, *metacognition*, in order to do this. To illustrate what I mean by that, I will begin by thinking about the ways in which anthropologists have understood apparently irrational beliefs, especially in the context of religion. They have mostly proceeded by distinguishing between different categories of representation or thought and arguing that different rules apply in each case. I will go on to argue that an analysis of Day's work shows that a similar process can be observed on his part. Since Day's work, and the alt-right movement of which it is characteristic, has its own metacognitive theories that are similar to but different in some respects from anthropological theories, care will need to be taken to give those theories due prominence in any attempt to provide an explanation.

Post-truth

The term *post-truth*, as readers will be aware, suddenly became ubiquitous in 2016 in response to political campaigns in the United States and United Kingdom in which some parties seemed to be prepared to turn a blind eye to the near-consensus conclusions of communities of experts such as climate scientists and economists. Many commentators found it particularly baffling that the voters seemed to be voting against their own interests. The term spread rapidly around the world and was translated into many languages. Columns were written on the topic in the popular press and by editors of scholarly journals, many of whom were prompted to reflect on the loss of authority of academic expertise. Social scientists and political commentators are still struggling to account for this phenomenon.

In a preliminary review of some early contributions from different disciplines (Mair 2017), I found that authors tended to blame the emergence of post-truth on one or more of three causes. First, they identified a new willingness on the part of politicians such as Trump and Nigel Farage to lie and not to be embarrassed when they are found out. Second, they pointed to transformations in the economy of information that mean that, in the presence of an unprecedented superabundance of information, people increasingly are exposed to a narrow silo that reflects and confirms their prejudices and those of the people they associate with. Finally, they argued that these silo effects and other factors such as the deterioration of education have led to the increased influence of universal cognitive biases such as confirmation biases.

In reading these articles, it immediately struck me that while these explanations are entirely plausible, they rely on external factors, leaving alleged post-truthers as passive subjects of powerful social forces and actors. The most revealing anthropology often works by explaining what ways of thinking and doing look like from the inside, from the point of view of an active, first-person subject. As well as seeing post-truth as a product of technological and social factors, there must, I thought, be an account of post-truth models and motivations that makes sense from the inside. This chapter should be considered an experiment in applying this approach to post-truth. I focus on the work of one prominent alt-right writer, Day, which has often been associated with the term *post-truth*. Since post-truth is a nebulous, mostly online phenomenon, it is hard to imagine what a conventional ethnographic approach would look like, but our attempts to understand it can profit by learning from generations of ethnographic work on apparently irrational beliefs in the anthropology of religion. Given this tradition, anthropologists in the twenty-first century ought to be well prepared to think about the apparently irrational phenomena of our time, including post-truth. However, to date, anthropologists have had very little to say on the topic.

Trying to explain post-truth serves as a salutary challenge to our established ways of understanding social life in general. Anthropology has established itself as an apologetic science, by which I mean that it serves to vindicate the other by explaining away the strange. Susan Harding famously observed that this approach is disrupted by some categories of subjects, that antiorientalizing tools of cultural criticism are better suited for some "others" and not other "others" (1991, 375). She was writing about Christian evangelicals whose politics made them, in her terms, "repugnant" to anthropologists. The same surely applies to the kinds of people who are described by others as post-truthers. In this chapter, I argue that trying to understand these kinds of subjects will allow us to move beyond apology and get back to explanation.

Explanation and Anthropological Theories of Cognition
Ethnography Challenges the Belief-Motivation-Action Equation

An important part of explanation in anthropological writing has always been the process of setting people's actions in the context of their beliefs, or knowledge. The aim is usually to explain behavior that might otherwise be hard to understand for an outsider who does not share the tacit assumptions, explicit theories, or experiences of the people whose lives the anthropologist is describing. Naturally, this means that collecting and presenting the beliefs and knowledge, including people's explanations of their own actions, has always been an important part of the work of ethnography.

This kind of explanation—setting action in the context of beliefs—is something more than description, but it is not, I suggest, usefully thought of as a theory. Instead, it would be appropriate to describe this procedure as analysis. On the other hand, explaining using thoughts and beliefs does *require* a theory, whether or not it is explicitly discussed, in order to explain the relationship between three terms on which such analyses are based: (1) action or practice, including speech and the production of other representations; (2) mind or thought; and (3) the content to which the mind can be applied: beliefs, knowledge, sensations, emotions, desires, and so on.

This tripartite schema must be in place regardless of the position one takes on the question of the relationship of representations to the world. It is still required, for example, for "ontological" approaches that deny there is a difference between mind and world—jaguars can have beliefs and be mistaken about them and be misled by cunning hunters (cf. Viveiros de Castro 1998). The underlying theory that explains the relationship of these three terms (action, mind, and content) is best described as a theory of cognition, however suspicious many anthropologists have come to be of that term. Those anthropologists who have explicitly called their work "cognitive anthropology" (e.g., Boyer 1994; Sperber 1996; Whitehouse 2004) have focused on representations (including imagistic ones), but cognitive content does not need to be representational (Bloch 2005). Other anthropological theories of cognition are often taken for granted and tacit, but they are no less theoretical for that, and no less cognitive. A theory of cognition might include emotions and affect as well as beliefs, knowledge, memory, the content of utterances, texts, ritual, and so on. And to have a theory of cognition does not necessarily commit us to the kind of mind-body dualism usually blamed on René Descartes, or to the individuality of minds; one might well defend a theory of cognition based on the Strathernian dividual (Strathern 1988) or the Durkheimian superorganism (Durkheim 1979), for instance. Many anthropologists have done just that, of course.

A simple and widespread theory of cognition is what philosophers have called the belief-motivation or belief-desire model of action (Elster 1986). This is the theory that action is the product of decisions that arise when preferences are considered in the light of beliefs about the world in which the actor is constrained to act (table 1).

For example, if we have observed people making an offering to a god, we might use this theory to offer an explanation by supplying information about relevant beliefs and desires. This could be based on ethnographic or other data, if we have them, or we might have to speculate in a way that would at least be helpful in driving further research. The result might look something like table 2.

Like a mathematical equation with three terms, the logic of this model is that if we know two of the terms, we can derive the third. For example, if we know what someone believes and what they want, we can predict what they might do. If we know what someone did and we know the beliefs they hold about the world, we can at least begin to think about what they want. Say that we know that someone is ill and wants to get better and they decide in that context to conduct an

TABLE 1   The belief-motivation model—in the abstract

$$
\left.
\begin{array}{c}
\text{preferences} \\
+ \\
\text{beliefs about the world}
\end{array}
\right\} \Rightarrow \text{decision} \Rightarrow \text{action}
$$

TABLE 2   The belief-motivation model—a concrete example

preference: *desire for good fortune* + belief: *the gods reward those who make offerings by giving them good fortune*	⟹ observed action: *making offerings*

elaborate ritual; we might conclude that they believe the ritual will help to heal their disease. Where the three elements are known but are not logically related to each other, then we might be looking at a case of irrationality.

Of course, the belief-motivation model, understood in this way, is a gross simplification. Its mechanistic form is also a turn-off for anthropologists who know that actions and representations are polyvalent. Real life is full of instances in which the belief-motivation model does not seem to apply, as ethnographers know only too well. The theory assumes too much about the consistency of beliefs over time and in different contexts, and about the relationship of action to habit and to the emotions.

From its beginnings, the Malinowskian fieldwork paradigm served precisely as an efficient way of finding examples of inconsistent statements of belief, or of statements of belief that were not consistently reflected in behavior. By observing life in its minutiae and collecting data over long periods, rather than simply relying on interviews or formalized accounts of mythology, ethnographers found that their subjects' accounts of their own lives were frequently inconsistent. Fieldwork also brought the realization that very different forms of life also made sense and were often practically efficient, despite these inconsistencies. So rather than simply diagnosing irrationality as previous generations of anthropologists had done, anthropologists from Bronislaw Malinowski's time on have increasingly sought to explain apparently irrational behavior or statements of belief by providing richer and more complex accounts of the relationship between action, mind, and content.

Multiplying the Terms of the Equation

The classic belief-motivation model relates the key terms—motivation, belief, and action—by assuming that each category is internally coherent and that the mind that works with all three is capable of drawing logical inferences. It works only to the extent that subjects have preferences that are not contradictory, for example, and only to the extent that beliefs are consistent over time, and only to the extent that people are capable of acting in a way that fulfills their decisions. I have said that ethnographic fieldwork led ethnographers to posit a more complex relation between minds, content, and action than that envisaged by the belief-motivation model. This is not the place for an exhaustive survey of these contributions, which are extremely diverse. What I want to highlight here is that one common way in which these more complex theories of cognition work is to split one or more of the terms of the belief-motivation model into multiple subcategories: different genres of thought and speech, different domains of action, different kinds of mind. As most anthropologists since the early twentieth century have accepted the psychological unity of all humans, their attempts to generate more complex accounts of cognition have focused on understanding multiple forms of content and action rather than suggesting that there are different kinds of mind. A widespread version of this approach that is still influential distinguishes between ordinary language on the one hand and religious language on the other. On this view, ordinary language reflects a person's beliefs and preferences in a straightforward way (that is, in the way the belief-motivation model would suggest), while the special genre of religious language must be understood in a different way. Perhaps religious representations are systematically metaphorical, or "symbolic," and must be translated into literal language before they can be understood. Perhaps speech in a religious context has a "performative" role. By adding genres in this way, it is possible to account for—to explain—important areas of thought and action that are apparently irrational while leaving subjects' capacity for pragmatic action intact.

Consider a classic example: Edmund Leach's essay "Virgin Birth," published in 1966. The Trobrianders and some Australian groups are said to believe that a woman can get pregnant without any involvement from a man. To interpret such statements in the same way as ordinary belief, argues Leach, is to treat these people as if they are stupid. Statements about the role of men in producing children, he goes on, should be treated as a special category of speech, which he calls "dogma." Dogma is a special genre of language that expresses consent to the prevailing social system. In matrilineal systems, the brothers of children's mothers and the progenitors of those children often come into conflict. When a Trobriander asserts the reality of virgin birth, that assertion serves to affirm the matrilineal social system by denying the validity of fathers' claims to rights in children. In other contexts, such as animal husbandry, the same people show themselves perfectly capable of understanding the biological conditions of paternity, Leach insists.

Leach's concept of dogma shows that it is possible to complicate the belief-motivation model by introducing a distinction between two subcategories of action, without giving up on the idea of explicability (table 3). Once the expressive

TABLE 3   The belief-motivation model—apparent irrationality explained by multiplying categories of action

preference: breeding strong domestic animals, having children, social solidarity + beliefs: that sex causes pregnancy; that denying physical paternity reinforces social solidarity	⇒	observed action: subcategory 1: pragmatic action and speech; subcategory 2: dogmatic speech

content of dogma is rendered in literal form ("I do not wish to challenge the prevailing social order"), it can be fed into the standard belief-motivation model like any other belief.

However, some other anthropological theories of mind do not preserve strict rationality in this way. Consider, for example, Pierre Bourdieu's (1977) theory of *doxa*. Bourdieu distinguishes between two modes of thought and action: objectified and unobjectified. Objectified thought is based on well-ordered, internally consistent, and ends-oriented beliefs and is associated with certain unusual activities, such as formal education or capitalist bookkeeping, in which establishing a disinterested view is valued. The content of what Bourdieu calls "practical" thought, by contrast, is not objectified; it is naturalized through its embodiment in habitus and is therefore unquestioned and perhaps unquestionable (table 4).

Though practical thought reflects economic or strategic interests, and therefore has a certain instrumental rationality when judged by its effects, it is not strictly rational when judged in terms of its content because it may not produce beliefs that are internally consistent or consistent over time. Kabyle determinations on questions of kinship are unstable because they depend on contextual calculations of cost and benefit that are not—and cannot be—apparent to the person making the calculation, if Bourdieu is right.

In this sense, then, Bourdieu's doxa is unlike Leach's dogma in an important sense. A further difference is the way the boundaries between different categories of content or action are mapped onto distinctions between groups in society or between societies. For Leach, dogma was a mode of speech in which anyone could participate some of the time, a mode, as he explicitly argued, that was just as available to Cambridge dons as it was to Melanesians. Bourdieu, by contrast, argued that objectified thought was more characteristic of particular classes of people—scholars and capitalists are two important examples. It is therefore more typical of societies in which members of such classes are numerous than of those in which they are few in number or absent. That still allows for a smooth gradation

TABLE 4   The belief-motivation model—two categories of thought in Bourdieu's theory of action

preference:	
pursuit of economic interests	
+	
beliefs:	⟹ observed action
subcategory 1: objectified thought, based on abstract rules;	
subcategory 2: doxa, based on a practical mastery of the social field in question	

of societies ranging from those with the least space reserved for objectified thought to those with the most.

Other anthropological theories of cognition draw a firmer distinction between different kinds of society determined on the basis of their forms of cognition. I have in mind here the influential idea that a certain kind of reflective belief is only found in societies influenced by Christianity, or more generally by monotheism. Malcolm Ruel (1982), for example, complained that anthropologists frequently assume that the people they study have, and are able to reflect on, well-formed, consistent propositional beliefs. This, he argued, betrays the formation of anthropology as a discipline with roots in Christian societies. Christianity is a tradition in which adherents are expected to hold such a set of propositional beliefs—the creed—and to be defined by them. Many societies have been deeply influenced by Christianity, but the ground rules of Christian belief do not apply in all societies or all religious traditions, Ruel warned.

Jean Pouillon (1979, 1982) argued along similar lines, although he thought that the key to the distinction is not Christianity, with its emphasis on acceptance of the creed, but the cosmological model shared by all the Abrahamic religions. These traditions, he reasoned, all feature a bipartite cosmology that distinguishes between the world we know through experience and the transcendent world "beyond," to which we have no direct access (table 5). Belief, in the religious sense, is what we do in respect of knowledge about that world beyond. It requires commitment and trust because we cannot ever verify its contents. Other religious systems, he claimed, such as animism and polytheism do not share this cosmological premise and therefore have no need for a fundamental distinction between knowledge and belief.

I could provide many other examples of anthropological theories of cognition, but these few examples will suffice for my current purpose, which is to draw attention to the common basis of different approaches with different conclusions. In each case, ethnography that challenges models of rationality is explained using

TABLE 5   The belief-motivation model—classic anthropology of religion

preferences + beliefs: subcategory 1: everyday beliefs or knowledge; subcategory 2: beliefs about the world "beyond" that is beyond evidence and requires "faith"	⟹	observed action: subcategory 1: everyday, practical action; subcategory 2: religious ritual and language

a theory of action, mind, and content that explains the complexity of relations between the terms by dividing one or more of them into multiple subcategories.

Metacognition

It is not only anthropologists who formulate complex theories of cognition in this way. Thinking about thought is such a fundamental and consequential phenomenon that psychologists have even coined a term for it. *Metacognition* was defined by educational psychologist John Flavell in a 1979 article as knowledge and cognition about cognitive phenomena. Flavell began from the observation that as children grow older, they acquire improved insight into their cognitive activities. They understand which tasks are difficult and which are easy, and they come to understand their own skill and limitations in relation to particular content and activities and in comparison to other children. This insight enables older children to devise more effective strategies for learning, so better (second-order) metacognition leads to better (first-order) learning outcomes.

In that seminal article, Flavell outlined a list of elements that make up any form of metacognition. They are the following: (1) metacognitive knowledge, (2) metacognitive experiences, (3) goals, and (4) strategies. Metacognitive knowledge includes theories about the kinds of content to which the mind can be turned, ideas about cognitive activities, and ideas about the mind, such as what different kinds of mind there are and how they fare when engaged in different cognitive activities. Metacognitive knowledge also includes knowledge about available cognitive and metacognitive goals and strategies. Metacognitive experiences are experiences related to cognitive tasks, such as clarity, bafflement, confidence, discomfort, achievement, and shame. Goals are the telos of metacognitive effort—they may be cognitive or metacognitive. An example of a cognitive goal is being able to recite a text from memory; an associated metacognitive goal might be understanding and mastering a particular technique for the memorization of texts. Strategies are the activities through which goals are to be achieved. The presence of goals and strategies means that metacognition has evaluative and ethical aspects.

The Cultural Nature of Metacognition and Its Importance for Anthropology

Flavell proposed that metacognition improves both according to a universal timetable in younger children *and* as a result of explicit education about metacognition in older children. For educators, this means that teaching needs to provide opportunities for students to learn to reflect on their learning. For anthropologists, though, there is another, and I think a very important, message. If metacognition can be taught, if it can be passed from one person to another, and if it can vary, then there can be *cultures* of metacognition. And if there can be cultures of metacognition, then there can be ethnography of metacognition. As far as I can tell, though there has been a profusion of work on metacognition by educational and developmental psychologists, it has taken an exclusively normative approach to metacognition; that is to say, they have been interested in establishing which pedagogies of metacognition are most effective in promoting learning in children. It falls to anthropologists, then, to make the full range of existing forms of metacognition into an ethnographic object.

The specifics of Flavell's model of metacognition have been debated and developed by educational psychologists and philosophers since he proposed it, and some have suggested the cake should be cut up in different ways. For anthropologists, however the elements are defined, the important point remains: thought and action often depend in consequential ways on how the people concerned think about thought. This is analogous but parallel to the ways in which anthropologists have long formulated their own theories of cognition. Just as Leach can speculate about different genres of language and Bourdieu can elucidate different forms of thought and action, all anthropological subjects are also doing the same thing, and the ways in which they think about their thought will be important for the way they actually think.

Anthropologists might still conclude that people are not aware of all the processes that govern their thought; that would not be surprising. I am by no means arguing for an ethnographic foundationalism (see introduction, this volume) when it comes to cognition, in which taking local or specific forms of metacognition seriously means giving up on formulating and refining a general theory of cognition. However, the role of metacognition in shaping people's actions in relation to the content they think about, and especially the potential for thought about thought to be part of ethical projects, means that whatever general theories of cognition we might endorse, specific forms of metacognition will often have to be an important part of our explanations. Let me now turn to post-truth to illustrate how this approach can work in practice.

Vox Day and Post-truth

Born in 1968 in Boston, Vox Day earned money as a musician and video game developer in his twenties before increasingly turning to writing. He first authored science fiction and then took on an opinion column that was syndicated to a variety of online news sites. That was the venue in which he first achieved notoriety, with a string of provocative pieces including one that ran under the headline "Why Women Can't Think." He has published a number of nonfiction works, including *The Irrational Atheist* (2008), which takes on Richard Dawkins and the New Atheists, and he was an editor of and contributor to an influential collection of essays titled *Cuckservative: How "Conservatives" Betrayed America* (Red Eagle and Day 2015). Day runs two popular blogs, *Vox Popoli* (*sic*), which he mostly uses to comment on politics and science fiction, and *The Alpha Game*, which is for discussion of his elaboration of the "sociosexual hierarchy" discussed by so-called pickup artists or proponents of "the Game." He was an influential advocate of #GamerGate in 2014 and has pursued a number of vendettas using print and social media, mainly against people who have criticized his writing on political grounds.

Day's politics are typical of the alt-right, in that he sees white men as being targeted by a liberal elite in a way that endangers America and Western civilization. Within the wider alt-right umbrella, he defines his approach as "alt-West" rather than "alt-white." The former category describes people who balk at explicit racial supremacism, and who think that people of different ethnic backgrounds can participate in Western civilization. In common with a number of other prominent alt-right thinkers, Day claims to be a member of a minority that is championed by his adversaries: he is descended in part from Native Americans, and he has mentioned this in his work as support for the idea that the benefits of Western civilization are open to all. However, his rejection of race as a central factor in the culture wars is by no means absolute. He has written that culture cannot be changed within a single generation, nor perhaps within many, so the distinction between ethnicity and culture is not cut and dried. He also sometimes promotes the idea that there are stark differences between different races when it comes to IQ.

I should say at this point that I remain at best cautious about the use of the "post-truth" category. It is clearly a normative category, as well as a descriptive one—no one who was sympathetic to a writer would describe his or her work as "post-truth." That alone should make us cautious about using it as a term of analysis, no matter what our politics are. Moreover, a term such as *post-truth* that is supposed to capture a general and global phenomenon, a zeitgeist, is bound to resist careful study, as it will always be unclear to what extent any alleged instance is really representative of the general class. Those caveats aside, anthropologists should at least be engaging in this discussion and doing what they do well: trying to find specific mechanisms at work in particular cases that may be of use in explaining other cases through comparison of similarities and differences, or if that is not possible, then showing through the examination of particular cases the weaknesses of the general category.

SJWs Always Lie

SJWs Always Lie, subtitled *Taking Down the Thought Police*, presents a straightforward argument—though there is a twist in the final chapter. It is written in a curious bathetic style that mixes grand world-historical claims with highly personal examples drawn from Day's quarrels with specific "social justice warriors." Day's central claim is that freedom of speech, logic, reason, and Western civilization are under attack. The aggressors are SJWs. They dominate the state, media, education, and other establishment institutions and are motivated by a highly simplistic moral narrative, or "the Narrative." Day writes, "The Narrative is the story that the SJWs want to tell. It is the fiction they want you to believe; it is the reality that they want to create through the denial of the problematic reality that happens to exist at the moment. And there is no one definitive Narrative. Instead, there are many Narratives, all of them subject to change at any time, thereby requiring the SJW who subscribes to them to be able to change his own professed beliefs on demand as well" (2015, 277).

In a cameo foreword that introduces Day's argument, Milo Yiannopoulos explains that, because the Narrative is aspirational, not representational, it "cannot survive contact with reality" (2015).[1] The Narrative abhors complexity, but real life is always complicated. This explains what Day calls the First Law of SJWs: SJWs always lie. (Day distinguishes SJWs from other groups of people who habitually lie: propagandists, marketers, and sociopaths [2015].)

As SJWs always lie, on Day's account, they must constantly face inconvenient evidence; it does not discourage them, because they display "a willingness to deny science, history, logic, their past words, or any other aspect of reality that contradicts their current Narrative" (2015). Apart from facing down evidence and reason, in order to defend their Narrative, SJWs must also contend with heroic refuseniks such as Day himself. This is why, Day asserts, SJWs are so hostile to freedom of speech in all the venues in which they seek to disseminate their Narrative (i.e., every venue in which they find themselves, since they do so at every opportunity).

Despite attempts to prohibit the free speech of dissenters who challenge the Narrative, Day avers that "a broad-spectrum, reality-based resistance to the mirage is now taking shape, a resistance that will eventually undermine and replace all the old institutions that have been invaded and captured by the SJWs. All it takes to be part of it is a refusal to accept the religion of social justice, a refusal to bow down before the gods of Equality, Diversity, Tolerance, Inclusiveness and Progress" (2015, 250).

Members of this resistance can expect to be attacked for their pains. Day explains that when SJWs are confronted with their lies, they will "double down" (this is the Second Law of SJWs) by elaborating on their lies and "project" (and this is the Third Law) by accusing their opponents of faults of which they are themselves guilty.[2]

Dialectic and Rhetoric

In the final chapter, Day abruptly changes tack. He begins by introducing a distinction—derived from Aristotle's *Rhetoric*—between different kinds of language. Both of these forms of speech are used, he explains, for persuasion. Dialectic is based on logic and proceeds by way of syllogism. Rhetoric is based on emotional appeal and works with false syllogisms that merely associate certain conclusions with particular emotions. Day explains that Aristotle defended the use of rhetorical language as a means of communicating with those who are not capable of understanding dialectic. He quotes Aristotle: "Before some audiences not even the possession of the exactest knowledge will make it easy for what we say to produce conviction. For argument based on knowledge implies instruction, and there are people whom one cannot instruct."

That does not mean, Day points out, that these people cannot be taught in any way, just that they can only be reached by playing on their emotions. Not surprisingly, he asserts that

> SJWs fall squarely into the category of people who cannot be instructed and cannot be convinced by knowledge. This is the key to understanding their astonishing ability to cling to their Narrative in the face of evidence that obliterates it as well as their insistence on clinging to it even as it shifts and contradicts itself. The reason SJWs can believe seven impossible and mutually contradictory things before breakfast is their inability

to be instructed by knowledge; as long as each of those seven things happens to be in line with whatever their emotions are at the moment, SJWs will not see the inherent contradictions that thinking people do.

Finally, halfway through this final chapter comes the surprising twist. Day gives a practical example in order to illustrate the difference between rhetoric and dialectic. "If I say 'SJWs occasionally lie' in response to an SJW's false statement," he writes, "this is proper dialectic but poor rhetoric, as it is likely to fail to persuade a rhetoric-speaker of the actual truth, namely, that the SJW is lying in the present circumstance. The better rhetorical statement is 'SJWs always lie,' which is not dialectically sound (or if you prefer, untrue), but despite its lack of soundness, it is more likely to persuade the rhetoric-speaker to believe the relevant truth, which is that the SJW is lying."

So Day concludes his book by saying that the argument he has been advancing is not after all true, in the logical sense, but is merely emotionally effective in persuading people who are incapable of being moved to change their position.

He goes on to explain that there are three kinds of people. There are those who can understand dialectic, who are "intellectually honest and capable of changing their minds on the basis of information." Then there are those who are only capable of understanding rhetoric, like the SJWs. If one tries to communicate in dialectic to a "rhetoric-speaker, he hears it as rhetoric. Or, not infrequently, as complete gibberish." Finally, a third category of person has the intelligence to be able to communicate in both modes, and to switch between them at will. Day, of course, sees himself as being in that superior category: "I speak dialectic to those capable of communicating on that level, and I speak rhetoric to those who are not." He continues, "However, because many SJWs attempt to cloak their rhetoric in pseudo-dialectic, you can use sound dialectic to strip them of that pseudo-dialectic cloak on behalf of those capable of following the real thing, while communicating directly in rhetoric to the SJWs. This requires a degree of fluency in both discourse-languages as well as the ability to switch back and forth between them at will, a skill that takes some time to develop."

On this view of the world, information presented by the mainstream media, or other establishment institutions, mainly serves a political or "ideological" purpose, rather than an informative one, so it can safely be ignored; in fact, it must be ignored. Day represents the "rebels" of the alt-right as soldiers in the info trenches, pitting propaganda against propaganda by providing competing representations that can win out over those promoted by the liberal establishment.

Of course, by the time he makes these claims about categories of person defined by intelligence and the information war, it is not at all clear to what degree we are to take any of what he says at face value. Indeed, as a result of his open admission that he is involved in a sort of Gramscian war of position, Day's alt-right sympathizers often appear confused about which of his statements are meant in earnest and which are merely designed to provoke social justice warriors. In other words, to put it in his terms, they are confused about whether he is speaking dialectic or speaking rhetoric. This gives the exchanges between Day and his followers on his websites a sense of vagueness, uncertainty, and playfulness, and a disinterested reader will be left wondering whether even Day has a firm handle on the boundary between his sincerely held beliefs and his attention-seeking posturing.

SJWs Always Lie as a Metacognitive Theory

SJWs Always Lie is typical of much of the discourse that characterizes the alt-right and other populist movements. It is intended as a manual for use in "resistance" to the allegedly dominant culture, and the tools it provides to do that are not really first order, in the sense that they are directly related to the content of the dominant culture that the protagonists find objectionable. Instead, Day addresses second-order questions about the way in which the opponents think. By multiplying terms just as the anthropologists I discussed earlier do, Day aims to provide an explanation, a key to unlock the secrets of rhetoric. Like Bourdieu, he introduces subcategories of belief (table 6). Like Bourdieu's doxa, the SJW Narrative is, in Day's telling, wishful thinking—and it is related to preferences in a way that is not epistemically justified. Like Leach, he also introduces subcategories of language: dialectical language for ordinary communication, and rhetoric, which, like Leach's dogma, has a political effect.

One important difference between Day's model and those of the anthropologists is that Day also multiplies the kinds of minds that have beliefs and preferences and act on them. For Day, there are three categories of mind, each of which apprehends rhetoric and dialectic in a different way. As I noted earlier, since the time of Malinowski, the "psychic unity" of human beings has been treated as axiomatic by most anthropologists. There are, however, anthropological

TABLE 6 The belief-motivation model—classic anthropology of religion

preferences + beliefs: subcategory 1: ordinary beliefs; subcategory 2: "The Narrative"	observed action: subcategory 1: ⟹ dialectical communication; subcategory 2: rhetorical communication

precedents for this kind of move, most notably in the anthropology of Lucien Lévy-Bruhl and James Frazer.

I want to draw two sets of conclusions from this brief discussion, first in relation to post-truth, and second in relation to anthropological explanations of behavior.

Day is only one moderately influential thinker in the American alt-right, and his thinking can hardly stand for all of the phenomena around the world that have been classified as "post-truth." However, I think this case is enough to suggest that paying attention to the metacognitive content of alt-right and post-truth discourse can bring certain insights to the specificity of post-truth thought that the explanations that I discussed briefly at the outset ignore. Day's account is not simply an expression of a failure of trust in politicians, nor of the operation of a paranoid imagination in the absence of the regulating virtues of critical thinking. It is an elaborate expression of thought about the nature of thought in the contemporary moment.

SJW's Always Lie is substantially taken up with what Flavell called metacognitive theories. There are theories about the kinds of content that we can encounter: representations are either rhetoric or dialectic. Then there are theories about the kinds of thinking agents that apprehend this content: there are social justice warriors and plucky rebels such as Day, and this distinction is crosscut by the distinction between the three levels of aptitude: those who can understand rhetoric only, those who can understand dialectic only, and those who can switch between the two.

It seems to me that any attempt to understand Day and his followers in terms of universal characteristics of thought such as cognitive biases, or in terms of the transformation of information economies, will have missed a significant part of the picture and will fail adequately to comprehend the differences between the cynicism of the contemporary alt-right and other forms of cynicism. It is hard to say how much generalization will prove possible, but less elaborate versions of elements of Day's scheme, such as the distinction between mainstream media and independent media are certainly very widespread. In order to understand the specificity of positions such as Day's, with all its irony and instability, it is necessary to understand the specific configuration of theories of minds, content, and motives that underlie them. In other words, in order to explain their thought and action, it is necessary to produce an account of *their own* explanations of their own and other people's thought and action, of their own *culture of metacognition*.

Understanding this aspect of post-truth, if it turns out to be widespread, will also be important for those who are concerned to counter it. The form of metacognition that Day is teaching could make his audience almost impervious to persuasion at the level of first-order content. Any challenging claim can be dismissed as rhetoric if its author can be identified as an SJW—in this sense it is a "closed predicament," in Horton's sense (1967), complete with processes of secondary elaboration. It seems to me that the system is more vulnerable to second-order criticism, that is, criticism that aims at the metacognitive theory.

For anthropology, there is an additional lesson. Our explanations of people's actions are likely to be lacking if we do not pay adequate attention to those people's own explanations, including their conceptualization and evaluation of mind, action, and content. Since metacognition is formally identical to anthropological theories of cognition, there is a danger that we will simply apply our own categories to the first-order content, overwriting local metacognitive schemas with our own favored theories. That would be a mistake, not because anthropological theory must be subordinated to the thought of anthropological subjects, as some ethnographic foundationalists would claim, but because the thought of any agent is significantly conditioned by his or her thought *about thought*.

NOTES

1. Quotations from *SJWs Always Lie*, Day 2015, are given without page numbers because the book was published (by Day's own publisher) without them.

2. The elaboration of the Second and Third Laws is based almost entirely on a bizarre and petty discussion of a feud that Day has been conducting with another science fiction writer.

REFERENCES

Bloch, M. 2005. *Essays on Cultural Transmission*. Oxford: Berg.

Bourdieu, P. 1977. *Outline of a Theory of Practice*. Cambridge: Cambridge University Press.

Boyer, P. 1994. *The Naturalness of Religious Ideas: A Cognitive Theory of Religion*. Berkeley: University of California Press.

Day, V. 2008. *The Irrational Atheist: Dissecting the Unholy Trinity of Dawkins, Harris, and Hitchens*. Dallas: BenBella Books.

——. 2015. *SJWs Always Lie: Taking Down the Thought Police*. Kouvola, Finland: Castalia House.

Durkheim, É. 1979 [2012]. *The Elementary Forms of the Religious Life*. London: Routledge.

Elster, J., ed. 1986. *Rational Choice*. New York: New York University Press.

Flavell, J. H. 1979. "Metacognition and Cognitive Monitoring: A New Area of Cognitive–Developmental Inquiry." *American Psychologist* 34 (10): 906–911.

Harding, S. 1991. "Representing Fundamentalism: The Problem of the Repugnant Cultural Other." *Social Research* 58:373–393.

Horton, R. 1967. "African Traditional Thought and Western Science." *Africa* 37 (1): 50–71.

Leach, E. 1966. "Virgin Birth." *Proceedings of the Royal Anthropological Institute of Great Britain and Ireland*, no. 1966:39–49.

Mair, J. 2017. "Post-truth Anthropology." *Anthropology Today* 33 (3): 3–4.

Pouillon, J. 1979. "Remarques sur le verbe 'croire.'" In *La fonction symbolique*, edited by M. Izard and P. Smith, 43–51. Paris: Gallimard.

——. 1982. "Remarks on the Verb 'to Believe.'" In *Between Belief and Transgression: Structuralist Essays in Religion, History, and Myth*, edited by M. Izard and P. Smith, translated by J. Leavitt, 1–8. Chicago: University of Chicago Press.

Red Eagle, J., and V. Day, eds. 2015. *Cuckservative: How "Conservatives" Betrayed America*. Kouvola, Finland: Castalia House.

Ruel, M. 1982. "Christians as Believers." In *Religious Organization and Religious Experience*, edited by J. Davis, 9–31 London: Academic Press.

Sperber, D. 1996. *Explaining Culture: A Naturalistic Approach*. London: Blackwell.

Strathern, M. 1988. *The Gender of the Gift*. Berkeley: University of California Press.

Viveiros de Castro, E. 1998. "Cosmological Deixis and Amerindian Perspectivism." *Journal of the Royal Anthropological Institute* 4:469–488.

Whitehouse, H. 2004. *Modes of Religiosity: A Cognitive Theory of Religious Transmission*. Walnut Creek, CA: AltaMira.

Yiannopoulos, M. 2015. Foreword to *SJWs Always Lie: Taking Down the Thought Police*, by V. Day. Kouvola, Finland: Castalia House.

FINDING REAL AND FAKE EXPLANATIONS

Sarah Green

Every time someone seeks asylum and then goes through the process of applying for refugee status, they have to explain the circumstances under which they ended up doing so in order to prove that they have the right to claim asylum under the terms of the 1951 Geneva Convention on Refugees.[1] According to the convention, a refugee is "someone who is unable or unwilling to return to their country of origin owing to a well-founded fear of being persecuted for reasons of race, religion, nationality, membership of a particular social group or political opinion" (UNHCR [United Nations High Commissioner for Refugees] 2011, Article IA(2)). In recent years in the European Union (EU) region, attempts to persuade immigration officials that an applicant satisfies this definition mostly fail, despite the fact that in the past, they mostly succeeded. Didier Fassin noted in 2012 that in France, the rate of acceptance of applications had dropped to below 10 percent, down from over 90 percent in the 1970s (Fassin 2012, 116, 143); Heath Cabot noted in 2014 that in Greece, the percentage of acceptances was dramatically worse than that (Cabot 2014, 5).[2] And as documented by both of them, along with almost everyone else involved in observing this process within EU member states, the reasons that an explanation is thought to be fake appear to be highly unpredictable: however hard the lawyers, experts, activists, nongovernmental organization (NGO) workers, or even the applicants themselves try to discern which explanation counts as a valid and convincing one, there seems to be no way to predict the outcome of each new application.

Some of the most harrowing ethnographic accounts in this field involve the ethnographer telling of repeated efforts of someone trying to persuade the authorities of the truth of their claim, only for it to be rejected in the end. For example, Fassin (2012, 128–129) tells the story of Elanchelvan Rajendram, a Sri Lankan Tamil who claimed asylum in France and was repeatedly turned down, even though he gave exactly the kind of medical and other evidence that should have proved that his claim was true. In the end, his claim was rejected as being "too stereotypical" and he was returned to Sri Lanka. A few months later, he was shot and killed in Sri Lanka.

From the French assessors' perspective, Rajendram's explanation had been judged to be a standardized account specially formulated for the purpose of gaining refugee status, rather than the true story of a unique individual. From that vantage point, whatever it was that motivated Rajendram's application for asylum in France, the assessors believed it was something other than a well-founded fear of persecution, and so his application was rejected. Nevertheless, what happened after Rajendram was returned to Sri Lanka suggests that it was not a fake.

The Importance of Location and Territory

This is a familiar situation now in many parts of the world. Yet despite all the media attention to the problem, there has been relatively little attention paid to a couple of its key characteristics, both of which have to do with the relationship between people and their location. First, the whole concept of a refugee is dependent on a particular legal and political understanding of territory. This understanding has developed historically, and its logic is not self-evident (Elden 2013). In order to become a refugee, a person has to cross a particular kind of border, one that distinguishes between territories to which people legally belong and those to which they do not belong. It is obvious, but it is also key to understanding claims to asylum: the whole system is based on certain assumptions about the relationship between geographical space and human beings, assumptions that are embedded within the legal regulations that establish different kinds of rights to be physically present in a territory. By definition, asylum seekers are people who come from somewhere else and are asking for exceptional leave to stay in a territory to which they do not normally legally belong. In that sense, claims to asylum are always exceptional. I will be suggesting later that this historically contingent legal condition of territoriality generates a sense of contradiction whenever the number of claims to asylum rises to a level that makes them appear to cease to be exceptional to the authorities processing the claims. What Fassin did not describe in his outline of changes in French policies on accepting claims to asylum is that the number of people seeking asylum in each of those periods was dramatically different. In 1972, the total population of refugees in

France was 98,900; in 2012, it was 217,865, or more than twice the 1972 number.[3] UNHCR figures show that in 2012, the number of applications for asylum to France was 97,637.[4] In stark contrast, between 1970 and 1974, asylum applications to France were approximately 5,100 (Van Mol and de Valk 2016, 37).

It is important to note that, in both cases, the number of people involved was miniscule relative to the whole population of France: in 1972, the French population was almost 53 million, and in 2012, it was 65.5 million, which means that refugees as a proportion of the French population were and remain entirely negligible.[5] The same is the case for the EU as a whole. In 2012, the EU population was just over 441 million;[6] applications for asylum in the EU region were 386,392, or 0.087 percent of the population.[7] This is not about the significance of the numbers of applications relative to the population as a whole—those figures have always been statistically insignificant, despite what some political parties or media reports might suggest. Rather, my focus is on the bureaucratic management of asylum claims, of the circumstances under which claims are heard. In those terms, what changed is that in 2012, the French migration authorities received an average of 267 claims to asylum every day, while in the 1970s, it was less than 3 claims per day. From a border management perspective, if claiming asylum is an exceptional breach of the contemporary principle of territory, then it cannot simultaneously be a common occurrence.

The second issue relates to how that basic principle of territoriality comes into conflict with ideas about human rights on the one hand and humanitarianism on the other. I suggest that the highly precarious existence in which asylum seekers regularly find themselves, and most particularly, the apparently endless waiting it involves, is at least partly the result of the mutual contradictions between these principles. The logic of humanitarianism is universal: it concerns a moral obligation to care for those who suffer, and it focuses mostly on bodily, physical suffering; the logic of human rights is also universal in principle, but it is based on legal rights bestowed on individuals and does not directly concern a moral obligation, but instead a legal obligation, which ties it to the logic of territory, as it is only states that can execute laws. The contradictions between these three principles—humanitarianism, universal human rights, and the particularistic and bordered logic of territory—often lead to the result that people who draw on universal principles in claiming a moral or legal right to enter a territory often find themselves placed in apparently endless moments of waiting and precarity, caught between contradictory logics. They end up with nowhere that they can either safely or legally put their feet on a patch of the earth.

This is somewhat different from a point made many years ago by Liisa Malkki (1992) in her study of Hutu refugees in Tanzania. Malkki suggested that the logic of the refugee camp was tied to the logic of the rootedness of the concept of nationality: the idea that people belong to a territory in the same way trees are rooted in the soil. This meant that refugees came to be understood as being uprooted, and thus placed in special places for those who are effectively "matter out of place," in Mary Douglas's famous phrase (Douglas 1976). While not questioning this approach (indeed, Malkki's pathbreaking scholarship was among those that inspired my interest in spatial aspects of social life), I am more concerned with the concept of location than I am with issues of people's identities in this chapter: what difference it makes that the ground upon which people walk is defined in such a way that it generates a condition of locals and foreigners.

Hospitality and Hostility

Anthropologists and others occasionally draw on Jacques Derrida's (Derrida and Dufourmantelle 2000) work on hospitality in attempting to build an explanation for the vexatious situation in which no asylum seeker's explanation will do.[8] For Derrida, the concept of hospitality, as an abstract concept, implies the simultaneous power to be *in*hospitable, as well as the potential requirement to accept even hostile strangers into your house in order to satisfy the requirements of being hospitable. A host must have control over the house in question; but also, the host must be morally obliged to use that power over the house to allow strangers in, even ones who might ruin the house. Derrida suggests that these mutually contradictory elements coexist within the concept of hospitality. Some scholars have called on Derrida's reasoning to try and explain why asylum seekers seem to be constantly let down by the widely reported cultural and social moral obligation to be hospitable toward strangers, while at the same time, current procedures for granting asylum in, for example, the member states of the EU seem to be deliberately designed to reject just about everybody. So how to square this circle? How can the border management processes of countries whose populations apparently publicly take pride in their adherence to the concept and moral obligations of hospitality (not to mention justice and freedom) constantly result in people being sent back to places where they fear that they will be jailed, tortured, and killed?

Greece, which, at the time of writing, is one of the locations of a particularly intense focus on the refugee question, is also the location of a much longer-term anthropological debate on the concept of hospitality in general, and these two debates have folded into each other in discussions of how the refugee question is being confronted there (see Cabot 2014, 99–102, for a summary of that debate). Here, explanation has to make ethnographic rather than philosophical sense. This is important: in anthropology, the abstractions that constitute philosophical reasoning cannot be simply "applied" in order to explain ethnographic events; there is no direct route between Derrida's ideas and whatever might happen next in Greece, for example. Derrida's commentary concerned the word *hospitality* and the thought that the word made possible in a particular language, at a particular moment in history, and that might explain the possibility of the meaning of that word. In his conceptual work, Derrida is never describing what occurs; his work is always "as if," not "what is."

Matei Candea (2012, S35) argues this point in looking at how Derrida's views on hospitality might help in understanding ethnographic details in Corsica. He concludes that in practice, "hospitality more often seems to be a common language in which to argue and disagree, a language of accusation and disappointed hopes, a language of insult and wounded pride" (S46). In coming to that conclusion, Candea carries out two anthropological twists in order to turn his account into an anthropological explanation. The first is that he notes Derrida was French and lived in Paris, and that he made direct interventions on questions of hospitality in French public and political arenas. This turns Derrida into an ethnographic resource for Candea's study of Corsica, rather than a conceptual resource. And the second is that Candea points out that in practice (or what might in Derrida's terms be called "in the event"), there is no final conclusion to be had about the meaning of hospitality, nor the best ways to practice it or express it, which means it cannot act as an explanation. In short, hospitality in practice is not only contingent on particular contexts (i.e., the idea will mean different things in different contexts); it is *also* the subject and object of agonistic debate, in Chantal Mouffe's (2013) sense: in any given context, how to interpret the word is a matter of disagreement between parties—indeed, it is used as a means to throw brickbats at each other. Candea suggests that this agonism is hidden in the publicly pronounced universalizing and generalizing platitudes about the French (or Corsican) peoples being, ipso facto, hospitable. Drawing on ethnographic description, Candea notes that this is demonstrably not the case, and to make the mistake of thinking that Derrida's understanding of hospitality can simply be "applied" to the Corsican case is, in Candea's view, to miss most of the point.

Counterfeits

In the rather different situation I am focusing on—the bureaucratic procedure and unpredictable outcome of asylum-seeking claims in the EU region—there is a different element of Derrida's work that might be helpful. This concerns the asylum-seeking process as such, rather than anthropological explanations for the practices of hospitality that might make such applications either acceptable or unacceptable. Within the EU at least, the asylum-seeking process is a prolonged (and infamously chronically delay-inflected) event, during which explanations are exchanged between different parties to this process: the applicants, the people who are trying to help the applicants (lawyers, NGO workers, activists, friends), and the people who are adjudicating the claim. As it is currently practiced within the EU, it is an inherently agonistic process as well, in which disagreements regularly occur about the meaning of asylum, of a refugee, and of the accounts given by the applicants. During this bureaucratic stage of the process, the social moral force of hospitality is not supposed to be involved at all: the officers are formally obliged to apply the law indifferently, objectively assessing the applications against a set of criteria (Herzfeld 1992).[9] In theory, this is supposed to ensure a just result as often as possible. Nevertheless, as the work of researchers such as Fassin and Cabot has shown, there is currently a very strong tendency for officers to assess applications negatively.

This is where Derrida's thought on performativity as outlined in "Signature Event Context" (1988) might prove helpful. That essay presents Derrida's ideas on writing as a performative act, which he developed in his engagement with, and critique of, J. L. Austin's concept of performative speech acts. In the course of this discussion, Derrida comments on the peculiar characteristics of a signature as a form of performative writing: "In order to function, that is, to be readable, a signature must have a repeatable, iterable, imitable form; it must be able to be detached from the present and singular intention of its production. It is its sameness which, by corrupting its identity and its singularity, divides its seal" (Derrida 1988, 20).

This implies that, in the process of authenticating that somebody is the author of a text and authenticating that what is contained in the text is the author's intention ("I, the undersigned, do hereby . . ."), there must always be the possibility of a fake, a counterfeit signature. The signature only works if the person signing can repeatedly reproduce it: if it looked completely different every time they signed, it could not be used as a form of authentication. This means that, by definition, the possibility that somebody else could produce a copy of this signature (a counterfeit) is always already there: it is a key part of how signatures work, how they become performative in (for example) making a document into a legal document.

I will return to this at the end; suffice it to say here that the process of claiming asylum constantly requires that the applicant authenticate themselves in this way, and as many have observed, that process of authentication has become ever more elaborate, ever more burdensome, with ever more demands for more authentication, and in recent years, with diminishing chances of success. Moreover, it is not only that the chances of having the asylum seeker's story accepted as authentic are quite slim: it seems almost impossible to predict which techniques will work.

The Rise of Humanitarianism, Security, and Precarity

As a result of all this uncertainty, there have been plenty of explanations offered by anthropologists and others about the *real* reasons for these dismal success rates (success in this case meaning being officially recognized as a refugee under the 1951 UN Convention on Refugees). There has been no shortage of events around the world in recent years that have generated a "well-founded fear of being persecuted for reasons of race, religion, nationality, membership of a particular social group or political opinion," to use the phrase from the convention (UNHCR 2011, Article IA(2)). And as outlined earlier, in recent years, the number of applications has increased considerably. For example, the UNHCR recorded that the number of applications to France between 2000 and 2010 was 885,487; between 2011 and 2021, it was 1,382,336, a 64 percent increase.[10] The acceptance rate went down during that period, but not dramatically: from an average of 17 percent to an average of 15 percent.[11] In 2012, the year mentioned by Fassin, UNHCR recorded a 9 percent success rate, an unusually harsh decision year, it would seem. Nevertheless, none of the 2000s figures are anywhere near the 90 percent acceptance rate of the 1970s that Fassin mentions. The acceptance rate in the EU as a whole in 2012 was 11 percent (43,834 positive decisions from a total of 383,216 decisions made), again nothing like a 90 percent success rate.[12]

On the basis of ethnographic fieldwork in France, including in the transit facility and camp at Sangatte near Calais, Fassin suggests that a shift away from a political definition of asylum, as drafted in the UN Convention, and instead toward a more humanitarian moral imperative to take care of people who are suffering, is part of the explanation: "The logic of compassion now prevailed over the right to protection" (Fassin 2012, 144). Fassin notes that simultaneously, there was a substantial rise in the suspicion that asylum seekers were lying about their suffering. He suggests that in the 1970s, during which time claims for asylum to France were rare relative to more recent years, applications were generally taken at face value, or at least not investigated very heavily (116). In recent years, at the same time as the rise in humanitarian approaches, no story seems to be believed, and even if it is, it does not necessarily mean a successful application.

This simultaneous rise in humanitarianism and increase in suspicion of migrants within the EU region has been described by many others. This notably includes Nick Vaughan-Williams (2015, 30), who draws on Michel Foucault,

Giorgio Agamben, Gilles Deleuze, Derrida, and (most particularly) Roberto Esposito to suggest that there has been a mutually reinforcing relationship between the ever-increasing securitization of the EU's borders and the EU's ever-increasing emphasis on a humanitarian response to what is often termed a "migration crisis." Vaughan-Williams's explanation is that the EU has effectively developed a kind of strong membrane at the outer edges of its territory, which simultaneously both compassionately permits "good people" in and strongly protects and repels "harmful outsiders." It is not accidental that this sounds a little like the contrast between "bad bacteria" and "good bacteria" that is often made in advertisements for yogurt: Vaughan-Williams explicitly suggests that a biopolitical (and racist) notion of "immunisation" is behind many policies toward the EU's outer borders: "'The border' does not exist as such beyond diverse biopolitical attempts to striate space and produce subjects," he says (2015, 10).

That latter comment, although relatively common within a range of scholarship on contemporary border dynamics, is of course somewhat of an overstatement. In practical terms, modern political borders (at least those) also have a formal legal existence, whose purpose is to demarcate territory in the manner outlined by Stuart Elden (2013): as a bounded space under the control of a group of people, which defines a historically specific form of power in relation to that space. The meaning, creation, enforcement, and experience of political borders may be a highly complex matter, and one that, within the EU, has some historically novel forms (Green 2012b, 2013); but they still follow the contemporary legal and discursive logic of territory. Christoffer Kølvraa and Jan Ifversen, in their discussion about the European Neighbourhood Policy, also point to this geopolitical condition when they comment on the habit of many researchers to refer to "deterritorialization" in discussing recent changes in border dynamics: "Deterritorialization does not mean the elimination of territory—which would be absurd—but is just another way of understanding the link between territory and state" (2011, 47).

This is an important point in what I want to suggest about explanation in relation to contemporary asylum-seeking processes: the whole process is based on the premise of a spatial and geopolitical difference between the place from which the asylum seeker fled and the place in which that person ended up. The separation of the two places, both in geographical terms and in terms of their relative value, is crucial: the asylum-seeking process occurs in one of the states that is a signatory to the UN Convention on Refugees, and the process always involves specific reference to a specific other state (the state from which the asylum seeker fled). This sets up distinct and historically changing conditions that define one of the fields (in Bourdieu's [(1990) 1995] terms) concerning what can, and cannot, count as a valid explanation in this process. Explanations that

focus strongly on the bodies of asylum seekers, or on processes of subject formation, tend to ignore this geopolitical territorial element in their explanations.

The key point here is that Vaughan-Williams's explanation for the failure of the
majority of asylum seekers to succeed in their efforts to be recognized as refugees
(even if they are given leave to remain, it is rarely as refugees) is that the biopolitics
of the EU basically regards the majority of people applying for asylum as somehow
toxic for the EU citizens' body politic, as it were. In this, Vaughan-Williams is suggesting a fundamental shift from territories to bodies as the focus of the operations of power—or rather, a confusion between bodies and territory, as if they were
the same thing.

A much more ethnographically grounded argument that also focuses on the
bodies of asylum seekers is provided by Miriam Ticktin. Like Fassin, Ticktin
studied the French case, and she also focuses her explanation on the idea of the
rise of humanitarian rather than political justifications for assisting those attempting to escape persecution (Ticktin 2011, 2016). She argues that the shift
from giving people political asylum to focusing on their bodies as a form of care
actually hides a move away from an earlier concern with political inequalities,
and toward a situation in which every case has to be judged, case by case, on the
grounds of levels of human, bodily suffering (Ticktin 2011). Like Fassin, she
argues that in France at least, the monitoring and assessment of the wounded
body has become the focus of the possibly successful applicant. Increasingly,
the paperwork for establishing that a person is worthy of being allowed to stay
requires demonstration of what could be called the stigmata of persecution.
Alternatively, there might be the right to compassion due to having a life-
threatening illness that cannot be treated in the country from whence you came.
That possibility is the result of a change in French immigration law in 1998
(Ticktin 2011, 2).[13]

More recently, Ticktin has argued that the humanitarian approach requires
those who have suffered to be innocent (victims), and preferably children, rather
than people who have the right to asylum because of a well-founded fear of persecution, irrespective of their moral worth. As Ticktin puts it, "Rather than
having access to rights or laws, humanitarian solutions depend on individual
sensibilities, which, in turn, are shaped by racialized and gendered ideas of who
is a worthy subject of compassion" (2016, 265).

In this kind of explanation, the level of precarity over what might or might not
succeed as an application for asylum is about as high as it gets, being dependent on
the most unpredictable of things: emotional responses to somebody's reported
plight, often based on highly biased assumptions drawn from historically fraught
and unequal relations between different parts of the world, and between different populations: postcolonialism, racism, gender bias, and prejudices regarding

sexuality all come into it. No surprise, then, that the outcome of each application appears to be individual—idiosyncratic, even.

Geopolitical Territorial Shifts

There is an important point here that many writers focusing on the rise of humanitarianism make: that the logic of humanitarianism is based on an abstract logic, an apparently universal moral principle that people should take care of their fellow human beings if they are suffering. There is no legal or spatial referent to this principle of humanitarianism. Yet as most of the authors I have mentioned emphasize, and as Malkki (1992) noted years before them, there is a rugged and often brutal territoriality in the evaluation of human suffering, and where that territorial principle is challenged, it is often violently reimposed, or at the very least has to be channeled through the contemporary geopolitical logic of territoriality. This is a point alluded to by Agamben (1998) at one end of the spectrum (notions of the camp, as special spaces taken out of normal territorial conditions) and Judith Butler (2004, 2009) at the other end (precarity and legibility): the abstract principle of humanitarianism not only turns out to have a spatial, religious, and political history, as Fassin has noted; it is also crosscut by the geopolitics, historical discourses, and the laws of borders. Yet humanitarianism, in being a universalizing principle, contradicts the particularizing logic of geopolitical borders. It is not simply, as Ticktin has forcefully argued, that humanitarianism "depoliticizes" the problem of asylum seekers and masks the highly power-inflected inequalities that exist across the world, as noted in the quote above (2016, 265); it is also that the logic of humanitarianism works against the territorial logic of contemporary border dynamics.

This has important implications for the explanations provided by asylum seekers: the people doing the assessments within the context of the EU are officers of the state, and they are implementing EU laws and protocols; their task is to decide whether to permit people to stay in the state territory, and their job is to defend the logic of the border. The 1951 UN Convention on Refugees provides a balancing act between these two: while evoking the idea of universal human rights, it is also based on the premise that a person needs the legal right to reside in a territory in order to be able to exercise those human rights. It could not be otherwise: its principles can only be applied by states who choose to sign the convention.

Hannah Arendt, who famously studied the refugee crises in Europe that eventually led to the drafting of the 1951 Convention on Refugees, noted the territorial basis of human rights many decades ago. She pointed out that human rights—although they have various principles (e.g., the right to life, liberty, and the pursuit of happiness in the US version, or equality before the law, liberty, protection of property, and national sovereignty according to French principles)—are also only guaranteed by law, and the law assumes a right to reside in a state (Arendt 1958, 295). The problem of the stateless person, Arendt said, "is not that they are not equal before the law, but that no law exists for them; not that they are oppressed but that nobody even wants to oppress them. . . . Even the Nazis started their extermination of Jews by first depriving them of all legal status (the status of second-class citizenship) and cutting them off from the world of the living by herding them into ghettos and concentration camps" (295).

Arendt is noting that in practice, rights only exist when a person has the right to reside within a political territory. In legal terms, all the procedures that are organized in terms of dealing with asylum seekers are based on that principle. It also sets up an implicit, and sometimes entirely explicit, relationship between the state that is receiving the asylum seeker and the state from which the applicant has arrived. The officer who makes the decision about the applicant is assessing not only the veracity of the applicant's claim but also the relative value of the territory from which the applicant has come, compared with the value of the territory into which the applicant wishes to move. In that comparison, it is more often than not assumed that the relative value of the host country across a range of measures (e.g., quality of life, economic conditions, and security) is far higher than the country from which the applicant arrived (a perceived relative value that both applicants and assessors often share).

Elsewhere, I have referred to this constant habit of placing different parts of the world in a hierarchy of value as "relative location" (Green 2012a): the idea that the value and significance of any given place are at least partly dependent on its connections to and separations from other places, defined by some kind of hierarchical classification system that locates a given place somewhere along its scale.[14] When an asylum applicant's case is assessed, it is not only the applicant who is being assessed: it is also the relative value of where they have come from. Both in terms of the underlying territorial logic of the law being applied in assessing the case and in terms of the relative value of the two territories being compared, there is no escaping the deep territoriality of this process, despite the apparently abstract and body-focused notions of suffering embedded within the principles of humanitarianism.

The Problem of Disproportion

Even without the advent of humanitarianism, the idea of asylum still poses a challenge to the modern logic of territoriality, as Arendt pointed out, and as others (e.g., Fassin, Ticktin, and Cabot) have also noted. This particular challenge has been repeated time and again historically. As Arendt noted, the First and Second World Wars generated huge numbers of displaced people who had been rendered stateless—their former states would not accept them back. Suddenly, there were millions of refugees in the world. Arendt suggests that the right to asylum was always intended to be exceptional, on the premise that almost everyone should be a citizen of somewhere. The right to asylum could not survive the mass loss of citizenship generated by those two world wars: "The first great damage done to the nation-states as a result of the arrival of hundreds of thousands of stateless people was that the right of asylum, the only right that had ever figured as a symbol of the Rights of Man [*sic*] in the sphere of international relationships, was being abolished" (Arendt 1958, 280).

The point is that this right to asylum was a borderless right, one that appealed to a universal (that is, covering the whole world) human right. Although the UN Convention on Refugees that was ratified shortly after Arendt wrote this was framed entirely within territorial logic, it also incorporated that universal principle of human rights. The implication is that, in recognizing a refugee as someone with a right to reside in a legal territory on the basis of having fled from somewhere else, it creates a category of person whose status is inherently based on them being from somewhere else. In noting this, Arendt is pointing toward a paradox: people who claim some right to reside in a country on the basis of either asylum or humanitarian grounds are in effect questioning the territorial logic of the nation-state. These are not temporary guests, as implied in discussions on hospitality; rather, they are claiming the right to stay as refugees, as people who, by definition, are not from there.

This paradox has not been lost on Cabot, who studied the often deeply paradoxical processes involved in Greece when people (both asylum seekers and others; the distinction was often somewhat blurry in practice) attempted to gain the right to reside. As she notes at the beginning of her study, "Refuge is awarded by the very virtue of their being 'alien': a citizen of another nation where citizenship has failed. Thus, while the law of protection is grounded on an ahistorical vision of humanity, a 'universal' citizenship invoked through the regime of international human rights, this framework simultaneously reinscribes the refugee's 'alien' origins" (2014, 7).

As Arendt and others have pointed out, so long as the number of asylum-seeking applicants remained exceptional, this underlying paradox would not present a problem. However, whenever the numbers have historically gone up sufficiently to draw the attention of the media and for the migration authorities to feel as if it is a regular occurrence, the underlying paradox becomes highly visible, and thus highly problematic. A couple of examples from what has been happening in Greece recently demonstrate how this reveals that there can be no possibility of an explanation that can square the circle for the applicant: the logical contradiction between the idea of refugee (someone who is axiomatically from somewhere else, by definition) and the territorial logic of the relation between people and location (citizenship, in which a person legally belongs in a territory) means that any explanation in terms of the one will contradict the terms of the other.

One example is provided by Katerina Rozakou, who has been researching the processing of spontaneous migrants on the island of Lesvos for some years now (Rozakou 2017). She noted that in 2015, at the height of what the media dubbed the "migration crisis" for that island, the UNHCR estimated that over half a million people arrived by sea. To provide a sense of the way this felt out of proportion on the island, Lesvos normally has around 85,000 inhabitants (Rozakou 2017, 37). That year, 2015, was not only a period of intense arrival of undocumented visitors; it was also at the height of the Greek financial crisis, during which there was a very real chance that Greece might crash out of the Eurozone. In the summer of 2015, when the number of undocumented people arriving on the island daily ranged between 1,000 and 3,000, the banks were closed and everyone was restricted to extracting a maximum of sixty euros per day (Green 2017).

The EU media seized on the optics of this situation: a small island being "overwhelmed" by undocumented travelers arriving just when the residents were on their knees financially. The way the Greek authorities struggled to cope was also widely reported, adding to the negative coverage of Greece as somehow being a problematic EU member state during that period.[15] Yet the arrivals were not traveling to Lesvos, nor even to Greece, really: they were entering the territory of the EU. The island was a transit point on the way to somewhere else. And having been on the island during the summers myself across those most intense years (2009–2016), I did not gain any sense of being overwhelmed by these travelers. In practice, the sense of crisis affected a relatively small part of the island: some of the villages on the coast where many of the boats landed; the port in the main town of Mytilene, where many of the travelers were processed for onward travel to Athens; the areas where the makeshift reception centers were set up. There was also an increased workload for the police and border authorities who had to process all the people who had arrived, and for the travelers themselves, who were perhaps more overwhelmed than anybody else.

Those last two groups of people, the border authorities and the travelers, did indeed experience it as being overwhelming, out of proportion, and anomalous. Rozakou recounts how, in the reception centers, the strain caused by the sheer numbers involved often overwhelmed the officers who were trying to process all these people, with the aim, once processed, of shipping them off to Athens. The idea was to provide them all with a piece of paper, an "expulsion order," which specified terms suggesting that the holder of the paper should leave voluntarily. For those from Syria, Somalia, and others classified as "nondeportable," the period before voluntary expulsion was six months; for all others, it was one month. Rozakou describes the way these papers were full of errors; how the backlog of processing developed; how there were enormous political efforts to clear the backlog; how representatives from EU agencies, especially Frontex and, later, UNHCR, came to inspect and assist; and how everyone complained that everything was creaking under the strain. Yet at the same time, these events were not overwhelming for those not caught up in the process. For most others on the island, they lived the intensity vicariously, by reading about it in the media and occasionally catching glimpses of people who had recently arrived, or seeing some of the debris of their crossings—damaged dinghies, tins of food, clothes, many other items—piled up in the harbor.

Nevertheless, in the media the events of 2015 were expanded to appear to be a generally overwhelming condition, implicitly affecting the entire EU area. It was also quickly recorded as a "humanitarian crisis" (to add to the migration crisis and financial crisis). The result was that Lesvos not only received thousands of undocumented travelers every day, it was also deluged with the world's media, and quite a few famous people, including Susan Sarandon and Pope Francis (Smith 2016). There was much more of this kind of media reporting, but that is enough to give a sense of the way that the logic of humanitarian reason (in Fassin's terms) was being applied in reporting about Lesvos. It could hardly have been any more extravagantly theatrical.

Eventually, the EU brokered a deal with Turkey in 2016, which allowed these "spontaneous migrants" to be sent back to Turkey, from which they had traveled to reach Lesvos. UNHCR, as well as a variety of other NGOs and activist organizations, complained that this deal was illegal under the 1951 Convention on Refugees, but the arrangement was maintained (Rozakou 2017, 45).

Rozakou argues that this situation did not represent the breakdown of state structures. On the contrary, it demonstrated the continued effectiveness by which the state reproduced itself, even if it was done somewhat chaotically on this occasion: it was still Greek police and other officers of the state who were dealing with all of this, who took responsibility. And I will also note that in this situation, part of the "solution" to the state authorities being overwhelmed with the number of people was to effectively close the border by expelling these travelers from Greek territory—irrespective of the law, or of the needs of those people who had made the journey to arrive on Lesvos. The fact that this reassertion of the territorial border (in this case, it was the EU border, not the Greek one, that was being reasserted) was likely to be in contravention of the Convention on Refugees seemed somehow irrelevant.

The second case involves Cabot's (2014) extensive study of the procedures carried out in Athens for handling asylum applications. Cabot notes that many people arriving in Athens had multiple reasons for leaving the country from which they came, a situation that is not really catered for in either the asylum application procedures or the standard migration application procedures. Cabot particularly looked at the extreme importance that almost everyone involved—the applicants, the NGOs helping the applicants, and the migration authorities—placed on a piece of paper generally referred to as the "pink card." This card was issued to asylum seekers and provided leave to remain for a period of time while the holder of the card's application for asylum was being processed. Cabot describes how the whole process was replete with paradoxes, informal practices, mutual misunderstandings, endless delays, and waiting, and with a sense on the part of the authorities that they were somewhat overwhelmed with numbers. Cabot also describes how the card became a highly important object, capable of being reinscribed in a variety of ways, often quite contrary to the formal status of the card itself. She notes, "The card cannot be easily located in zones of legality or illegality, but rather, moves unpredictably through the shifting spectrum or 'continuum' between illegal and legal status and practice" (2014, 46–47).

Cabot goes on to describe how the card simultaneously appeared as a means to control and render the holder visible, while there were also all kinds of space for negotiation on every side (official, applicant, unofficial) about the meaning and the use of the card. Often, it was an important form of legitimation for applicants; at times, it was effectively used as a residence permit by the police. Drawing on this ethnography, Cabot resists any of the studies that would suggest that there was any single explanation of, cause for, or power over what she observed happening. Instead, she concludes, "Governance, thus, emerges as an evolving, unruly nexus of persons, practices, and things, constantly redirected toward variously overlapping, conflicting, or even unrelated ends" (62).

The Gray Area of the Exercise of the Law at Borders: Fakes, Counterfeits, and Paradoxes

That brings me back to the question of fakes and counterfeits, and the impossibility of any stable explanation in this situation. Both Rozakou and Cabot point to the way that the line between what is legal and what is not, what is real and what is fake, is a highly gray area. In the process of dealing with asylum claims, nobody was exactly following the rules, and it was often physically, logistically, or even formally impossible to do so. Laws were broken, partial truths and outright lies were told, and compromises and creative solutions were found all the time. This is unlikely to be solely the outcome of the extreme conditions in Greece at the time. Madeleine Reeves (2013), in her study of Kyrgyz migrant workers in Moscow, whose arrival was in no way overwhelming for the Russian migration authorities, also describes the very gray area between legality and illegality in her study of how the workers prove, or fail to prove, that they are legally in Russia. That situation is particularly notable because during Soviet times, these same workers did not need any visas at all, since both territories were within a single legal jurisdiction.

Given this combination of legal grayness at borders in general and the paradoxical position of the refugee in relation to territory in particular, I have suggested that asylum seekers are collectively placed under suspicion when the number of applicants for asylum rises beyond the level of being exceptional from the perspective of officers of the state who process these claims (as noted earlier, these numbers have not been significant in terms of the whole population of France or even the EU for the periods being discussed). That shift from a general acceptance of the explanation the applicant gives to one that is assumed to be fake reveals an underlying contradiction between the idea of the refugee (always already from somewhere else, and granted asylum on the universal grounds of human rights or humanitarian principles) and the logic of territoriality upon which contemporary formal border management relies (the integrity of the bordered territory is paramount). What appears to happen regularly in practice is that the figure of the refugee is rendered exceptional again by other means: whatever the applicants say, whatever they demonstrate about the validity of their case, the vast majority must be counterfeits; people will only be admitted exceptionally.

Finally, I return to Derrida's "Signature Event Context." The asylum application procedure plays an important performative role: if successful, it transforms a citizen of another country, or a stateless person, into a refugee. The process through which this occurs follows the application of particular laws, bureaucratic procedures, and protocols and thus, in principle at least, satisfies the requirement of iterability: there are specific, repeatable, and citable procedures that must be followed in order to enact the transformation from the one status to the other. As Tuija Pulkkinen outlines, Derrida's understanding of performativity relies on this element: "We are able to understand what an utterance means and what it performs, not because of the intention of the speaker, but because of a known cultural procedure, which is present in the given culture by virtue of its constant repetition. The meaning of an utterance and its performative force derive from the possibility of iterability" (2000, 187).

Here, there is an implication that neither the intentions of the applicant nor the intentions of the officials examining the case should be important in establishing whether it will be successful: it is the repeatability of the procedure, the standardization, that should, in principle, create the result that, most of the time, if applied correctly, will succeed. Yet in the case of refugees, I have described how the same procedure has resulted in dramatically different success rates at different historical moments. The iterability, which means the possibility of a fake copy must always be present, seems to be generating almost no fakes at one moment and endless fakes at another. I have argued that this historical instability is related to the way applications for asylum have to be exceptional to avoid challenging the logic of territory that gives people the right to apply for asylum in the first place. By focusing on the historically shifting logic of location and the law of territory rather than on the person (or body) of the undocumented traveler and whether he or she is welcome, what emerges is a spatial contradiction that is ultimately unresolvable: unlike other kinds of travelers, the refugee can only ever be an exception. No explanation will do unless that condition is met.

This provides a different argument from that of researchers such as Fassin and Ticktin, who have identified a significant shift in whether the utterances of the refugee are taken at face value, are accepted by the authorities as a signature of their own life rather than a counterfeit, and one that authentically involves a well-founded fear of persecution. For Fassin and Ticktin, the move away from human rights and toward humanitarianism has effectively been a cultural change: the perceived likelihood of the signature being authentic has radically dropped. Nowadays, instead of looking out for the fake in a sea of authentic signatures, there is an attempt to find the authentic signature in a sea of fake ones. My argument has been that this shift marks different historical moments during which the people tasked with protecting the logic of state territorial borders attempt to find the exception, and they shift their practices when applications becomes too numerous or too frequent, so as to maintain the exceptional status of the refugee.

That could make more sense of Cabot's and Razakou's rich ethnographic accounts, which tell of the messy, chaotic spontaneity involved in this process, showing repeatedly that things do not proceed according to the formal rules and regulations. The implication is that the paradox of the figure of the refugee, caught in between two contradictory locational principles (the principle of universal humanity and the principle of state territoriality), and thus always having to be exceptional, could never produce a stable explanation; it all depends on when and where someone claims that status.

NOTES

1. The research for this text has been carried out with funding from European Research Council Advanced Grant 694482, Crosslocations. See https://www.helsinki.fi/en/researchgroups/crosslocations.

2. As will be discussed further, the actual numbers of refugees accepted by France changed significantly in different time periods, so the percentages hide a wider story.

3. The source for refugee numbers is World Bank data: "Refugee Population by Country or Territory of Asylum," World Bank, accessed February 13, 2023, https://data.worldbank.org/indicator/sm.pop.refg.

4. Source: Asylum Applications, 2012–2021, Refugee Data Finder, UNHCR, accessed February 13, 2023, https://www.unhcr.org/refugee-statistics/download/?url=vM7h6M. These statistics are calculated in different ways by different organizations. Eurostat shows a very different figure for asylum applications to France in 2012: 61,440. "Asylum Applicants by Type of Applicant, Citizenship, Age and Sex—Annual Aggregated Data," Eurostat, accessed February 13, 2023, https://ec.europa.eu/eurostat/databrowser/view/migr_asyappctza/default/table?lang=en.

5. Source: "Population, Total—France," World Bank, last accessed February 20, 2022, https://data.worldbank.org/indicator/SP.POP.TOTL?locations=FR.

6. Source: "Population, Total—European Union," World Bank, last accessed February 13, 2023, https://data.worldbank.org/indicator/SP.POP.TOTL?locations=EU.

7. Source: Asylum Applications, 1970–2021, Refugee Data Finder, UNHCR, accessed February 13, 2023, https://www.unhcr.org/refugee-statistics/download/?url=lQOoW9.

8. See also discussion on this use in Candea 2012 and Fassin 2012, 135.

9. Of course, as many ethnographic accounts have shown, such indifference is rare in practice; see, for example, Jordan and Duvell 2002.

10. Source: Asylum Applications, 1970–2021, Refugee Data Finder, UNHCR.

11. Calculated from UNHCR data: Asylum Decisions, 2016–2021, Refugee Data Finder, UNHCR, accessed February 13, 2023, https://www.unhcr.org/refugee-statistics/download/?url=Pvbv61.

12. Calculated from UNHCR data: Asylum Decisions, 1970–2021, Refugee Data Finder, UNHCR, accessed February 13, 2023, https://www.unhcr.org/refugee-statistics/download/?url=InEht6.

13. See also Ticktin 2006 for a discussion of the history of Médecins Sans Frontières.

14. This means, of course, that it is very important to have control over the logic of the classification, as noted by both Herzfeld (2004) and Wilk (1995).

15. Dalakoglou and Agelopoulos 2018 provides a wide range of perspectives on that moment in Greek history.

REFERENCES

Agamben, G. 1998. *Homo Sacer: Sovereign Power and Bare Life*. Translated by D. Heller-Roazen. Stanford, CA: Stanford University Press.

Arendt, H. 1958. *The Origins of Totalitarianism*. New York: Meridian Books.

Bourdieu, P. (1990) 1995. *The Logic of Practice*. Translated by R. Nice. Cambridge, UK: Polity.

Butler, J. 2004. *Precarious Life: The Powers of Mourning and Violence*. London: Verso.

———. 2009. *Frames of War: When Is Life Grievable?* London: Verso.

Cabot, H. 2014. *On the Doorstep of Europe: Asylum and Citizenship in Greece*. Philadelphia: University of Pennsylvania Press.

Candea, M. 2012. "Derrida en Corse? Hospitality as Scale-Free Abstraction." *Journal of the Royal Anthropological Institute* 18:S34–S48.

Dalakoglou, D., and G. Agelopoulos, eds. 2018. *Critical Times in Greece: Anthropological Engagements with the Crisis*. Abingdon, UK: Routledge.

Derrida, J. 1988. "Signature Event Context." In *Limited Inc*, edited by G. Graff, 1–24. Evanston, IL: Northwestern University Press.

Derrida, J., and A. Dufourmantelle. 2000. *Of Hospitality: Anne Dufourmantelle Invites Jacques Derrida to Respond*. Translated by R. Bowlby. Stanford, CA: Stanford University Press.

Douglas, M. 1976. *Purity and Danger: An Analysis of Concepts of Pollution and Taboo*. London: Routledge and Kegan Paul.

Elden, S. 2013. *The Birth of Territory*. Chicago: University of Chicago Press.

Fassin, D. 2012. *Humanitarian Reason: A Moral History of the Present Times*. Berkeley: University of California Press.

Green, S. 2012a. "Replacing Europe." In *The Sage Handbook of Social Anthropology*, edited by R. Fardon, O. Harris, T. Marchand, M. Nuttall, C. Shore, V. Strang, and R. Wilson, 286–307. London: Sage.

——. 2012b. "A Sense of Border." In *A Companion to Border Studies*, edited by T. M. Wilson and H. Donnan, 573–592. Oxford: Wiley-Blackwell.

——. 2013. "Borders and the Relocation of Europe." *Annual Review of Anthropology* 42:345–361.

——. 2017. "When Infrastructures Fail: An Ethnographic Note in the Middle of an Aegean Crisis." In *Infrastructures and Social Complexity: A Companion*, edited by P. Harvey, C. B. Jensen, and A. Morita, 271–283. London: Routledge.

Herzfeld, M. 1992. *The Social Production of Indifference: Exploring the Symbolic Roots of Western Bureaucracy*. Oxford: Berg.

——. 2004. *The Body Impolitic: Artisans and Artifice in the Global Hierarchy of Value*. Chicago: University of Chicago Press.

Jordan, B., and F. Duvell. 2002. *Irregular Migration: The Dilemmas of Transnational Mobility*. Cheltenham, UK: Edward Elgar.

Kølvraa, C., and J. Ifversen. 2011. "The European Neighbourhood Policy: Geopolitics or Value Export?" In *The Frontiers of Europe: A Transatlantic Problem?*, edited by F. M. Bindi and I. Angelescu, 45–69. Washington, DC: Brookings Institution Press.

Malkki, L. 1992. "National Geographic: The Rooting of Peoples and the Territorialization of National Identity among Scholars and Refugees." *Cultural Anthropology* 7 (1): 24–44.

Mouffe, C. 2013. *Agonistics: Thinking the World Politically*. London: Verso.

Pulkkinen, T. 2000. *The Postmodern and Political Agency*. Jyväskylä, Finland: University of Jyväskylä.

Reeves, M. 2013. "Clean Fake: Authenticating Documents and Persons in Migrant Moscow." *American Ethnologist* 40 (3): 508–524.

Rozakou, K. 2017. "Nonrecording the 'European Refugee Crisis' in Greece: Navigating through Irregular Bureaucracy." *Focaal—Journal of Global and Historical Anthropology* 77:36–49.

Smith, H. 2016. "Pope Francis Takes Refugees to Rome after Lesbos Visit." *Guardian*, April 16, 2016. https://www.theguardian.com/world/2016/apr/16/pope-francis-flies-to-lesbos-to-highlight-humanitarian-crisis-in-europe.

Ticktin, M. 2006. "Medical Humanitarianism in and beyond France: Breaking Down or Patrolling Borders?" In *Medicine at the Border: Disease, Globalization, and Security, 1850 to the Present*, edited by A. Bashford, 116–135. Basingstoke, UK: Palgrave Macmillan.

——. 2011. *Casualties of Care: Immigration and the Politics of Humanitarianism in France*. Berkeley: University of California Press.

——. 2016. "Thinking beyond Humanitarian Borders." *Social Research* 83 (2): 255–271.
UNHCR (United Nations High Commissioner for Refugees). 2011. *The 1951 Convention Relating to the Status of Refugees and Its 1967 Protocol*. Geneva: UNHCR.
Van Mol, C., and H. de Valk. 2016. "Migration and Immigrants in Europe: A Historical and Demographic Perspective." In *Integration Processes and Policies in Europe: Contexts, Levels and Actors*, edited by B. Garcés-Mascareñas and R. Penninx, 31–55. Cham: Springer International.
Vaughan-Williams, N. 2015. *Europe's Border Crisis: Biopolitical Security and Beyond*. Oxford: Oxford University Press.
Wilk, R. 1995. "Learning to Be Local in Belize: Global Systems of Common Difference." In *Worlds Apart: Modernity through the Prism of the Local*, edited by D. Miller, 110–133. London: Routledge.

EXPLAINING MINDFULNESS IN POLITICAL ADVOCACY

Joanna Cook

. . . a way of being in wise and purposeful relationship with one's experience.

—Jon Kabat-Zinn, foreword, *Mindful Nation UK*

But does it work?

—National Health Service service commissioner, 2015

In 2015 a report called *Mindful Nation UK* (Mindfulness All-Party Parliamentary Group [MAPPG] 2015) was launched in Westminster. Its publication marked the culmination of an APPG inquiry established to investigate the policy potential of mindfulness, an awareness training practice originating in Buddhism, across multiple policy areas. And it had been written by a group of unpaid nonpolitical advocates over an eight-month period. The report cited research that identifies an ongoing mental health crisis in Britain, outlining the character and scale of challenges in health, education, the workplace, and the criminal justice system, as well as the existing evidence for mindfulness-based interventions. It did this by setting out the economic case for preventive mental health support, calling for targeted interventions in each area and funding for further research. As a complement to this, each section of the report contained two to four pages of case studies from people who had benefited from mindfulness. These were written in the first person and were personal stories of the lived impact of mindfulness practice. In short, the efficient collation of econometric and statistical research findings and qualitative accounts in the report presented a troubling picture of a costly mental health crisis, beginning in the health sector and extending through the education system, the criminal justice system, and the workplace. The report recognized and costed problems in society, it identified policy objectives, and it made a case for mindfulness as a scientifically appropriate and economically responsible solution. In effect, mindfulness was presented as both instrumental (it could be used) and goal oriented (it would work).

While the report went on to influence political policy (see the discussion later in this chapter) and, to date, has been downloaded over thirty thousand times, it also received criticism. For example, it was critiqued by two reviewers for promoting mindfulness as "a method that 'works'" (Moloney 2016, 283) in the service of "specific operational objectives" (Hyland 2016, 134). In his review of the report, Terry Hyland argues that the "transformational function" of mindfulness has been "co-opted in order to achieve specific *operational* objectives, and such pragmatic purposes have obscured the links with the foundational moral principles" (2016, 134–135) as mindfulness has "swept virus-like through academia, public life and popular culture" (133). Similarly, Paul Moloney thinks that mindfulness is "at the forefront of an official utilitarian 'mental health' movement, sweeping through the health and social sciences" (2016, 270). He describes the report as blending "a declared humanitarian commitment with a strong fiscal case for psychological treatment—(in this case, 'mindfulness')—as a means of reducing healthcare bills through the prevention of psychological distress, and by getting the disturbed and disabled back to work and off the state sickness benefits roster" (271). And he argues that "mindfulness could never be a treatment or method that 'works' in a relatively straightforward way, like swallowing a medicinal pill" (283).

Analysis of the report divorced from the social processes through which it was created and to which it contributes might render mindfulness as an instrumentalized tool of governance. In this chapter, I focus on how the *Mindful Nation UK* report was drafted in order to provide an ethnographic account of explanatory practices in an era of evidence-based policymaking. An abstract denunciation (or celebration) of "instrumentalization" and "evidence" makes little sense in anthropological terms because the mere fact of instrumentalization tells us very little about the causes and effects of practices of governance in any given context (cf. du Gay 2005). Like many others, I am cautious of the effects of instrumentalization and the utilitarian logics of audit and accountancy measures (see, for example, Hoggett 2005; Miller 2005), and yet, dwelling on the reduction of ethical practices to an instrumentalist agenda misses the opportunity to explore the ways in which such agendas are developed and the creative effects that they generate. What can an ethnographic account of political advocacy reveal about explanatory practices? What kinds of case are compelling? What makes an explanation persuasive? And how is this achieved?

The report was written by volunteer advocates who were motivated by their personal ethical commitment to mindfulness practice and who did not have any previous experience with political advocacy. Mindfulness practitioners were motivated to become political advocates by their conviction that mindfulness is a personally transformative practice and is foundational for living well. At the same time, in order to make mindfulness intelligible as a policy object, it had to be framed in utilitarian and economic terms. With an analytic focus on the social practices of advocacy, I examine how volunteer advocates resolved the (potentially) uncomfortable relationship between the ethical value that mindfulness held for them and their use of governmental technologies, political discourses, and economic logics. The relationship between the ethopoetic processes associated with self-cultivation and larger economic and political logics raises significant ethnographic questions about the negotiation and coordination of different kinds of knowledge, values, and interests. How do political advocates negotiate conflicting values? How do they integrate their motivating values with their knowledge about action? And what do they think of as the right way to coordinate in order to reach their goal? In what follows, I unpack the practices of knowledge management by which explanations of the policy potential of mindfulness were made persuasive. And I show that in the process of drafting the report, volunteer advocates learned to navigate political technologies and discourses and to negotiate a balance between ethical and economic values.

In a series of papers, Michael Lambek makes a persuasive case for maintaining a clear analytical distinction between the meaning of "value" in ethical and economic practice and cautions against conflating the two (see also Tambiah 1990, 150).[1] Ethical and economic values are incommensurable because they are constituted in distinctly different ways and there are places where they just do not meet; they are "isomorphous and each leaves a remainder" (Lambek 2008b, 139). For Lambek (2008b), ethical value is characterized by the exercise of judgment in ongoing personal practice and is contingent on context and multiple considerations. In contrast, liberal economic value is characterized by its "utility" (Lambek 2008a) and informs concepts of abstract reasoning, economic rationalizing, and bureaucratic justification (Lambek 2000, 310). Ethical values are absolute and incommensurable, expressed as practices of judgment, while economic values are commensurable and relative.[2]

Lambek's distinction helpfully puts a finger on an ethnographic puzzle at the heart of the *Mindful Nation UK* report. Utility theories of value do not account for the experience, value, and effect of learning to relate to oneself mindfully that motivated volunteer advocates to write the report. Volunteers described mindfulness as "a way of being," and their passion for mindfulness came much closer to Lambek's theory of moral judgment and ethical value, because it gave them "the practical means to engage ethically with the present and to anticipate the future by means of practices established and dispositions cultivated in the past" (Lambek 2008a, 125). At the same time, however, political advocacy itself is *necessarily* instrumentalizing; it is an effort to effect change in the world, however that might be conceived. Furthermore, the presentation of mindfulness in the report and the evidence gathered for its efficacy were clearly informed by a utility theory of value. At its simplest, it is unlikely that mindfulness would be being discussed in Parliament as a "way of being" if it were not for the development of an evidence base for its efficacy. In order to ask, "Does it work?" means and ends must be separated, and ends must be framed as measurable objects, rather than as qualities of acts (virtue) or of actors (character) (Lambek 2008b, 136).

In what follows, I develop an ethnography of explanation by examining the explanatory requirements attached to making a case for mindfulness in a policy context. I ask, by what means is such a case produced, and whom does it serve? How is authority constructed in political advocacy, and through what technologies is it made persuasive? And how do people relate political practices to understandings of ethical life? This chapter is inspired, in part, by a Foucauldian concern with the relationship between forms of political rationality and specific technologies of government, encapsulated in Michel Foucault's theory of governmentality. But whereas governmentality is seen by some as purely an instrument of coercion (e.g., Shore and Wright 2000), I argue that engagement with technologies of government opens up new spaces of reflection and political negotiation (cf. Born 2002). As such, this chapter illustrates the simple point that explanatory practices may be constituted by multiple, and sometimes competing, types of value. I focus on the interrelationship between personal ethics, normative imperatives, and new technologies of government in order to explore the processes of knowledge management that are central to bureaucratic practice and political advocacy. Over the eight months that it took to get the document right, volunteer advocates learned to navigate political technologies in order to be "heard"—that is, to shape mindfulness as a credible policy object. This recursivity, explaining mindfulness and transforming mindfulness in the process, suggests that policy development and advocacy are nonlinear processes, and that they are informed as much by ethical and normative as by epistemological or economic agendas.

Learning Advocacy and Drafting the Report

The volunteer advocates who wrote the *Mindful Nation UK* report were brought together by their enthusiasm for mindfulness. Collectively, they made up a group of highly professional people, including a senior journalist, senior academics, the chief operating officer for an educational trust, the clinical lead for a National

Health Service trust, a director of the Royal Society of Arts, a director from the corporate sector, a chief executive from the probation service, clinical psychologists, and others. Each of them had experience with mindfulness in their respective professional worlds and all of them had committed personal meditation practices, in some cases extending for decades, but none of them had been involved in political advocacy before. Political advocacy and participation in the MAPPG were thrilling. Volunteers were excited that the MAPPG and the drafting of the report were powered by a groundswell of grassroots support by passionate independent practitioners.

Immediately after the eighteen-month MAPPG inquiry process, the volunteers drafted a brief twelve-page interim report, which was launched in Parliament a month later to muted applause. The interim report summarized the findings of the inquiry process and referred to the considerable popularity of mindfulness in the United Kingdom, including widespread media coverage, high demand for mindfulness courses, and the popularity of books and CDs that draw on mindfulness-based interventions. In all, the brief document provided information on the outcomes of the hearings but contained few references to research on mindfulness. And while it referenced concerns about the economic cost of a mental health crisis, it placed emphasis on the possibilities of "transformation" and "wisdom" that the volunteers believed arose through mindfulness practice. As they wrote, "We find that mindfulness is a transformative practice, leading to a deeper understanding of how to respond to situations wisely. We believe that government should widen access to mindfulness training in key public services, where it has the potential to be an effective low-cost intervention with a wide range of benefits" (MAPPG 2015, 1).

The parliamentarians were not happy, and they summoned representatives of the volunteers to Parliament for a meeting. The volunteers reported back to the group that they had (figuratively) had their wrists slapped: the interim report just did not work as an advocacy document. The parliamentarians wanted to see evidence of the scales and costs of the problems to be addressed, as well as the evidence for mindfulness-based interventions in each case, and for all of this information to be embedded in existing political narratives. In addition to the policy challenges presented by mental health, mindfulness also needed to be framed in terms of alternative metrics such as well-being, resilience, and flourishing. That is, problems had to be identified, evidenced, and costed, and mindfulness had to be couched in already-existing political and economic narratives. As Susan, a senior journalist, told me, "They were applying a very New Labour policy framework to it. Everything that we do in terms of social spending has to be absolutely bottomed out in terms of its impact, value for money: 'this is how much you spend, this is how much you save.'"

The parliamentarians' feedback on the interim report reflects a dominant strand of contemporary governmental culture. In an era of evidence-based policymaking, governmental agendas increasingly rest on evidence for efficacy and accountability. In the later decades of the twentieth century, political decision making became increasingly dependent on scientific knowledge and experts, informed by the assumption that the empirical tools of randomized controlled trials, advanced statistical analysis, and social science could improve public policy. Explanatory cases for policy development increasingly rested on scientific evidence for "what works" (Davies, Nutley, and Smith 2000). This "scientization of politics" (Maasen and Lieven 2006, 400) is reflected in the increasing dominance of evidence-based medicine and the demand that clinical practice and increasingly all health policy and practice (and indeed other areas of social policy) be based on systematically reviewed and critically appraised evidence of effectiveness (see Lambert 2005).[3]

The volunteer advocates felt deeply frustrated by the parliamentarians' response. They had intended the interim report to act as a placeholder while they began the big job of drafting the final report. But the comments from the parliamentarians raised important questions about what ought to go into the report and what it was for. What kind of explanation of mindfulness would be persuasive? And could mindfulness be presented as an evidenced technique without detracting from the value that it held for volunteers? Volunteer advocates felt that, while they clearly *could* make an evidenced and economic case for mindfulness-based interventions, such utilitarian terms were ill suited for explaining the ethical value of mindfulness. They felt strongly that econometric justification needed to be balanced by a representation of mindfulness as an ethical practice with the potential to transform society. The challenge of the writing process for the volunteers was to produce an account that struck a balance between the ethical value of reflective self-awareness and the economic value of pragmatic and measurable outcomes.

On the day of the first drafting meeting, I walked to the sandwich shop with Danny, a National Health Service senior executive, and I asked him what he thought success would look like: What would it mean to live in a "mindful nation"? Danny had been practicing meditation for thirteen years. He first came across mindfulness while he was doing a cognitive behavioral therapy training course and started practicing mindfulness on his commute to work. Danny told me that, for him, a mindful nation would be "a society that is more awake, compassionate, more interested in processes than results." Returning to the meeting with our sandwiches, though, he told me that if the report was going to have any political impact, it would need to propose targeted recommendations with specific outcomes that were economically and statistically justified. Recommencing the drafting process after lunch, he said to the group, "As a health professional, I'm a secularized philosopher in a way, and we're asking the question, what is a good life? How do we lead a good life?" Reflecting on the challenge ahead, he noted, "In this thrust to get mindfulness into policy, we need to do it pragmatically but without losing its transformative potential. That's why this is such a difficult one to pin down."

Personal Ethics versus Political Evidence

For volunteer advocates, the value of mindfulness lay in both the experience and effect of developing a relationship with one's own mind: a relationship that they thought resulted from meditation practice. Tom was keen to emphasize this in our discussions over the writing period. Tom worked in education and had been practicing meditation for twenty years. In the pub one evening he told me that, for him, the real value of mindfulness lay in cultivating metacognitive awareness.

"It feels like what it's seeking to create is metacognitive space, isn't it, and that capacity for reflection. In that Viktor Frankl bit . . . you know, about stimulus and response and the gap, and the gap is our power to choose, and in that power to choose is our growth and our freedom. It feels like that capacity for metacognition is the name of the game. It's the name of the game."[4]

In Tom's view, people might learn to relate to themselves with mindful awareness, and this was of value because it led to the freedom to discern a wise response to experience. Others shared this view. They thought that having an ongoing mindful relationship with the mind was valuable, not as a goal of practice but for its own sake. As Danny told me when we met up for tea in the British Library, "I think mindfulness connects us to being human, and being part of the species *sapiens sapiens*. It's sad that we're all going to get old and ill and die, and it requires a huge amount of compassion. And we all have to somehow support each other and be in a community that supports us with that existential reality." For Danny and others, learning to relate to oneself and others with mindful awareness was an important motivator in their voluntary work. For Marjorie, for example, this pointed to a possible societal sea change if mindfulness were widely practiced.

> The thing that's really lighting me up at the moment is the potential for this work to stimulate systemic change and the sense that the human mind is at the basis of everything we do. And if we can, as a society, really get skillful about how we think about and use and cultivate our minds, well, that's going to have an impact across all sectors. So, it's something about just really being explicit on a societal level that this is

important and that it's not just about mindfulness as a tool, but mindfulness is one tool that can support skillful use of the human mind.

Marjorie was a cognitive psychologist who had been practicing mindfulness for twenty-five years. She was motivated to volunteer her time to drafting the report by personal conviction and a sense of shared ethical feeling with other advocates. Similarly, Adam Reed has highlighted the relationship between private moral enthusiasm and an ethics of professionalism in his ethnography of a Scottish animal protection charity (see Reed 2017a, 2017b). Reed (2017a) demonstrates that participation in the charity is based on a convergence of private and organizational values, and the success of the charity is thought to rest on the moral enthusiasm of its staff. Mindfulness advocates were motivated by their personal meditation practice and their professional experience. This drove enormous commitment to the advocacy process, which was at times in tension with the work of advocacy itself.

For many of the volunteers, instrumental explanations of the effects of mindfulness did not capture why it was important to them. For example, the idea that living well might be understood in instrumental terms did not sit well with Teresa, a mental health professional. As she told me, "If we were just farm animals, it would be fine. A lot of NICE [National Institute for Health and Care Excellence] guidance for later life is like that. Look after the 'old person animal.' Exercise, nutrition, warmth. But the things that make people live independently, have quality of life, and look after themselves are feeling valued, feeling they've got something to give, to get up for . . . all those things that are about us as feeling human beings with a sense of self, identity, or purpose.'"

After a meditation practice at the beginning of a drafting meeting, she turned to me and asked, "Really, how are you going to measure this?" Furthermore, volunteers thought that the tension they felt between ethical and economic values was reflected in parliamentarians' engagement with mindfulness as well. As Marjorie told me in a formal interview during the drafting process,

> There's something really interesting about that whole Parliament thing. It's almost as if there were two parallel things happening for those politicians. The reason I think that some of them really got behind this was because of their own personal mindfulness practice. That awakened something in them. You'd need to inquire with them, but I suspect it was something about reconnecting to personal values, personal meaning, a sense of sanity about how we can live our lives. So there's that element, but alongside that there's this other element which they have to buy into about policy development and looking at mindfulness in a

much more instrumental way, about the sorts of things that policymakers have to talk about like cost effectiveness and productivity and presenteeism and efficiency and use of attentional resources. So, they're both true, but I think there's potentially a hazard with majoring on the instrumental aspect of it. Because actually they're not what's going to sustain the reasons for practicing this.

This relationship between ethical commitment and evidence was reflected in the development of the *Mindful Nation UK* report, and volunteer advocates navigated what they saw as the ill fit between the "intangible," ethical nature of mindfulness and the standard categories used to identify policy areas and the measures used to assess outcomes.

Political Narratives

In a privately written anonymous document circulated to the group, the head of a national charity provided volunteers with advice about how to think about their work. In developing the report, volunteers were encouraged to think carefully about *why* mindfulness might be a policy issue. For example, were there specific policy "asks": two or three specific areas in which they hoped to make an impact? They were asked to consider how these might fit in a devolved system environment, in which executive control is increasingly local or regional. The document suggested, "Rather than generating interest that isn't already there, find conversations that are already going on and be part of them. Be part of existing conversations around mental health, wellbeing economics or procedural fairness in criminal justice, for example." Articulating mindfulness in relation to broader political narratives became a central focus of the eight-month writing period. As anthropologist Maia Green argues of her work as a development policy analyst and adviser, in order to explain why policy objectives should receive funding, development categories have to be reordered and worked out so that they can become "thinkable, malleable and ultimately real" (2011, 41). Quite consciously, mindfulness was incorporated into political narratives focused in different ways on the mind, which were supported by alternative metrics. Volunteers worked to explain mindfulness in terms of emerging political narratives about mental health, character, attention, happiness, well-being, and resilience. Each of these buzzwords referenced wider social interests at the time and offered a way of embedding mindfulness in conversations that were already taking place. Drafting the report involved researching these conversations, marshaling scientific evidence on mindfulness, and establishing a relationship between the two.

Such narrative framings were not a fabrication of the advocates—these were already widespread in academic and political literature. For example, "well-being" has emerged as a key economic and development focus (cf. Clark 2002; Crisp and Hooker 2000; Dasgupta 2001; Griffin 1986; Sen 1999). It was incorporated into the United Nations Development Index and informed the development of the metrics of quality- and disability-adjusted life years by the World Health Organization (Cummins 2005). Well-being has comfortably become a standard narrative and metric in political models of prosperity and development. As a political narrative, it enables the marriage of wide-ranging ideas about health, education, opportunity, empowerment, and capability, with broader metrics such as affluence, gender, or the environment. Linked to this are broader issues of "quality of life" (Nussbaum and Sen 1993; Offer 1996), leading some to describe well-being and quality of life as a "global morality dictum" (Strathern 2005). Similarly, "resilience" became a part of mainstream development language in Britain after it was placed "at the heart" of the UK government's *Humanitarian Emergency Response Review* in 2011 (Ashdown 2011, 4). The term *resilience* was developed in the physical sciences to describe the qualities and capacities that enable a community to recover from a catastrophic event (Barrios 2016), focusing on the mechanisms that enable a system to return to equilibrium after a stress or the ability to absorb change (Gordon 1978; Holling 1973, 14). The concept of resilience was soon extended from political interest in infrastructure to a focus on human capacity, becoming a core part of Department for International Development work and education policy. Political focus on resilience is informed by concerns about mental health and psychological vulnerability. Here, *resilience* indicates psychological characteristics that enable individuals to "bounce back" from challenging circumstances and to weather the everyday stresses of life (Ryff et al. 1998).

The value of mindfulness could easily be explained in the language of well-being or resilience. Psychological research suggests that mindfulness practice plays a role in psychological well-being (e.g., Brown and Ryan 2003; Josefsson et al. 2011). Attention and impulse control have been linked to social well-being indicators as wide ranging as criminal record, addiction, ability to maintain committed relationships, and body mass index (cf. Moffitt et al. 2011). Mindfulness is believed to help those who practice it cope with life (from stress, anxiety, and depression to impulse control, emotional regulation, and intellectual flexibility) through the cultivation of psychological resilience (see, for example, Bajaj and Pande 2016; Shapiro, Brown, and Biegel 2007).

As a political narrative for mindfulness, well-being had many advantages. It had formed the basis of previous policy work that had led to important changes in the provision of and training in mental health services in the United Kingdom and had been treated as an object of empirical knowledge informed by value judgments about the good life (Alexandrova 2017). But as a narrative, well-being was also felt to come with its own challenges. The multifaceted nature of well-being makes it a useful tool in qualitative research but made it hard for the volunteer advocates to develop a clear, workable presentation of its value, its measurement, and its outcomes in relation to mindfulness as a narrative bed for advocacy. For example, in shadow cabinet discussions about mindfulness in the run-up to the 2015 election, it was anticipated that a framework of well-being might be critiqued as being too "fluffy" by opponents on both the right and the left, and that it did not present an economically credible focus for investment. On May 7, a general election saw the Conservatives gain an outright majority, unshackling the conservative government from their unpopular coalition with the Liberal Democrats and confounding the predictions of opinion polls and political analysts alike. In their manifestos, each of the political parties had made a strong commitment to increased provision for mental health, and the Labour Party went further in promising that mental health would be given the same priority as physical health. In the Labour Party manifesto, the party hedged their narrative bets by pledging to introduce mindfulness as a support for young people's well-being *and* resilience (Labour Party 2015, 47).

Volunteers could draw on this existing language to explain the value of mindfulness for parliamentarians, and they were confident that these claims were factually accurate. But they thought that these kinds of explanations, while true and important, did not provide a full representation of mindfulness. Reflecting on the different political narratives through which mindfulness could be explained, Tom commented that, while mindfulness could not be reduced to resilience or well-being, the fact that different narratives could be used to frame it reflected its foundational nature: "That's part of the versatility of narrative and the best articulation is a nuanced understanding that includes this array of character, grit, resilience, that kind of language, and recognizes that we're dealing with complex concepts, because we're talking about a human potential that is multidimensional."

For Susan, narratives such as well-being and resilience did not capture the value of her personal practice.

> It's interesting, isn't it? Because I'm not sure I desperately connect with any of those words if I think about mindfulness and my own practice. Maybe *well-being*, but it's quite a vague term. *Happiness* is an interesting one. Am I any happier through mindfulness? I'm not sure I'd use the word *happy*. Happiness doesn't particularly resonate for what mindfulness does for me. *Resilience* in some ways connects, but something around self-care and resilience rather than just that ability to bounce

back. Perhaps for me "resilience" in the past has been slightly brutal . . . "come on now, get back on the horse." I think mindfulness in a way can enhance any of these different things. So, mindfulness might help happiness or resilience but I'm not sure it *is* resilience, or increased happiness.

Nonetheless, she thought that engaging skillfully with political narratives could point to a larger concern with "living well": "It isn't closing down. In some moments, resilience is what's needed, in other moments compassionate openness is what's needed. We need all these different qualities to actually navigate our lives and it's about flexibility and responsiveness and wider perspective taking, seeing what's most need moment by moment. Yeah. And it's a nice way of framing it. . . . That's maybe moving it towards a bit of a narrative: what is it to live well."

Throughout the drafting process, the need to explain mindfulness in terms of pragmatic outcomes and personal transformation remained present for volunteer advocates. Peter and I took a walk along the canal in East London in the run-up to the general election of 2015. Peter had a long-term meditation practice and had been a key figure in the development of a popular meditation app. The towpath was busy with weekenders enjoying the spring weather, and we stopped for a cup of tea on a narrow boat that had been refitted as a café. At this point in the drafting process, volunteers were struggling to find a language that would explain the value of mindfulness in political circles, to present mindfulness in such a way that what members thought of as its profoundly transformative potential could be understood by others. As he told me, "What's starting to happen is we're finding words for why it is that much more important, but we're only just starting to do that. And so, you start by using the language that you *have* got like *well-being* or *resilience*. . . . And that's pretty visionary and big and cross sector, but it's still kind of one set of language, one kind of frame."

Useful Knowledge

The ethical value that mindfulness held for volunteers motivated commitment to advocacy and helped them maintain belief in the broader political project of promoting mindfulness, but it occupied a subordinate position in the discursive hierarchy of the report itself. What made evidence for mindfulness "useful" in the report was its ability to be communicated to and consumed by others (Strathern 2006, 75), and this was shaped by an idea of its "users": the parliamentarians. The success of the document rested on its ability to assess mindfulness, provide accountability for political decisions that might be made as a result of it, and demonstrate value for money. As Susan told me in an interview after the report had been launched, "What the politicians wanted was credibility. Something you could take to a minister and they would say 'this is really interesting.'" The report needed to show that mindfulness was clearly evidenced and costed for specific and targeted objectives.

For volunteer advocates, then, the presentation of mindfulness through econometric data and the evidence of randomized controlled trials did not feel disingenuous, but it did feel strategic. For example, Peter understood the use of instrumental data as a way of communicating something of the value of mindfulness to people who had never practiced it. He told me, "Trying to describe mindfulness is a bit like trying to describe the taste of an orange. How do you do that? Ok, so it's hard to describe the taste of an orange, but you can point out the benefits of vitamin C. It protects you against colds, improves your skin, that sort of thing. That's sort of what we're doing: describing why it's socially important and the mechanisms it influences. But I think we can do better." Peter understood the measurable effects of practicing mindfulness, such as reduced cognitive reactivity or emotional regulation, as secondary but important benefits of practice. But he focused on these measurable secondary benefits when presenting mindfulness as a policy object. Similarly, Teresa and others thought of mindful awareness as foundational for human flourishing, and they did not think that the value of this could be completely accounted for by the evidence and targeted recommendations that they were compiling in the report. But equally, they did not think of these metrics or the evidence that supported them as misleading or untrue. As Teresa said to me, "That's the language you speak if you want to be part of the conversation."

Over the course of drafting the report, volunteer advocates learned appropriate ways to represent mindfulness that were simultaneously moral and technical (cf. Harper 2000). They acted as knowledge brokers, bringing together information from think tanks, universities, research divisions, and mental health institutes in order to provide ideas and solutions with which policymakers could work. Drafting the report involved months of effort in reading research reports and collating their findings, discussing drafts, and developing the text (cf. Harper 1998). The sheer amount of time and effort that went into getting the document "right" is worth emphasizing. I think of drafting the report as an ongoing social process, which was notable not only for the way in which volunteer advocates learned how to navigate the policy landscape but also for the ways it shaped mindfulness as a policy object. That is, through the writing process, the "parameters of the thinkable" (Green 2011, 42) were shaped. Explanatory practices were not just representational; they contributed to an iterative process that made it possible for mindfulness advocacy to develop, contributing to and shaping policy discussion in turn. In the service of explanation, evidence was marshaled and managed in order to establish "what is the case" (ontological), to demonstrate "how we know this is the case" (epistemological), and to develop a persuasive argument for "what we think should be done" (normative). In the process, mindfulness *became* a policy object.

The final report made specific and supported recommendations for how mindfulness could be introduced across UK services and institutions. In each policy area, the recommendations spoke to identified policy objectives and were couched in emerging political narratives. Divided into four sections, the report presented a dizzying amount of research. It provided pages of references detailing the nature and extent of problems identified in each area of the inquiry, as well as econometric data on the forecasted cost of these problems to the state. What had begun as a broad inquiry into mindfulness and mental health in the United Kingdom had now become an eighty-page comprehensive summary of much of the academic research on mindfulness at the time. The collation of this research had taken months to achieve and had brought together the orchestrated efforts of a highly professional group of people. Mindfulness was presented as an evidenced civil society recommendation with clear policy potential as a preventive health-care intervention. It was framed as a possible solution to costed social problems, based on academic research that suggests that it "works": statistical, social scientific, and psychological research was marshaled to support the claim that mindfulness is an appropriate and positive intervention.

In addition to this, the report was prefaced with a two-page foreword by Jon Kabat-Zinn, the originator of mindfulness-based stress reduction, and each of the key sections contained two to four pages of case studies from people who had benefited from mindfulness. The volunteers thought that both the foreword and the case studies were essential for the success of the document. Kabat-Zinn wrote that mindfulness "has the potential to add value and new degrees of freedom to living life fully and wisely" (MAPPG 2015, 9). Volunteers saw this representation of mindfulness as a "way of being" that was cultivated "wisely and effectively through practice" as a vital complement to the evidenced recommendations that made up the bulk of the report. In addition to the efficacy of mindfulness as a targeted intervention, it was also, and importantly, represented as "a way of being in wise and purposeful relationship with one's experience, both inwardly and outwardly" (9). The case studies from people with health issues, a schoolgirl, a teacher, workers, a policeman, an ex-offender, and a prisoner drew portraits of people who had learned to "re-connect to life" and find time to "simply be," in some cases in very challenging circumstances (57, 58). Tom told me that, for him, these case studies really explained the value of mindfulness: sharing personal stories of the lived impact of mindfulness practice powerfully hit home. As he said, "My hunch is that nobody really is inspired for a lifetime of mindfulness practice by randomized controlled trials and 'resilience,' that it's as much a poetic enterprise as a scientific enterprise."

In the animal protection charity that Reed (2017b) studied, personal ethical positions were articulated in political lobbying through the combination of scientific and moral techniques. Although photographic images and video footage of creatures caught in snares did not count as "proper evidence" in political lobbying, campaigners presented both quantified evidence and representations of suffering animals in order to spark empathy in politicians. Similarly, Deborah thought that the case studies in the report were important because they were *more* persuasive than the scientific evidence. As she said to me, "What persuades who? Personal testimony. Because we're human beings, our hearts are engaged first and then our heads and we always think we're persuaded by evidence but actually we seek the evidence once the case has caught us. But once we're persuaded, we need the evidence in order to go off and persuade others. But that gives us the confidence person to person to make it connect."

One effect of the creation of this document had been to shape a representation of mindfulness as an effective and evidenced contribution to policy discussion not only about mental health but also about well-being and resilience. Mindfulness was presented as a way of "supporting wellbeing and resilience across the population as a prevention strategy to keep people well" (MAPPG 2015, 19). This presentation of mindfulness as a preventive health measure was complemented by multiple research findings on the positive effects of mindfulness on cognitive and emotional processes, and a correlation was drawn between these processes and living a well-adjusted and happy life.

The Ethics and Economics of Mindful Nation

I return to Lambek's distinction between ethical and economic value. As mindfulness is incorporated into political discussion, does it take on external values, rather than goods that were previously internal to it? Does a practice that was previously integrated into a total way of life come to be valued for the ends that it effects? One possible response might be that mindfulness is instrumentalized in the process of advocacy and comes to be valued for its goal-oriented efficacy. An alternative response might be that the presentation of mindfulness in utilitarian terms is disingenuous and its *real* value is as an ethical practice. I hope to have shown that neither interpretation is sufficient to account for the motivation for and ongoing process of political advocacy. My interest in this chapter has been to ethnographically examine the ways in which ethical and economic values (in Lambek's terms) intersect, and the efforts taken in different moments to maintain or reduce the distance between them. That is, rather than assuming that advocacy reduces the meaning of ethical value to a relative economic or utility value, I have asked, what is the ongoing relationship between ethical and economic value in the social process of advocacy? The oil and water of ethical and economic values may be characteristic of contemporary political practice in the United Kingdom more broadly, and the incommensurability between the two may itself be productive. In the context of political advocacy, capacity and utility values are mutually reinforcing: if it were not for the evidence that it "works," mindfulness would not be being discussed as a policy intervention; if the only value mindfulness had were extrinsic to it, advocates would not have sufficient moral conviction to campaign for it.

In accounting for the efforts that volunteer advocates made to draft the *Mindful Nation UK* report, I have sought to move away from a linear representation of political decision making. Rather, political advocacy is revealed to be an ongoing and iterative social process. As Peter told me recently, "Political policies are like sausages: you wouldn't want to see how they get made." Participation in mindfulness advocacy for nonstate enthusiasts was motivated by personal moral conviction, and by marshaling multiple sources of evidence in the report, volunteers sought to contribute to cultural change. Volunteer advocates' efforts to explain the value of mindfulness in political conversations were intended as a political intervention. Advocates did not just describe things in the world but sought to explain to parliamentarians why they mattered and what should be done about them, and this explanation was achieved through the *management* of different kinds of evidence, drawing relationships between them and embedding them in broader political narratives. Volunteers learned to explain the value of mindfulness as a policy object through the collation of quantitative research, econometric data, and the reproduction of what they understood to be prominent and salient discourses of the state. This led to what Thomas Kirsch has referred to as a "mimetic incorporation of bureaucratization" (2008, 237), as volunteer advocates responded to the perceived nature of policy development and political conversation. I argue that, motivated by personal ethics and located in broad normative agendas, engagement with governmental techniques is informed by, coexists with, and leads to multiple forms of rationality and ethics (cf. Born 2002). The report may be thought of as a "living document" (Green 2011, 33), a way of maintaining a place in an evolving conversation about policy, of navigating ongoing disputes and future possibilities. As such, it is alive with the social processes that produced it, and it continues to have a "performative quality" even though the discursive form that it takes masks this "politics of interaction" (see Green 2011; Riles 2006).

By the end of my fieldwork in 2016, the inquiry process and the report had had relatively little impact on the policy landscape.[5] Nonetheless, the volunteers felt that their work had been a success: mindfulness had been put on the table and had become a staple in conversations about mental health in the United Kingdom. The massive public interest in mindfulness generated around the MAPPG and the *Mindful Nation UK* report was informed by and reflected in its uptake in the British press and in Parliament. Volunteers saw advocating for mindfulness as part of a wider project of societal transformation, which was to be achieved by working with, rather than against, dominant political forms. As Peter told me after the launch, "This is our starter for 10 and then we begin the messy business of ongoing relationship building and policy development over a number of years." It is hard to know what the long-term effects of the *Mindful Nation UK* report will be in political terms, but at the time of the launch, Britain seemed to be on its way to becoming a mindful nation. Ironically (given the labor that went into collating the evidence), this had less to do with the development of specific policy "asks" and more to do with a normalization of debate about mental health and mindfulness that had occurred as a result of the process. At the end of the day, the promotion of the instrumentalized goals and targeted recommendations of the report had, in fact, led to a broad discussion about mental health and mindful awareness as constituent aspects of living well, an outcome that was in alignment with the ethical aspirations that had inspired the process of advocacy in the first place.

NOTES

1. Tambiah warns of similar effects of rationalization when he writes, "Science invades the economy, the economy invades politics, and now politics is alleged to inform us on morality, choice and the values to live by. And there's the rub" (1990, 150).

2. Lambek argues that ethical values are posited in respect of absolute standards (the value of a life), while economic values fluctuate (economic value is negotiable). Furthermore, absolute values cannot be substituted for one another.

3. Critics of evidence-based medicine have argued that a drive toward quantification and statistical analysis risks the loss of sensitivity to context and responsiveness to circumstance or individual patients (see Ecks 2008), with "best evidence" increasingly defined by the data and analysis of randomized controlled trials (Williams and Garner 2002). Contrastively, those in favor of evidence-based medicine respond that preserving clinical autonomy perpetuates bias and personal preference in treatment protocols, thereby putting patients' health at risk. As Lambert (2005: 2640) points out, arguments both for and against evidence-based medicine often claim the moral high ground in representing the greater good.

4. Viktor Frankl, an Austrian psychiatrist and Holocaust survivor, is commonly cited as writing, "Between stimulus and response there is a space. In that space is our power to choose our response. In our response lies our growth and our freedom." Despite the frequent attribution, the quote is not found in Frankl's writings. Frankl wrote a

psychological memoir, *Man's Search for Meaning* ([1959] 2004), in which he reflects on his experiences in Auschwitz, the purpose of life, and courage in the face of difficulty. The quote was attributed to Frankl by Stephen R. Covey in his best-selling self-help book *The Seven Habits of Highly Effective People* (1989), and it may be that the attribution entered common usage from there. See O'Toole 2018.

5. Within three years of the launch of the report, a series of actions had been taken that were indirectly linked to it. Two recommendations from the health chapter had been acted on: mindfulness-based cognitive therapy had become a mandated therapy through the Improving Access to Psychological Therapies program, and Health Education England was funding mindfulness-based cognitive therapy training. The Department for Education began funding a research trial on mindfulness and mental health interventions in schools. All of the report's recommendations in criminal justice were acted on. The National Offender Management Service (now Her Majesty's Prison and Probation Service) convened a steering group and conducted research on mindfulness among staff.

REFERENCES

Alexandrova, A. 2017. *A Philosophy for the Science of Well-Being.* New York: Oxford University Press.

Ashdown, P. 2011. *Humanitarian Emergency Response Review.* https://www.preventionweb.net/go/18663.

Bajaj, B., and N. Pande. 2016. "Mediating Role of Resilience in the Impact of Mindfulness on Life Satisfaction and Affect as Indices of Subjective Well-Being." *Personality and Individual Differences* 93:63–67.

Barrios, R. E. 2016. "Resilience: A Commentary from the Vantage Point of Anthropology." *Annals of Anthropological Practice* 40 (1): 28–38.

Born, G. 2002. "Reflexivity and Ambivalence: Culture, Creativity and Government in the BBC." *Cultural Values* 6:65–90.

Brown, K. W., and R. M. Ryan. 2003. "The Benefits of Being Present: Mindfulness and Its Role in Psychological Well-Being." *Journal of Personality and Social Psychology* 84 (4): 822–848.

Clark, D. A. 2002. *Visions of Development: A Study of Human Values.* Cheltenham: Edward Elgar.

Covey, S. R. 1989. *The Seven Habits of Highly Effective People.* New York: Simon and Schuster.

Crisp, R., and B. Hooker, eds. 2000. *Well-Being and Morality: Essays in Honour of James Griffin.* Oxford: Oxford University Press.

Cummins, R. A. 2005. "Measuring Health and Subjective Wellbeing: Vale, Quality-Adjusted Life-Years." In *Rethinking Wellbeing,* edited by L. Manderson and R. Nile, 69–89. Perth, W.A.: API Network.

Dasgupta, P. 2001. *Human Well-Being and the Natural Environment.* Oxford: Oxford University Press.

Davies, H., S. Nutley, and P. Smith, eds. 2000. *What Works? Evidence-Based Policy and Practice in Public Services.* Bristol: Polity.

du Gay, P. 2005. "The Values of Bureaucracy: An Introduction." In *The Values of Bureaucracy,* edited by P. du Gay, 1–13. Oxford: Oxford University Press.

Ecks, S. 2008. "Three Propositions for an Evidence-Based Medical Anthropology." *Journal of the Royal Anthropological Institute* 14:S77–S92.

Frankl, V. E. (1959) 2004. *Man's Search for Meaning.* London: Rider.

Gordon, J. E. 1978. *Structures: Or Why Things Don't Fall Down.* Harmondsworth, UK: Penguin Books.

Green, M. 2011. "Calculating Compassion: Accounting for Some Categorical Practices in International Development." In *Adventures in Aidland: The Anthropology of Professionals in International Development*, edited by David Mosse, 33–56. Oxford: Berghan.

Griffin, James. 1986. *Well-Being: Its Meaning, Measurement and Moral Importance*. Oxford: Oxford University Press.

Harper, R. 1998. *Inside the IMF: An Ethnography of Documents, Technology and Organisational Action*. San Diego: Academic Press.

——. 2000. "The Social Organization of the IMF's Mission Work: An Examination of International Auditing." In *Audit Cultures: Anthropological Studies in Accountability, Ethics and the Academy*, edited by M. Strathern, 23–53. London: Routledge.

Hoggett, P. 2005. "A Service to the Public: The Containment of Ethical and Moral Conflict by Public Bureaucracies." In *The Values of Bureaucracy*, edited by P. du Gay, 165–190. Oxford: Oxford University Press.

Holling, C. S. 1973. "Resilience and Stability of Ecological Systems." *Annual Review of Ecology and Systematics* 4:1–23.

Hyland, T. 2016. "Mindful Nation UK—Report by the Mindfulness All-Party Parliamentary Group (MAPPG)." *Journal of Vocational Education and Training* 68 (1): 133–136.

Josefsson, T., P. Larsman, A. G. Broberg, and L.-G. Lundh. 2011. "Self-Reported Mindfulness Mediates the Relation between Meditation Experience and Psychological Well-Being." *Mindfulness* 2:49–58.

Kirsch, T. G. 2008. *Spirits and Letters: Reading, Writing and Charisma in African Christianity*. New York: Berghan Books.

Labour Party. 2015. *Labour Party Manifesto 2015*. London: Labour Party. https://www.telegraph.co.uk/multimedia/archive/03265/LabourPartyManifes_3265486a.pdf.

Lambek, M. 2000. "The Anthropology of Religion and the Quarrel between Poetry and Philosophy." *Current Anthropology* 41 (3): 309–320.

——. 2008a. "Measuring—or Practising Well-Being?" In *Culture and Well-Being: Anthropological Approaches to Freedom and Political Ethics*, edited by A. Corsín Jimenez, 115–133. London: Pluto.

——. 2008b. "Value and Virtue." *Anthropological Theory* 8 (2): 133–157.

Lambert, H. 2005. "Accounting for EBM: Notions of Evidence in Medicine." *Social Science and Medicine* 62:2633–2645.

Maasen, S., and O. Lieven. 2006. "Transdisciplinarity: A New Mode of Governing?" *Science and Public Policy* 33 (6): 399–410.

MAPPG (Mindfulness All-Party Parliamentary Group). 2015. *Mindful Nation UK*. London: Mindfulness All-Party Parliamentary Group. https://www.themindfulnessinitiative.org/mindful-nation-report.

Miller, D. 2005. "What Is Best 'Value'? Bureaucracy, Virtualism and Local Governance." In *The Values of Bureaucracy*, edited by P. du Gay, 233–254. Oxford: Oxford University Press.

Moffitt, T. E., L. Arseneault, D. Belsky, N. Dickson, R. J. Hancox, H. Harrington, R. Houts, et al. 2011. "A Gradient of Childhood Self-Control Predicts Health, Wealth, and Public Safety." *Proceedings of the National Academy of Sciences* 108 (7): 2693–2698.

Moloney, P. 2016. "Mindfulness: The Bottled Water of the Therapy Industry." In *Handbook of Mindfulness: Culture, Context, and Social Engagement*, edited by R. E. Purser, D. Forbes, and A. Burke, 269–292. Basel, Switzerland: Springer.

Nussbaum, Martha, and Amartya Sen, eds. 1993. *The Quality of Life*. Oxford: Clarendon Press.

Offer, Avner, ed. 1996. *In Pursuit of the Quality of Life*. Oxford: Oxford University Press.

O'Toole, G. 2018. "Between Stimulus and Response There Is a Space. In That Space Is Our Power to Choose Our Response." Quote Investigator, February 18, 2018. https://quoteinvestigator.com/2018/02/18/response/.

Reed, A. 2017a. "An Office of Ethics: Meetings, Roles, and Moral Enthusiasm in Animal Protection." *Journal of the Royal Anthropological Institute* 23 (S1): 166–181.

——. 2017b. "Snared: Ethics and Nature in Animal Protection." *Ethnos* 82 (1): 68–85.

Riles, A. 2006. "Anthropology, Human Rights, and Legal Knowledge: Culture in the Iron Cage." *American Anthropologist* 108 (1): 52–65.

Ryff, C. D., G. Dienberg Love, M. J. Essex, and B. Singer. 1998. "Resilience in Adulthood and Later Life." In *Handbook of Aging and Mental Health*, edited by J. Lomranz, 69–96. New York: Plenum.

Sen, Amartya K. 1999. *Development as Freedom*. Oxford: Oxford University Press.

Shapiro, S. L., K. W. Brown, and G. M. Biegel. 2007. "Teaching Self-Care to Caregivers: Effects of Mindfulness-Based Stress Reduction on the Mental Health of Therapists in Training." *Training and Education in Professional Psychology* 1 (2): 105–111.

Shore, C., and S. Wright. 2000. "Coercive Accountability: The Rise of Audit Culture in Higher Education." In *Audit Cultures: Anthropological Studies in Accountability, Ethics and the Academy*, edited by M. Strathern, 57–89. London: Routledge.

Strathern, M. 2005. "Resistance, Refusal and Global Moralities." *Australian Feminist Studies* 20 (47): 181–193.

Strathern, M. 2006. "Useful Knowledge." *Proceedings of the British Academy* 139:73–109.

Tambiah, S. 1990. *Magic, Science, Religion and the Scope of Rationality*. Cambridge: Cambridge University Press.

Williams, D. D. R., and J. Garner. 2002. "The Case against the 'Evidence.'" *British Journal of Psychiatry* 180:8–12.

EXPLAINING THE POLITICS OF THE AUTHOR

Adam Reed

I want to begin with an extract from a conversation with one of the first Henry Williamson readers I ever met—a lovely man, now sadly deceased, called Ted. It is important to note that the dialogue reproduced here marked a noticeable shift in the tone of our exchange, from a previously easygoing and confident accounting of a life spent reading the literary works of a favorite author to a much more sober reflection, a cautious and at times uncertain stance.

> "But Henry Williamson was his own worst enemy. Er you've probably heard about the political involvement?"
>
> "In the thirties?"
>
> "Yeah, yeah. People find this quite unforgiveable. Anne [the author's official biographer] gives an excellent explanation of why he felt and how he felt the way he did. But he was a person, I think once he'd sort of locked onto an idea he would never give it up, no matter how people tried to explain to him or how events were shown to be the opposite of what he believed, he still clung to this idea right up to the very end. He felt that Hitler had, I won't go into the political side because that's not of interest, but he felt Hitler had been misled by his generals and that he was really a good bloke at heart. You know, he was terrifically loyal to people like Oswald Mosley."
>
> "Yes."
>
> "It didn't do him any good at all, and he was ostracized by the BBC, and publishers wouldn't publish his books, and all because of his attitude.

I think that's why people branded him so much as a right-wing writer and that's why people just don't want to know him."

[*Pause; we both take a sip of tea.*]

"So, it's a great embarrassment to the society. It's an embarrassment to me [*Ted bows his head*], and I think it was very foolish, but I don't think a writer should be judged by his private life."

As is immediately apparent, this part of our conversation was full of references to explanation. Ted pointed out, for instance, the "excellent explanation" of the author's politics available to readers in the official biography. He conceded that Williamson (1895–1977) was known to be resistant to the counterexplanations of fascism and of historical events offered by his contemporaries. Finally, Ted presented a few comments of his own, as a rather reluctant explaining subject. These centered on the kind of person he assessed the author to be and on his interpretation of why the works of Williamson were no longer widely read.

While it's probably the case that Ted raised the author's politics with me in anticipation that I might ask him about it—this was one of my first meetings with a member of the Henry Williamson Society—I soon came to realize that such exchanges were entirely commonplace. Indeed, the offering of explanation about Williamson's politics was a regular occurrence, especially but not exclusively if members came across someone new. This was brought home to me when later that year, in early October 1999, I headed down to North Devon to attend my first annual meeting of the literary society.

Since I was without a car, the society's committee had arranged for me to be picked up from Barnstaple station. The instruction was that someone named Anna, who would be driving up from her home in Dorchester, would stop en route and provide a lift to the hotel venue. Much younger than I expected, certainly in comparison with Ted, who was in his seventies, Anna greeted me casually dressed in jeans and a pink oversize shirt. After she apologized for the mess, which she blamed on young children and the pressures of running a homemade jewelry business, we set off. Throughout the drive, a lively discussion about football and peace campaigning—I learned that Anna was the chairperson of her local Campaign for Nuclear Disarmament group—was interspersed with observations about the countryside around us. Indeed, she was able to point out various locations linked to the novels and the life of the writer.

Passing through the small village of Georgeham, for instance, Anna told me that this was where Williamson and his family had lived for many years and where he wrote many of his books. She revealed that she had herself met "Henry" there in the late 1960s when she was only seventeen years old; the author had invited her to pay a visit after receiving a letter from Anna full of enthusiastic praise for one of his novel series. There followed what she could only describe as a wonderful, crazy couple of days in the old man's company. At this point, Anna turned and asked if I knew about Williamson's fascist past. The question was hurriedly followed by an assertion that she didn't think the writer was a "real" fascist. His politics, Anna explained, came out of the experience of serving as a soldier through the First World War and from his determination never to see such a conflict happen again. "He was a very stubborn man, too loyal to people," she went on. "That's why, even after the Second World War, he refused to fully condemn Mosley or Hitler." Anna shook her head and then laughed. She revealed that when she joined the literary society, her husband teased her remorselessly, prophesying that its members would turn out to be a "bunch of old fascists"! However, when she went to her first meeting, Anna found everyone was friendly and agreeable. "There was one old man though," she reflected as we turned into the hotel drive, who in her opinion talked about the connection between Williamson and Mosley just a little too much and seemed like he might be "a bit dodgy."

Similar kinds of conversations occurred across the annual meeting. For instance, as we assembled in the main hall of the hotel the following morning in preparation for a planned visit to Williamson's writing hut, at the time conserved by the society, I met a member called Frank. Tall, gray haired, and balding, he introduced himself as coming from the seaside town of Worthing in West Sussex and informed me that before his retirement he used to work as a manager in the National Health Service. Frank said that compared with most members of the literary society, he came to the novels very late in life, just twenty years ago; so he had never had the chance to meet the writer, which was a great regret. And next, rather abruptly, had I heard about Henry's fascism? Frank then narrated a story he had been told about Williamson responding to the news of the outbreak of war in 1939 by speeding through a nearby town with a Union Jack flying out of one car window and a swastika flag out the other. "Needless to say," he chuckled, "this did not make him popular with the locals." But, Frank explained, Williamson was a genius and one has to be single-minded and extreme to be a writer. "You only need to look at the way Henry treated his family," he added. Frank invited me to consider the writer's decision to buy a rundown farm on the other side of the country during the 1930s. "Just on a whim! You know Henry came home one day and suddenly declared that they were all moving to Norfolk!" Frank chuckled again. "His fascism was just idealism," he explained to me. "I think Henry must have been horrified when he later heard about the Holocaust and what happened in Nazi Germany and occupied Europe during the war."

Another member took up the issue of the author's politics with me later in the day. This conversation began at the hotel bar, after the formal dinner and traditional evening talk. Initially focused on a shared interest in Williamson's stories of school days in South London, our discussion soon became diverted toward the issue of fascism. Clearly by now a little worse for wear—it had been a long day followed by a fair amount of beer and wine—my companion started to expound on how unfair it was that the writer continued to be judged on his politics rather than his literature. "Maybe Henry didn't get it so wrong," he threw out in deliberate provocation. "After all, many people are saying it was a mistake for Britain to go into the Second World War. All that happened was that we got into terrible debt to the Americans and lost our empire." Energized by the statement, he ventured, "It's possible that atrocities like the Holocaust might not even have happened had we stayed out, that we might have been able to use our influence to stop it." The intensity in his words died down and he sighed. "Anyway, we have not got rid of prejudice. Just look at how Asians are treated today." He sighed again. "Why pick on Williamson?"

As I quickly came to realize, members of the literary society perceived the need, however hesitantly, to say *something* about the author's politics and particularly to address the question of the historical relationship between the man, his works, and the ideology of fascism. On occasion united by a shared belief in the idea that *the* explanation did exist somewhere out there or alternatively by shared recognition of actual explanations of Williamson's fascism, individual readers were just as likely to test out or innovate their own explanations. At a very basic level, then, this was a society of explanations. In fact, I want to propose that the realization of the necessity for explanation was identified by Williamson readers as one of the chief outcomes of joining the literary society. For some members, this was quite simply the case because before they came across the Henry Williamson Society, they had absolutely no knowledge of the writer's links to historical fascism; the connection only surfaces in the content of a few novels and nonfiction writings (but see Reed 2022). For other members, it was because the awareness of Williamson's politics as a problem that might require an explanation *from them* only arose in the context of committing to the literary society's aims: "to encourage interest in and deeper understanding of the life and work of the writer Henry Williamson." So while they might have initially joined the society out of a love of the novels and from a curiosity to know more about the writer who created them (and perhaps also from a desire to gain access to out-of-print books), solitary readers soon found themselves drawn into a wider struggle to defend a literary reputation.

The interjected comments of Ted and the other Williamson readers cited earlier were just the beginning of a series of explanatory musings on the author's politics that I collected over the ensuing years. Sometimes these were presented to me directly or received in the context of being an audience member at society talks; other times, I read the explanations in the articles and letters authored by readers and published in the society's journal. In this chapter I am first and foremost concerned to describe these explanations in action. This includes a consideration not just of how they worked but also of what they were for and how they interacted. As we will see, explaining the author's politics involved readers moving between positions within the same order of explanation as well as shifting between apparently incommensurate scales of explanation. A *big* explanation, for instance one taken to be capable of encompassing or addressing the issue in its entirety, would sit alongside a whole host of intermediate and little explanatory moves and could even operate in tandem with anti-explanatory moves. I am also interested in exploring at what point an explanation of the author's politics satisfied or disappointed, and how a sense of unease could simultaneously generate and curtail an impulse to explain. As already alluded, Williamson readers often reported that explanation was drawn forth from them; its status as self-initiated action was far from straightforward. Indeed, their situation regularly led members of the literary society to ask themselves not just who explains and who prompts that explanation but who listens to explanation. It additionally led them to inquire why certain stances, events, and associations linked to the author or his works seemed to automatically demand explanation and why others clearly did not.

The Autonomy of Literature

Although the kinds of explanation for the author's politics offered by Williamson readers such as Ted, Anna, and Frank were generally fragmentary in form and apparently incomplete, it is important to note that sometimes members of the literary society highlighted explanatory moves of an entirely different order. After giving his hesitant thoughts on the origins and consequences of the author's politics, Ted, for instance, stated that he didn't agree Williamson's works should be judged on this basis. The final line of our quoted conversation makes reference to a broader argument about the proper treatment of literary authors and their works. "I don't think," Ted told me, "that a writer should be judged by his private life." While the comments of certain society members could be interpreted to mean that someone who writes oughtn't to be held up to the same moral account as others—Frank suggested that Williamson's politics or "idealism" might be excused on the basis of his genius—I read Ted as focused on a very different claim.

In its English coinage, the sphere of "private life" is typically invoked to distinguish certain activities or opinions from the public expressions of the person—that is, from those activities or opinions that are the appropriate object of public scrutiny and for which someone should be publicly held to account. By this measure, the writer's political views were a private matter, equivalent, say, to the issue of how he treated his family; or, reaching for an equivalence at the level of political opinion that society members could understand, to the issue of how someone voted in a general election. Just as the membership would not expect to be publicly interrogated on which political party they supported, so the author should not be interrogated for his politics. However, as we will see, Williamson's political views and allegiances were also at times very public. In fact, I suggest that the allusion was really invoked to demarcate something else, less the policing of a boundary between a private and public life and more an insistence on the autonomy of the domain of literature. Here Ted was concerned with the positive claim that a writer should principally be judged by his or her writings, or alternatively by the ideal that those writings should not be judged by the extraliterary practice (private or public) of the author.

Such a defense is very familiar. Indeed, as Pierre Bourdieu (1991, 72) points out, claims for the autonomy of works, often linked to modes of textual interpretation that seem to enable those works to "dictate the terms of their own perception," operate across the histories of art, literature, and philosophy. Bourdieu's observation is motivated by a specific desire to understand the philosophical defense of Martin Heidegger, which can include a disciplinary resistance to a political reading of his philosophical works. Bourdieu (1991, 5) highlights that to the charge of Heidegger's affiliation to Nazism, some respond by seeking to "localize him in the 'philosophical' arena"; for instance, through an account of Heidegger's particular position (against neo-Kantians) in the broader history of philosophy. This kind of explanatory move crucially assumes that "on the one hand we have Heidegger's biography, with its public and private events," and "on the other hand, we have the intellectual biography," somehow "'laundered' of all reference to events in the everyday life of the philosopher" (4). In the latter version, "the thinker becomes completely identified with his thought, and his life with his work—which is thus constituted as a self-sufficient and self-generating creation" (4). One might counter that Bourdieu's phrasing itself assumes a good deal; for instance, that intellectual matters *are* natural emanations of "everyday life" or that the detachment of one from the other must be a trick or, more neutrally, an achievement of some kind. It would surely be possible to reverse the problem and examine how much work, and perhaps trickery, is actually involved in making those connections appear (i.e., Bourdieu had to write a whole book). However, for our purposes I want simply to register the attention given to the apparent power of that explanatory move.

Indeed, more generally Bourdieu is interested in how this autonomy stance and the wider move to "the imposition of form" gets shored up by a specialized systematized language and expert practice, "which keeps the layman at a respect-able distance" and thus "protects the text" from being trivialized (1991, 89). What is perhaps immediately relevant here is Bourdieu's insistence that through this expert practice and in particular the formalist aesthetics of an internalist reading, the distinction between politics and philosophy gets enacted or experienced as a "genuine ontological threshold" (36). For example, Bourdieu is fascinated by the professional "alchemy" that allows "passage into another order, which is inseparable from . . . a change of social space which supposes a change of mental space" (36). Like the expert practice of mathematics that can "transmute" or convert "speed into a derivative or an area into an integer" or the alchemy of the judiciary that can transform "a quarrel or conflict into a trial," the imposition of philosophical form, Bourdieu argues, can convincingly alter the ontological status of the thing in front of one (at least for the philosopher) (36).

As must already be evident, in many ways Ted was far closer to a version of the "layman" whom Bourdieu recognizes as the figure precisely kept at bay by the specialized systematized language that typically supports the imposition of form. In fact, like his companion readers, Ted generally preferred to distance himself from the break with ordinary language, which most members associated with both critical and wider academic readings of literary texts. "We are not eggheads," one member once told me, echoing a widely expressed sentiment. "For us, enthusiasm is what matters, not erudition." This was evident not just because of the alienation toward critical reading practices that Williamson readers sometimes expressed but because, as the fragmentary explanations of Ted, Anna, and Frank also testify, most readers were heavily invested in the project of uncovering "the man behind the writings," or in reconnecting the books they read and loved with the life of the writer. Nevertheless, I don't believe that the principle of autonomy was invoked in bad faith. For there remained a strong sense in which Ted meant to seriously realize that ontological threshold between politics and literature. At least in the moment of uttering the phrase—"I don't think that a writer should be judged by his private life"—he sought to inhabit a recognizable version of that distinction.

Indeed, members of the literary society quite regularly highlighted claims for the autonomy of literature. Ted was certainly not the only Williamson reader to suggest that the writer shouldn't be judged by his private life, and the literary society often promoted its activities as explicitly "non-political . . . dedicated solely to its literary aim" (Henry Williamson Society, n.d.a). That these explanatory moves could be made without serious reference to the introduction of a thoroughgoing internalist reading of text or any expert practice capable of imposing form never seemed to particularly bother the readers I knew. Perhaps this was because in truth the principle was usually uttered without much elaboration, or perhaps it was because Bourdieu is partly wrong—that is, it doesn't necessarily take that much expert work to separate the literary from the political. But either way, I regularly suspected that the chief value of the ideal of the autonomy of literature lay more in the full stop it momentarily placed on further discussions of the author's politics. For me this was not so much a means of explaining his politics away or of cynical evasion as of self-protection. I liked to imagine the action of this explanation as akin to an umbrella opening, a move that provided the explaining subject with a space of respite or shelter from accusations concerning "Henry's fascism." It was in this regard very much outward facing, usually made in response to a specific charge against the writer or his works, or in anticipation of such. The apparent contradiction—between an assertion that a writer should only be identified with his writings and the widespread enthusiasm for authorial biography both as a basis for explaining the author's politics and as a popular explanatory device for reading the novels—needs to be understood in these terms, the invocation of the principle of autonomy placed in the time and orientation of its telling.

Because

If the claim that a writer should be completely identified with his writings didn't come from or generate forms of erudition that could support it, what forms of explanation did attach to the reading practice and activities of literary society members? The question returns us to the explanatory fragments that I collected. For these explanations of the author's politics, typically grounded in the assumption that a writer and his works could not be understood without a strong sense of his ordinary life and times, dominated the discussions between Williamson readers. They regularly exchanged such explanatory moves at society meetings. These explanations were *little* in the sense that they rarely seemed to connect to wider structures of argument or to strive toward a grand conclusion or even reach a detectable point of resolution.

In searching for a methodological language that might enable a descriptive fleshing-out of these little explanations, I have found the work of W. G. Runciman (1983) useful. I am particularly intrigued by Runciman's close attention to the mundane mechanics of "because" (1983, 155), those micro-shifts in the invocation of cause or condition for explanation that Runciman identifies at work in an anthropological, sociological, or historical register and that I also think animate much of the explanatory work of Williamson readers. This includes the ways in which what Runciman terms an "event, process or state of affairs" can become articulated as due to "something else" (155), which may itself be another event, process, or state of affairs; and Runciman's consideration of the specific aspect of the thing that is identified either as needing explanation or, in the guise of a something else, as providing that explanation. Indeed, it is that emphasis on the manner by which explanation can draw deceptively simple but nevertheless quite intense relations—"an explanation in terms of what?" (1983, 157)—that I here want to take forward.

In his wider four-stage schema of "understanding," Runciman observes that explanation always rests on a prior act of "reportage" (1983, 15). This is the apparently simple noticing of an event, process, or state of affairs whose identification leads its observers to propose that an explanation is necessary; for instance, as in my example, the noticing by members of the literary society of the author's politics or historical links to fascism. Runciman usually presents this as a relatively straightforward volitional act, but as this chapter has already well illustrated, it may also be something that the explaining subject is made to notice. Either way, the important thing is that the reported action takes on the status of "facts," in the sense that it is the thing that remains, at least initially, incontestable, out of the realm of dispute across competing explanations, and hence what makes "contrasts" available to consider or view. Reportage then is not just the noticing "of what has been observed to occur or be the case" (15), but also more specifically the noticing of actual or concrete objects of reportage (in our case, concerning the author's politics or links to fascism) that can or must be acknowledged by others.

Among society members, a much-cited example is the one-line quote by the writer found in the foreword to the 1936 edition of his tetralogy *The Flax of Dream*, which reads, "I salute the great man across the Rhine, whose life symbol is the happy child" (H. Williamson 1936, 7). This greeting, a clear nod by Williamson to Hitler and the then-new National Socialist regime in Germany, has since gained considerable notoriety. Its undeniable material existence on the page means that it continues to be an item those outside the society notice and hence that Williamson readers must respond to regularly with explanation. But that line sat alongside other objects of reportage commonly accepted by members of the literary society. Everyone I met recognized, for instance, the fact that Williamson was a member of the British Union of Fascists, that he attended some of their rallies and published occasional pieces in their party newspaper, *Action*. It is important to highlight that these are not just things that are *known*; they are also, à la Runciman, actions of reportage whose minor eventfulness should not disguise their crucial animating role in making little explanations possible. Indeed, as well as reporting this and other facts to me, members of the literary society were constantly reporting and re-reporting what was observed to be the case about Williamson's links to fascism to each other. Here reportage could also merge into forms closer to anecdote, storytelling, and gossip. At society meetings, members loved nothing better than sharing or passing on snapshot accounts from the life of the writer, including tales that could be taken to illustrate his politics—Frank's story about Williamson's provocative and very public reaction to the news of the outbreak of the Second World War being a perfect example of this kind of more vivid noticing.

For Runciman the shift from reportage to explanation involves a sensation of moving from observing what has taken place to a comprehension "of what caused it, or how it came about" (1983, 15). Among Williamson readers, one of the most conventionally identified causes for the author's politics, mentioned by Anna and often repeated, was the writer's experience as a trench soldier in the First World War. They regarded that to be one of those events but for which his politics might have been other than it was, a compelling example of a something else that for them had an explanatory effect as a result of being brought into alignment with objects of reportage. Indeed, the notion that the First World War could explain "Henry's fascism," that he became a fascist because of the influence on him and his generation of that conflict, was the basis for a plurality of little explanations. In what follows, I want to use that much-invoked explanatory move to illustrate the dynamism both within and between those little explanations, the intensity of attention thrown on the apparently straightforward sideways maneuver between two sets of events, processes, or states of affairs.

The relationship between the author's politics and the First World War could be invoked through accounts of typification—that is, Williamson's politics was expressive of the attitudes and beliefs of a trench generation—or alternatively it could be invoked by emphasizing the specific and exceptional experiences of the writer. In fact, micro-shifts often occurred between those positions; very quickly, the identification of a cause that might explain how Williamson's particular engagement with fascism came about turned into an explanation of the man as a product of his time and cohort, and vice versa. Many readers liked to highlight, for instance, the impact on Williamson of personally witnessing the famous Christmas Truce of 1914, which saw German and Allied soldiers briefly leave their trenches to shake hands and greet one another. For some, that and other experiences of trench warfare left Williamson determined at all costs to avoid a second war; it also led the writer to be suspicious of any postwar demonization of Germany and to have a natural sympathy for other frontline men, including political leaders such as Hitler and Mosley. Such observations could be accompanied by individual thickenings of explanation, through reference to authorial biography, which could also provide a rationale for further reportage of what was taken to have occurred.

Ted, for instance, subsequently chose to expand his explanation for the influence of the First World War on Williamson's politics by describing the writer's family history:

> When people criticize him you can only try and explain why he felt the way he did and what the influences were. The biggest influence was the First World War. And he had a German great grandmother, so he was sort of German stock, you could say, on his mother's side, and he had this affinity towards Germany. He also had a German nurse when he was very young, who had been his father's nurse. He went through the war, he did his bit as a soldier and there was no sort of pro German influence, but he was greatly perturbed afterwards the way the German nation was treated. The fact that they were bled white in reparation for the cost of the war, and that sort of thing, and he believed that it was because of that that Hitler rose to power and the [next] war resulted from it.

This narrative introduced new secondary causes for the author's politics, such as his German ancestry, but in a fashion that on this occasion didn't mark a path of divergence between little explanations. The oscillation between typification and original biography could also result in debates about the limits of the war's influence on the author's politics. Take for example the frequent reflections of Williamson readers, including Ted and Anna, on the writer's heightened sense of "loyalty" as an explanation for his reluctance to recant his past politics or unequivocally condemn fascist leaders. Society members regularly switched between putting that quality down to the effects of trench comradeship—in one talk an invited speaker told us that "it was no longer loyalty to their country or cause that moved the majority of men in the trenches but loyalty to their friends at the front"—and putting it down instead to just an ordinary aspect of the writer's character, such as the stubbornness reported by Anna.

The causal assumption that Williamson's politics came about because of the impact of the First World War could also feed into theories of diminished responsibility. Society members exchanged versions of this kind of argument all the time; while very rarely offering a defense of fascism, they did advocate their little explanations as forms of greater understanding. A sense of mitigation could be achieved by putting the author's politics "in the context of the time"—once again a move to typification—or alternatively by zooming in on the diagnosis of a specific flaw in the writer; Anna's highlighting of Williamson's stubbornness suggested that his political stance was to a degree involuntary. Indeed, all kinds of variances on these shifts could be innovated. I recall one society member, for example, telling me, "I think the reason that Henry didn't go back on his views on Hitler is because I don't think he blamed him as an individual, I think he blamed circumstances and everything else." In this account, the reader invited me to see Williamson's politics in context but then attributed the actual case for diminished responsibility—that is, the influence of the First World War on a whole generation—to the writer himself. Here, the individual was not the proper unit of blame but "circumstances," and Williamson was not just a product of those circumstances but also a victim of explanation itself, or at least of the theory of mitigating circumstance, which, in this account, prevented him from blaming Hitler or any other individual in the manner expected.

As already mentioned, Runciman is interested in the dynamism between rival explanations but also in the "contrasts" within "the causal field on which a given explanation rests" (1983, 160). The First World War may chiefly explain Williamson's politics for society members, but it is not the only influence that readers recognize. Indeed, as we have seen, they sometimes offer other kinds of little explanation. These can present as complementary, as with Ted's invocation of the writer's German ancestry, but they can also be figured in competition with or even as eclipsing other little explanations. For instance, one society member I met asserted, "I think that Henry got involved with fascism because he supported Mosley's agricultural policies when he was a farmer, and I think that was as far as it [the author's politics] went." More elaborate bases for convergence or tension between explanations could also be found by appealing to the relatively sparse number of secondary commentaries on the writer and his works. Readers could cite the familiar claim that Williamson's fascism was in fact shaped by "two catastrophic historical experiences: the First World War and the economic and political events of the 1930s" (Higginbottom 1992, 2–3) or the less familiar claim that his fascism was a product of the writer's constant need for a prophetic figure (Yeates 2017; also see Cunningham 1989). They could invoke the official biography, much praised by Ted, in order to stress the coeval influence on the author's politics of Romanticism (A. Williamson 1995, 196–197). But even if their little explanations were in divergence, each one was still generally concerned to spotlight clusters of contrasts or modulations between identifications of how something came about.

For Runciman, the play between such contrasts within a causal field also draws out the need to distinguish between at least two ordinary uses of *because*: one to identify a "cause" and the other to identify something perhaps better described as a "constraint" (1983, 156). "Causes," Runciman elaborates, are perceived to be "the contingent antecedent conditions, both immediate (or 'proximate') and background (or 'ultimate'), by which outcomes are determined; constraints are rather, necessary limitations on the outcomes which any combination of causes is able to effect" (156). That difference, between identifying what determined Williamson's politics and what constrained it, was constantly coming in and out of focus in the little explanations of society members. This was the case both in terms of which assembly of causes any member privileged and in terms of the degrees of autonomy she or he wished to attribute to the author's character. So some readers, including the official biographer, would identify Romanticism itself as a cause but also a constraint on his politics, perhaps because it was ultimately "a concept of freedom, an opening of horizons" (A. Williamson 1995, 196). Others would speak of the necessary limitation placed on Williamson's fascism by the writer's humanity or writerly capacity for sympathy, which they experienced and understood through reading the novels (Reed 2022).

Although these little explanations did not add up, in any cumulative sense, to a total explanatory apparatus for interpreting the author's politics, there was, I believe, something satisfying in considering the fragments in a dynamic system. Indeed, the movement internal to a little explanation—whether figured through shifting identifications of cause and constraint or through transformations or reversals in which event, process, or state of affairs gets marked as the thing to be explained or as the "something else" with explanatory power—necessarily coexisted with the movement between explanations. This was obviously the case when the same reader invoked a new explanatory move or when readers directly exchanged explanations in conversation. However, it might also be reasonable to include the interactive status of seemingly more dissociated explanatory fragments. One can do this in a strong sense, by for instance finding an immediate point of connection between them. The explanations expressed by Ted, Anna, and Frank may have occurred separately, but they were also all told to me; each society member was likewise the custodian of multiple little explanations offered to them by diverse Williamson readers. It can also be done in weaker fashion, by appeal to the ecology of such explanatory moves—the fact, for instance, that little explanations no doubt got repeated, reproduced, and innovated as they continually circulated between explaining subjects over the years.

Just Dad

But what of the politics of the explanations (of the author's politics) offered by Williamson readers? There is a literal question to answer here but also perhaps a much broader one; I take the latter first. According to Gayatri Spivak (1990, 380), at the most "general level" any likelihood of explanation always "carries the presupposition of an explainable (even if not fully) universe and an explaining (even if imperfectly) subject." More specifically, Spivak argues, every actual explanation "must secure and assure a certain kind of being-in-the-world, which might as well be called our politics" (380). That political dimension especially revolves around the issue of what gets articulated as being inside or at the center of a particular explanation and what gets pushed outside it or to its "prohibited margins" (381). If "the centre is defined and reproduced by the explanation that it can express," Spivak posits, then it is beholden on us to consider that explanation from the perspective of its points of exclusion (381).

It is of course immediately possible to identify the margins of at least some of these little explanations. When the Williamson reader I met at the hotel bar suggested that "maybe Henry didn't get it so wrong," his argument rested in part on the supposition that the costs of fighting fascism had been too high "for Britain." The possibility that loss of empire could still be a cause of regret, at least occasionally or for some literary society members for some of the time, spoke to normative ways in which both race and nation got more broadly invoked among the white men and women who made up the membership. Take for example those explanations that rested on accounts of typification. The claim that Williamson's political orientation was expressive of the attitudes and beliefs of a trench generation risked obscuring the fact that the politics of that generation was itself deeply polarized. But it also assumed that the effects of trench comradeship had naturalized endpoints. Readers who put forward this explanation generally understood that Williamson's politics was expressive of wider attitudes and beliefs among British veterans, assumed to be white, and not for instance of attitudes and beliefs among the trench generation as a whole. On the British side, that included men from all parts of the empire; as well as troops from white settler colonies, there were colonial troops from India, the Caribbean, and West Africa. Although it was true that a sense of solidarity across traditional lines of enmity could also be identified as an explanation for the author's unwillingness to automatically condemn Hitler and the politics of National Socialism in the 1930s, it is noteworthy that this kind of explanation was often backed up by appeal to the principle of ancestry. So Williamson's "affinity towards Germany" was also sometimes assumed to have arisen from the fact that he was at least partly "of German stock." To many in a literary society whose members largely identified as English, a status taken for granted precisely on the grounds that common ancestry naturally attached one to nation or place and hence to each other, this kind of explanation seemed self-evidently compelling, if never sufficient.

Other little explanations relied on different blind spots. However, I think it is worth reiterating that, as explaining subjects, the readers I knew generally considered themselves to be occupying a place at the margins of other people's explanations. In fact, joining the literary society was often an education in how a

certain kind of center, sometimes identified as the literary establishment, ex-
cluded through explanation. As generally reluctant explaining subjects, Williamson readers felt compelled to explain the author's politics precisely because
they felt the power of explanation's effects—for them, manifest not just in the
neglect of a favorite author but also in the resulting marginalization of their own
enthusiastic reading practice. Indeed, individual readers and the literary society have been periodically stung by just such kinds of explanatory practices, most
notoriously in 1980 when the fledgling society was asked to contribute to a BBC
documentary, which purported to be sympathetically reassessing the works of
the writer. In the end the program chose to present the faces and words of a group
of readers interviewed by the documentary makers alongside black-and-white
images of Hitler speechifying and shots of marching jack boots. More recently,
a political reading of Williamson and his works published in a popular literary
magazine dismissed anyone who still admired the writings or supported the author as a "small band of cultists" (Law 2012, 7); this article was still causing
consternation among society members five years later.

But that sense of exclusion came from other, more troubling directions too.
As well as explanations that denounced the writer and his works because of his
politics, readers had sometimes to grapple with explanations that positively em-
braced the author on the same basis. In the early days of the literary society,
this occasionally included explanations sourced from within its own ranks. Indeed, a few old members of the British Union of Fascists and its postwar rein-
carnation, the Union Movement, initially joined; this included Mosley's longtime
secretary Jeffrey Hamm, who occasionally contributed to the letters section of
the journal and who acknowledged the author and the society in his memoir
(Hamm 1983). An early journal issue also contained a brief essay by Diana Mosley. Even more troubling for present-day society members was the growing
awareness, especially because of the way internet search engines responded to
the entry of the author's name, of the fact that neo-Nazi or extreme English nationalist groups with explicitly racist agendas were increasingly claiming the
writer and his works as part of the new Far Right canon. Not surprisingly, this
news generated anxieties among readers about how these groups might also explain them, and how the general public might in turn read those explanations.
In 2011, this concern led the literary society to post a "Statement on Fascism"
on its website. Addressed to those whose "prime reason for visiting this site"
might be an interest in the author's politics, it read, "The Henry Williamson Society does not support nor promote Fascism in any way whatever and entirely
dissociates itself from any organisations which have misrepresented it as doing
so" (Henry Williamson Society n.d.b).

Indeed, part of the appeal of the dynamic system of little explanations, for instance its inherent resistance to any stable identification of cause or constraint, was precisely that it enabled explaining subjects to constantly shift and hence differentiate themselves from unwanted associations or other explaining subjects. This might include differentiations from historical fascist figures such as Diana Mosley; her short essay remained uncomfortable reading precisely because she invoked a range of very familiar little explanations. This included an insistence that Williamson's fascism was chiefly due to sympathy for her husband's agricultural policies and support for his "dedication to peace" or antiwar campaign (1981, 21). Within the literary society, the dynamic system allowed individual members to share an explanatory move while simultaneously distinguishing themselves on the basis of a divergence within the terms of that something else or by reference to the explanatory potential of an alternative event, process, or state of affairs. Neither Anna nor Ted would have been comfortable with a little explanation for the author's politics grounded in imperial nostalgia; however, they might happily have united in sentiments of exasperation with my hotel bar companion when he asked, "Why pick on Williamson?" Likewise, the outburst at the hotel bar should not obscure the fact that in this member's calmer, more sober reflections he too chose to privilege the claim that Williamson was a fascist *because* of the First World War. I suspected that the same work of dissociation often took place within explaining subjects; each one, so it seemed to me, constituted by their own moving field of little explanations regularly foregrounded and then withdrawn, invoked, and then displaced.

But this constant uneasy shifting between little explanations could also exhaust. There was never the moment of respite or space of shelter that Williamson readers sometimes felt, despite the air of unreality around it, as a result of embracing the principle of the autonomy of literature. The unsustainability of that latter big explanation and the never-ending micro-shifts of the dynamic system might be expected to generate some despondency. However, there was another explanatory or anti-explanatory resource available to members of the literary society, an outlook on the writer and his works that seemed on occasions to provide them genuine relief from their largely unwanted status as explaining subjects.

As already explored, a number of members identified character traits in the author as an explanation for his politics. In this move, rather than typification, the focus fell on political attitudes or beliefs as an expression of the temperament of the man. That invitation could work by drawing attention to flawed aspects of Williamson's personality (his reported stubbornness, for instance) or to aspects that might otherwise be adjudged more positively (his reportedly fierce loyalty toward friends, for instance). But each of these explanations additionally relied on a broader explanatory move, which worked by simultaneously highlighting both the ordinary and extraordinary qualities assigned to the individual. Here the author's politics was another, albeit embarrassing, instance of what made "Henry" distinctly Henry, the remarkable, sometimes infuriating, unpredictable, yet engaging character that he was usually appreciated to be. "Oh, that's just Henry," members frequently offered by way of a refrain. Alongside it, however, one commonly heard a reminder that Williamson was also "just a person." Closely tied to the complaint that the author was being unfairly singled out, perhaps best embodied in that exasperated utterance, "Why pick on Williamson?" the appeal this time was to the fact that Williamson lacked the kind of distinctiveness that warranted special criticism.

Describing a seemingly very different context for acts of explanation, Jacqueline Nassy Brown (2005) points out how this appeal can further work as a form of self-recusancy. Among "Liverpool-born Blacks" (LBB), who sometimes claim to be "the oldest Black community in Britain" (5), Nassy Brown reports, explaining subjects occasionally express the desire to resist the positioning or explanatory logics tied to a dominant politics of race, place, and class. "She prefers to be 'just a person,'" Nassy Brown observes of one interlocutor, in this case a white woman recognized as part of that LBB community by dint of marriage and children (206). As well as "refusing racial distinctions," the woman concerned insisted that she in turn treated others in like fashion. Friends were "just her friends and kids just kids." In this explanatory or anti-explanatory universe, other forms of explanation were surplus to requirement; in particular, to say someone was Black or white explained nothing essential about who they truly were. There was an equivalent kind of move, I believe, in the preference expressed by Williamson readers to regard the author as just a person. Here Henry was Henry alone, not something more. To call him fascist likewise explained nothing essential about him. Indeed, it rang false precisely because members knew Henry as Henry, a knowledge that affirmed, to requote Anna, that the writer was not a "real" fascist (i.e., because he was Henry).

But in Nassy Brown's account the appeal to be regarded as just a person also remained unsustainable. This was partly because, as Nassy Brown points out after Frantz Fanon, "a chief consequence of race" was exactly "the unfulfillable desire to be 'just' a self" (2005, 201). More pertinently, in the example provided, the woman's desire risked evading the issue of white privilege—that is, that the refusal of racial distinctions in favor of just being a person might not appear a viable option to others within the LBB community. In fact, as Nassy Brown goes on to describe, that explaining subject's project failed most dramatically at home, where her daughter insisted not only on identifying as Black but also on identifying her mother as "decidedly White" (207). While on one level the problems with such a comparison are self-evident—responses to the author's politics or to explanations of his fascism hardly equate with responses to the politics of race, particularly those grounded in the historical experience of racism—nevertheless I find Nassy Brown's descriptions apt. For the just-a-person appeal offered by Williamson readers, which included an invitation to refuse political distinctions, also didn't really work as an anti-explanatory resource. Indeed, it failed for much the same reasons: because others found it unconvincing or kept insisting on holding the author's politics in mind. "But wasn't he a fascist?" remained the recurring question that individual members and the literary society as a whole had to keep on addressing.

However, as Nassy Brown further testifies, that was not necessarily the end of the matter. While the white mother just discussed might have had her preference to be regarded as just a person pointedly rejected by her daughter, in different cases it was that very type of kin relation that provided a template for an apparently effective limit on explanations, at least those derived from the politics of race. For as Nassy Brown recounts, some other sons and daughters of white mothers in the LBB community insisted that race didn't come into that relationship. This was not because they regarded their mothers as just people but rather because they viewed them as "just me mum" (2005, 77). Indeed, the particularity of that relationship seemed to be central to its effectiveness as an anti-explanatory resource. Nassy Brown reports that for these sons and daughters, the "kinship role is paramount and determining: it nullifies race altogether" (76). Although Nassy Brown's wider emphasis falls on the contested nature of this nullification and the broader interactions between all available explanations—members of the LBB community were on occasion capable of identifying the same white women as Black based on the perception of a shared politics (203)—I find the observation once again instructive.

For among literary society members, the shift of outlook on the author's politics that resulted from adoption of a borrowed stance of son or daughter (and sometimes of wife) could be crucial. Or put another way, it was when Williamson readers imaginatively refigured the writer as father (or husband) rather than just a person that I believe they came closest to finding the kind of respite from continual explanation that they desired. Such a move was not entirely speculative. In fact, one of the distinguishing features of the literary society for many members was precisely that it brought them into contact with the writer's grown-up children and, before her death, with Williamson's first wife (in addition to running the literary estate, several of these sons and their wives regularly attended society meetings [see Reed 2011]). The appreciation and initial excitement generated by this contact, especially for new members, may have been further enhanced by the fact that family members also featured as minor characters in the novels and some of Williamson's nonfiction (see Reed 2019). However, what interests me more, by way of conclusion, is the way in which the perspective offered by these family members seems to have had the effect (or illusion) of finally making explanation appear unnecessary.

It was as if the introduction of that kin perspective in some mysterious sense settled something. Notably, Williamson's sons told innumerable stories about their father, many of which ended with the punchline, "To us, that's Just Dad." Perhaps those stories, quite often critical in tone, were reassuring because the concrete particularity of the kin relations invoked resisted co-optation. Extreme nationalist groups might claim the writer as part of their Far Right canon and critics might explain the author and his works through his politics, but neither could ever make an explanatory claim on Williamson quite like that. Alternatively, the relief that members clearly felt on hearing those stories and receiving that punchline might have been the result of the effect of shifting between kin terms. If each perspective (that of wife, son, or daughter-in-law) inevitably prompted awareness of these other possible kin perspectives on the writer, then this might render the person of the author too multifaceted to be contained by any accusation. Phrased another way, it might nullify Williamson's politics by drawing attention to something far more encompassing and momentarily incontestable—that is, the writer's status as Dad and the corresponding status of his sons, who apparently couldn't help but frame their explanations of the writer from the perspective of this relation.

NOTE

I wish to thank all the members of the Henry Williamson Society I spoke with, both for their frankness and for their continued companionship over the years. Special thanks to Matei Candea (especially for his comments on assumptions of ontological continuity in Bourdieu) and to Paolo Heywood for inviting me to contribute to this book. As well as presenting a version of this chapter at the original conference, I gave a version to the Anthropology Department seminar at Aarhus University; I thank both audiences for their constructive feedback. In addition, I wish to express my gratitude to Brian Alleyne, Jon Bialecki, Deidre Shauna Lynch, Marilyn Strathern, and Tom Yarrow, who each provided valuable commentary at various stages.

REFERENCES

Bourdieu, P. 1991. *The Political Ontology of Martin Heidegger*. Stanford, CA: Stanford University Press.
Cunningham, V. 1989. *British Writers of the Thirties*. Oxford: Oxford University Press.
Hamm, J. 1983. *Action Replay*. London: Howard Baker.

Henry Williamson Society. n.d.a. "About the Society." Accessed January 13, 2023. https://www.henrywilliamson.co.uk/society/aboutus.

Henry Williamson Society. n.d.b. "Statement on Fascism." Accessed January 13, 2023. https://www.henrywilliamson.co.uk/aboutus-57?id=55.

Higginbottom, M. D. 1992. *Intellectuals and British Fascism: A Study of Henry Williamson*. London: Janus.

Law, J. 2012. "Tarka the Rotter." *Slightly Foxed* 35:7–9.

Mosley, D. 1981. "The Politics of Henry Williamson." *Henry Williamson Society Journal* 3:21–22.

Nassy Brown, J. 2005. *Dropping Anchor, Setting Sail: Geographies of Race in Black Liverpool*. Princeton, NJ: Princeton University Press.

Reed, A. 2011. *Literature and Agency in English Fiction Reading: A Study of the Henry Williamson Society*. Manchester: Manchester University Press; Toronto: University of Toronto Press.

——. 2019. "Minor Character Reading: Tracing an English Literary Society through Its Culture of Investigation." *PMLA* 134 (1): 66–80.

——. 2022. "Sympathy for Oswald Mosley: Politics of Reading and Historical Resemblance in the Moral Imagination of an English Literary Society." *Comparative Studies in Society and History* 64 (1): 63–90.

Runciman, W. G. 1983. *A Treatise on Social Theory*. Vol. 1. Cambridge: Cambridge University Press.

Spivak, G. C. 1990. "Explanation and Culture: Marginalia." In *Out There: Marginalization and Contemporary Cultures*, edited by R. Ferguson, M. Gever, T. T. Minh-ha, and C. West, 377–394. Cambridge, MA: MIT Press.

Williamson, A. 1995. *Henry Williamson: Tarka and the Last Romantic*. Gloucestershire: Alan Sutton.

Williamson, H. 1936. *The Flax of Dream. A Novel in Four Books*. London: Faber.

Yeates, G. 2017. *Henry Williamson: The Artist as Fascist*. Independently published.

Contributors

Jon Bialecki is a continuing lecturer in the University of California San Diego Department of Anthropology; he has previously taught at Reed College and the University of Edinburgh. His first monograph, *A Diagram for Fire: Miracles and Variation in an American Charismatic Movement*, is a study of the miraculous and differentiation in American religion, with a focus on ethics, politics, language, and economic practices; it was awarded the 2017 Sharon Stephens Prize by the American Ethnological Society and Honorable Mention for the 2018 Clifford Geertz Prize by the Society for the Anthropology of Religion. A second book, *Machines for Making Gods: Mormonism, Transhumanism, and Worlds without End*, addresses religious transhumanism.

Matei Candea is professor of social anthropology at the University of Cambridge. He is the author of *Corsican Fragments* and *Comparison in Anthropology*. His website is www.candea.org.

Joanna Cook is a reader in anthropology at University College London. She is the author of *Meditation in Modern Buddhism: Renunciation and Change in Thai Monastic Life* and *Making a Mindful Nation: Mental Health, Metacognition and Governance in the Twenty-First Century*.

Sarah Green is professor of social and cultural anthropology at the University of Helsinki. She has spent her academic career studying issues of space, place, location, and borders, starting with research on safe space among radical and revolutionary feminist separatists in London. She moved on to study the reopening of the Greek-Albanian border following the end of the Cold War; and to look at the introduction of internet and digital technologies to Manchester. More recently, she has studied how diverse borders and locations overlap in the Mediterranean region, for a European Research Council Advanced Grant project she leads called Crosslocations. She is currently working on the regulation of cross-border livestock trade, the cross-border tracking of wild animals, and attempts to control the spread of animal-borne infectious disease. The aim of that work is to stretch understanding of border dynamics and location to more than human mobility.

Paolo Heywood is assistant professor of social anthropology at the University of Durham. Before this he was a junior research fellow in social anthropology at the University of Cambridge, where he took his undergraduate and doctoral degrees. He is the author of *After Difference* and of a number of contributions to debates over anthropology's "ontological turn."

Tanya M. Luhrmann is the Albert Ray Lang Professor at Stanford University, in the Anthropology Department (and Psychology, by courtesy) Her work focuses on the anthropology of mind and the way different representations of mind affect spiritual and psychiatric experience—in particular, the voices of spirit and the voices of madness. She was elected to the American Academy of Arts and Sciences in 2003 and received a John Guggenheim Fellowship award in 2007. She is the author of *Of Two Minds*, *Our Most Troubling Madness*, *How God Becomes Real*, and other books, and she is currently at work on a book entitled *Voices*.

Jonathan Mair is currently visiting researcher in the Department of Applied Communication Studies at the Complutense University, Madrid. His research has focused on ethics and cultures of belief and knowledge, and it has been based on fieldwork among Buddhist groups in northern China, Taiwan, and Europe.

Nigel Rapport is emeritus professor of Anthropological and Philosophical Studies at the University of St. Andrews and founding director of the St. Andrews Centre for Cosmopolitan Studies. He has also held a Canada Research Chair in Globalization, Citizenship and Justice. His most recent books are *Cosmopolitan Love and Individuality: Ethical Engagement beyond Culture* and (as editor) *Anthropology and the Enlightenment: Moral Relations Then and Now*. His current work centers on Emmanuel Levinas and how his philosophy might align with anthropological science.

Adam Reed is a reader in the Department of Social Anthropology at the University of St. Andrews. He conducts research in Papua New Guinea and the United Kingdom and is the author of *Papua New Guinea's Last Place: Experiences of Constraint in a Postcolonial Prison* and *Literature and Agency in English Fiction Reading: A Study of the Henry Williamson Society*. As well as continuing to work with an English literary society, his most recent UK project centers on animal activism.

Gildas Salmon is a CNRS research fellow at the Laboratoire Interdisciplinaire d'Études sur les Réflexivités (LIER-FYT). His work focuses on the philosophy and history of social sciences. After a first project devoted to French and American anthropology in the twentieth century, he is now working on a genealogy of comparative sciences within the framework of the British Empire. He has published *Les Structures de l'esprit: Lévi-Strauss et les mythes* and edited *Comparative Metaphysics: Ontology after Anthropology* (with Pierre Charbonnier and Peter Skafish) and *La Dette souveraine: Économie politique et État* (with Julia Christ).

Richard Staley is a historian of the physical sciences—broadly construed—who has developed a project on "physicist anthropologies" by examining the cultural history of mechanics and relations between a small group of physicists and anthropologists in the late nineteenth and early twentieth centuries who bridged two disciplines often defined in part by the contrast between them. He holds professorships at both the University of Cambridge and the University of Copenhagen and has recently helped lead a Mellon Sawyer Seminar titled "Histories of AI: A Genealogy of Power." In addition to studies of the history of economic anthropology, he is currently engaged in the collaborative Leverhulme Trust–funded project Making Climate History, examining the relations between making and knowing in the climate sciences over the past two hundred years.

Thomas Yarrow is a professor in social anthropology at Durham University. His research mostly focuses on expert knowledge, built space, and heritage, sometimes in conjunction. His books include *The Object of Conservation* and *Architects*.

Index

Abbot, Andrew, 4, 13
abduction, 9–10
absorption, 49–50, 75, 78
actor-network theory, 5
Agamben, Giorgio, 46, 47, 188, 190
Agar, Jon, 134–35
agnosticism, 71, 77
All-Party Parliamentary Group, 18
alterity, 30, 66
alt-right movement, 163, 173–79. *See also*
    right-wing politics
analysis, 85, 86, 165
Anscombe, Elizabeth, 46
anthropological explanation. *See* explanation
anthropological problems: approaches to,
    25–27; "category mistake," 29–30, 40–41;
    dissolution of, 14–15, 26–34, 37–38, 41;
    empirical resolution of, 26–27; explanation
    and, 30–42. *See also* ethnographic puzzles
anthropology: anti-explanatory mood in, 2–8,
    27, 104–5; classical, 19, 45, 104–5, 121;
    epistemology of, 5–8, 19; mixed methods,
    49–50. *See also* description; ethnographic
    foundationalism; ethnography; interpretation
antifoundationalism, 5–6
Appadurai, Arjun, 126, 133
Archetti, Eduardo, 31
Arendt, Hannah, 190–92
arguments: normative, 214; singularizing,
    84–86, 90, 94–99
Aristotle, 11, 175
artwork: distortion in, 145–47, 149–58; divine
    nature of, 157–58; miracles and, 155–56
asylum-seeking process, 17, 19, 181–97; hospital-
    ity and, 184–86, 192; hostility and, 184–85;
    location and, 182–84, 191, 197; territoriality
    and, 182–84, 188, 190–92, 196–97
atheism, 71, 77, 173
audiences, 13, 45, 93, 147, 159, 175, 179, 224
Augustine, 59
Aulino, Felicity, 58
Austen, Jane, 84
Austin, J. L., 186
Authors: politics of, 221–39; private life, 225–28
Avenarius, Richard, 129

Badone, Ellen, 68
"because," 228–33
behavior: belief and, 165, 167; explanations of,
    11, 13, 51, 87, 104; individual, 146; mental
    states and, 54–55; metacognition and, 179;
    miracles and, 72, 75; postmodernism and,
    121; rules and, 107; symbolic capital and,
    109; worldview and, 148
behaviorism, 117
belief: apparently irrational, 163–64, 167–69;
    behavior and, 165, 167; belief-motivation-
    action equation, 165–71, 177–78; knowledge
    and, 170 (*see also* knowledge); language and,
    168–69; miracles and, 71–78; monotheism
    and, 170; philosophers on, 47; reflective,
    170; truth and, 54, 56
Bialecki, Jon, 2, 15, 63–78
Bloch, Maurice, 45
Boas, Franz, 20n6, 108, 112, 138
Boddy, Janice, 68
bodies: absorption and, 50; artistic distortion
    of, 145–47, 149–58; of asylum seekers,
    189–91, 197; displacement of, 115, 117–18;
    mental events, 57, 59–60; mind-body dual-
    ism, 54, 166; in modern societies, 120.
    See also cognition; mental health; mental
    illness
borders, 182–84, 188, 190, 192–97
Borofsky, R., 45
Bourdieu, Pierre, 15, 107–22, 169, 172, 177,
    188, 226–28
Boyer, Dominic, 83, 96–97
Boyer, Pascal, 47
bracketing, 88
Brahinsky, Josh, 58
British Union of Fascists, 229, 235
Bücher, Karl, 129–31
Butler, Judith, 190
by-product explanation, 93–98

Cabot, Heath, 181, 186, 192, 195–97
Callon, Michel, 126, 137
Cambridge University, 46
Candea, Matei, 2, 15, 19, 27, 35, 65–67, 73–76,
    81–100, 185

www.ingramcontent.com/pod-product-compliance
Lightning Source LLC
Chambersburg PA
CBHW030358270326
41926CB00009B/1156

* 9 7 8 1 5 0 1 7 7 1 5 7 6 *